ROME

Directed and Designed by Hans Hoefer
Produced by Udo Gümpel
Edited by Dr. Heinz Vestner
Photographs by Patrizia Giancotti and others

APA PUBLICATIONS

THE INSIGHT GUIDES SERIES RECEIVED SPECIAL AWARDS FOR EXCELLENCE FROM THE PACIFIC AREA TRAVEL ASSOCIATION.

ROME

First Edition

© 1988 APA PUBLICATIONS (HK) LTD
Printed in Singapore by APA Press Pte. Ltd.
Colour Separation in Singapore by Colourscan Pte Ltd

APA PUBLICATIONS

Publisher: Hans Johannes Hoefer
General Manager: Henry Lee
Marketing Director: Aileen Lau
Editorial Director: Geoffrey Eu
Editorial Manager: Vivien Kim
Editorial Consultants: Adam Liptak (North America)
Brian Bell (Europe)
Heinz Vestner (German Editions)

Project Editors

Helen Abbott, Diana Ackland, Mohamed Amin, Ravindralal Anthonis, Roy Bailet, Louisa Cambell, Jon Carroll, Hillary Cunningham, John Eames, Janie Freeburg, Bikram Grewal, Virginia Hopkins, Samuel Israel, Jay Itzkowitz, Phil Jaratt, Tracy Johnson, Ben Kalb, Wilhelm Klein, Saul Lockhart, Sylvia Mayuga, Gordon MaLauchlan, Kal Müller, Eric Oey, Daniel P. Reid, Kim Robinson, Ronn Ronck, Robert Seidenberg, Rolf Steinberg, Sriyani Tidball, Lisa Van Gruisen, Merin Wexler.

Contributing Writers

A.D. Aird, Ruth Armstrong, T. Terence Barrow, F. Lisa Beebe, Bruce Berger, Dor Bahadur Bista, Clinton V. Black, Star Black, Frena Bloomfield, John Borthwick, Roger Boschman, Tom Brosnahan, Jerry Carroll, Tom Chaffin, Nedra Chung, Tom Cole, Orman Day, Kunda Dixit, Richard Erdoes, Guillermo Gar-Oropeza, Ted Giannoulas, Barbara Gloudon, Harka Gurung, Sharifah Hamzah, Willard A. Hanna, Elizabeth Hawley, Sir Edmund Hillary, Tony Hillerman, Jerry Hopkins, Peter Hutton, Neil Jameson, Michael King, Michele Kort, Thomas Lucey, Leonard Lueras, Michael E. Macmillan, Derek Maitland, Buddy Mays, Craig McGregor, Reinhold Messner, Julie Michaels, M.R. Priya Rangsit, Al Read, Elizabeth V. Reyes, Victor Stafford Reid, Harry Rolnick, E.R. Sarachandra, Uli Schmetzer, Ilsa Sharp, Norman Sibley, Peter Spiro, Harold Stephens, Keith Stevens, Michael Stone, Desmond Tate, Colin Taylor, Deanna L. Thompson, Randy Udall, James Wade, Mallika Wanigasundara, William Warren, Cynthia Wee, Tony Wheeler, Linda White, H. Taft Wireback, Alfred A. Yuson, Paul Zach.

Contributing Photographers

Carole Allen, Ping Amarand, Tony Arruza, Marcello Bertinetti, Alberto Cassio, Pat Canova, Alain Compost, Ray Cranbourne, Alian Evrard, Ricardo Ferro, Lee Foster, Manfred Gottschalk, Werner Hahn, Dallas and John Heaton, Brent Hesselyn, Hans Hoefer, Luca Invernizzi, Ingo Jezierski, Wilhelm Klein, Dennis Lane, Max Lawrence, Lyle Lawson, Philip Little, Guy Marche, Antonio Martinelli, David Messent, Ben Nakayama, Vautier de Nanxe, Kal Müller, Günter Pfannmuller, Van Philips, Ronni Pinsler, Fitz Prenzel, G.P. Reichelt, Dan Rocovits, David Ryan, Frank Salmoiraghi, Thomas Schollhammer, Blair Seitz, David Stahl, Bill Wassman, Rendo Yap, Hisham Youssef.

Distributors:

Australia and New Zealand: Prentice Hall of Australia, 7 Grosvenor Place, Brookvale, NSW 2100, Australia. **Benelux:** Utigeverij Cambium, Naarderstraat 11, 1251 AW Laren, The Netherlands. **Brazil and Portugal:** Cedibra Editora Brasileira Ltda, Rua Leonidia, 2-Rio de Janeiro, Brazil. **Denmark:** Copenhagen Book Centre Aps, Roskildeveji 338, DK-2630 Tastrup, Denmark. **Germany:** RV Reise-und Verkehrsuerlag Gmbh, Neumarkter Strasse 18, 8000 Munchen 80, West Germany. **Hawaii:** Pacific Trade Group Inc., P.O. Box 1227, Kailua, Oahu, Hawaii 96734, U.S.A. **Hong Kong:** Far East Media Ltd., Vita Tower, 7th Floor, Block B, 29 Wong Chuk Hang Road, Hong Kong. **India and Nepal:** India Book Distributors, 107/108 Arcadia Building, 195 Narima Point, Bombay-400-021, India. **Indonesia:** Java Books, Box 55 J.K.C.P., Jakarta, Indonesia. **Israel:** Steimatzky Ltd., P.O. Box 628, Tel Aviv 61006, Israel (Israel title only). **Italy:** Zanfi Editori SRL. Via Ganaceto 121, 41100 Modena, Italy. **Jamaica:** Novelty Trading Co., P.O. Box 80, 53 Hanover Street, Kingston, Jamaica. **Japan:** Charles E. Tuttle Co. Inc., 2-6 Suido 1-Chome, Bunkyo-ku, Tokyo 112, Japan. **Kenya:** Camerapix Publishers International Ltd., P.O. Box 45048, Nairobi, Kenya. **Korea:** Kyobo Book Centre Co., Ltd., P.O. Box Kwang Hwa Moon 1 658, Seoul, Korea. **Philippines:** National Book Store, 701 Rizal Avenue, Manila, Philippines. **Singapore:** MPH Distributors Pte. Inc., 601 Sims Drive #03-21 Pan-I Warehouse and Office Complex, S'pore 1438, Singapore. **Switzerland:** M.P.A. Agencies-Import SA, CH. du Croset 9, CH-1024, Ecublens, Switzerland. **Taiwan:** Caves Books Ltd., 103 Chungshan N. Road, Sec. 2, Taipei, Taiwan, Republic of China. **Thailand:** Asia Books Co. Ltd., 5 Sukhumvit Road Soi 61, P.O. Box 11-40, Bangkok 10110, Thailand. **United Kingdom, Ireland and Europe (others):** Harrap Ltd., 19-23 Ludgate Hill, London EC4M 7PD, England, United Kingdom. **Mainland United States and Canada:** Graphic Arts Center Publishing, 3019 N.W. Yeon, P.O. Box 10306, Portland OR 97210, U.S.A. (The Pacific Northwest title only); Prentice Hall Press, Gulf & Western Building, One Gulf & Western Plaza, New York, NY 10023, U.S.A. (all other titles).

French editions: Editions Gallimard, 5 rue Sébastien-Bottin, F-75007 Paris, France. **German editions:** Nelles Verlag GmbH, Schleissheirner Str. 371b, 8000 Munich 45, West Germany **Italian editions:** Zanfi Editori SLR. Via Ganaceto 121 41100 Modena, Italy. **Portuguese editions:** Cedibra Editora Brasileira Ltda, Rua Leonidia, 2-Rio de Janeiro, Brazil.

Advertising and Special Sales Representatives

Advertising carried in Insight Guides gives readers direct access to quality merchandise and travel-related services. These advertisements are inserted in the Guide in Brief section of each book. Advertisers are requested to contact their nearest representatives, listed below.
Special sales, for promotion purposes within the international travel industry and for educational purposes, are also available. The advertising representatives listed here also handle special sales. Alternatively, interested parties can contact Apa Publications, P.O. Box 219, Orchard Point Post Office, Singapore 9123.

Australia and New Zealand: Harve and Gullifer Pty. Ltd. 1 Fawkner St. Kilda 3181, Australia. Tel: (3) 525 3422; Tlx: 523259; Fax: (89) 4312837.
Canada: The Pacific Rim Agency, 6900 Cote Saint Luc Road, Suite 303, Montreal, Quebec, Canada H4V 2Y9. Tel: (514) 9311299; Tlx: 0525134 MTL; Fax: (514) 8615571.
Hawaii: HawaiianLMedia Sales; 1750 Kalakaua Ave., Suite 3-243, Honolulu, Hawaii 96826, U.S.A. Tel: (808) 9464483.
Hong Kong: C Cheney & Associates, 17th Floor, D'Aguilar Place, 1-30 D'Aguilar Street, Central, Hong Kong. Tel: 5-213671; Tlx: 63079 CCAL HX.
India and Nepal, Pakistan and Bangladesh: Universal Media, CHA 2/718, 719 Kantipath, Lazimpat, Kathmandu-2, Nepal. Tel: 412911/414502; Tlx: 2229 KAJI NP ATTN MEDIA.
Indonesia: Media Investment Services, Setiabudi Bldg. 2, 4th Floor, Suite 407, Jl. Hr. Rasuna Said, Kuningan, Jakarta Selatan 12920, Indonesia. Tel: 5782723/5782752; Tlx: 62418 MEDIANETIA; Mata Graphic Design, Batujimbar, Sanur, Bali, Indonesia. Tel: (0361) 8073. (for Bali only)
Korea: Kaya Ad Inc., Rm. 402 Kunshin Annex B/D, 251-1 Dohwa Dong, Mapo-Ku, Seoul, Korea (121). Tel: (2) 7196906; Tlx: K 32144 KAYAAD; Fax: (2) 7199816.
Philippines: Torres Media Sales Inc., 21 Warbler St., Greenmeadows 1, Murphy, Quezon City, Metro Manila, Philippines. Tel: 722-02-43; Tlx: 23312 RHP PH.
Taiwan: Cheney Tan & Van Associates, 7th Floor, 10 Alley 4, Lane 545 Tun Hua South Road, Taipei, Taiwan. Tel: (2) 7002963; Tlx: 11491 FOROSAN; Fax: (2) 3821270.
Thailand: Cheney, Tan & Van Outrive, 17th Floor Rajapark Bldg., 163 Asoke Rd., Bangkok 10110, Thailand. Tel: 2583244/2583259; Tlx: 20666 RAJAPAK TH.
Singapore and Malaysia: Cheney Tan Associates, 1 Goldhill Plaza, #02-01, Newton Rd., Singapore 1130, Singapore. Tel: 2549522; Tlx: RS 35983 CTAL.
Sri Lanka: Spectrum Lanka Advertising Ltd., 56 1/2 Ward Place, Colombo 7, Sr Lanka. Tel: 5984648/596227; Tlx: 21439 SPECTRM CE.
U.K., Ireland and Europe: Brian Taplin Associates, 32 Fishery Road, Boxmoor, Hemel Hempstead, Herts HP 1ND, U.K. Tel: (2)215635; Tlx: 825454 CHARMAN.

APA PHOTO AGENCY PTE. LTD.

The Apa Photo Agency is S.E. Asia's leading stock photo archive, representing the work of professional photographers from all over the world. More than 150,000 original color transparencies are available for advertising, editorial and educational uses. We are linked with Tony Stone Worldwide, one of Europe's leading stock agencies, and their associate offices around the world:
Singapore: Apa Photo Agency Pte. Ltd., P.O. Box 219, Orchard Point Post Office, Singapore 9123, Singapore. **London:** Tony Stone Worldwide, 28 Finchley Rd., St. John's Wood, London NW8 6ES, England. **North America & Canada:** Masterfile Inc., 415 Yonge Sr., Suite 200, Toronto M5B 2E7, Canada. **Paris:** Fotogram-Stone Agence Photographique, 45 rue de Richelieu, 75001 Paris, France. **Barcelona:** Fototec Torre Dels Pardais, 7 Barcelona 08026, Spain. **Johannesburg:** Color Library (Pty.) Ltd., P.O. Box 1659, Johannesburg, SOuth Africa 2000. **Sydney:** The Photographic Library of Australia Pty. Ltd., 7 Ridge Street, North Sydney, New South Wales 2050, Australia. **Tokyo:** Orion Press, 55-1 Kanda Jimbocho, Chiyoda-ku, Tokyo 101, Japan.

This guide to Rome is a new title in the *Apa Productions Insight Cityguides* series on the world's most beautiful cities. The idea grew out of the *Insight Guides*, a concept developed by the West German photographer Hans Hoefer in the 70s. His approach laid a new emphasis on photography and made the

Hoefer   *Gümpel*   *Vestner*

places where people live and work today the starting points for the guides—even for cities as multi-layered and full of history as Rome.

The first *Insight Guides* were limited to South-East Asia, but soon grew to cover all five continents. The worldwide success of the *Insight Guides* series on individual countries led to the development of the idea of *Cityguides*. *Cityguide: Rome* is one of the first titles.

The camera never lies, they say, and 180 color and black-and-white photographs offer you a visual guide to the city. The authors know their subjects and the city, and accompany you on your way around, without prescribing fixed routes. Given the size and the complexity of Rome, it would be ridiculous to claim that this guide is complete, and equally ridiculous to suggest that you could gain even a brief impression of this city in a few days. Rome simply invites return visits. Just one or two of the city quarters portrayed here offer endless fascinating information, and more images than the eye can take in. Works by art historians—mostly unread—fill up many bookshelves, and scholarly works full of dates of emperors' reigns and the murder of tyrants generally share the same fate. When looking for authors, we looked for journalists and people who knew Rome, who wouldn't try to hide their personal opinion, and who could show the reader Roman life from an unexpected point of view. We wanted them to write about the people of Rome and their streets, squares and city districts, information less well known than the date of Caesar's murder in the Theatre of Pompey.

Seven authors contributed to the book, all of whom have lived for years, in some cases for decades, in Rome and worked in Rome and Italy as correspondents for the international media. However, affection for their adopted home has not robbed them of their critical faculties.

Editor **Udo Gümpel** wrote the greatest number of contributions to the book. He also persuaded the other authors to take part and co-ordinated their work—no easy task, considering the number of guides to Rome already published and the impossibility of re-inventing the wheel. The new concept of the book, giving more weight to places, streets, squares and districts, letting photographs tell their own story, and not least the rapid changes which Rome has undergone in the last few years, all worked together to persuade the authors to have another go at writing a book on Rome.

Udo Gümpel, a Roman by choice, finally left his native city of Hamburg, where he was born in 1954, and settled down beside the Tiber in 1983. Since then he's been reporting for German weekly papers (e.g. *Deutsche Volkszeitung* and *Deutsches Allgemeines Sonntagsblatt*) and for various radio and TV programs on Italy.

Author **Werner Raith** was born in Regensburg, West Germany, in 1940. He is well known as a correspondent for the German paper *tageszeitung* and as the author of several books on Italy. Since his graduation in 1966 Werner Raith has concentrated on Italy and his name is now a byword for open and accurate reporting on Italian affairs. He lives in Terracina near Rome.

Henning Klüver, born in 1949 in Hamburg, is also well known, having worked from Rome as a newspaper and radio correspondent for many years. He's now followed the call of the weekly *Deutsches Allgemeines Sonntagsblatt* and come back to be its foreign news editor, but he hasn't lost his love for the country south of the Alps. He has already published a guide to Rome, *Anders Reisen*. Here he's responsible for describing the underground world of Rome, the part that lies under our thoughtless feet, while we walk on looking up at the domes of the churches. Kluver re-adjusts our point of view.

Responsible for the section on modern history is **Peter Kammerer**, born in Offenburg, West Germany, in 1938. For many years he has led an Italian commuter's life, working in Rome as a newspaper and radio reporter and in Urbino as Professor for Sociology. A co-author of *Anders Reisen*, Peter Kammerer let himself be persuaded, despite pressure of work, to contribute—driven by the delight mixed with the distaste familiar to all new citizens of Rome.

Uli Friedhof, born in Cologne in 1956, got to know Rome from an archaeologist's point of view during his time as a student, and later while working for his doctorate. To make the history of places come alive, he feels the need to look further than the facts, even if it is impossible to manage without naming one or two emperors. He's also concerned to link the Then very much with the

Now, so that we end up understanding more than the past.

Horst Schlitter is, with Peter Kammerer, the other representative of the older generation. He is well known as the Italian correspondent of the leading German paper *Frankfurter Rundschau*. His contribution to this book looks at the world of the grassroots Christians, Protestants, Jews and those of other faiths, all very active in this most Catholic city.

Raith   *Klüver*

Maria Morhart was born in 1953

Kammerer   *Friedhoff*

in Aschaffenburg, West Germany. After 12 years of living in Berlin, where she studied theatrical arts, she followed her first love in 1984 and now lives in Rome, where she writes for theatrical magazines and works with theater groups. "On the side" she manages to be the artistic organizer of the summer festival of the German Academy in the Villa Massimo. In Rome these two jobs are obviously not as wearing as they would be elsewhere—she spends much of her free time in exploring the Roman night life, which she describes most vividly.

Nearly all the photos in this book were taken by **Patrizia Giancotti**, a 29 year old photographer who comes from Turin, but nonetheless remains true to her Neapolitan mother and Calabrian father. She has published photo reports in the major Italian magazines such as *Epoca, Panorama, l'Illustrazione Italiana, Atlante, Gente Viaggio*. In the last few years she has become famous for her reports on Brazil and Argentina. An editor for the TV channel *Tele Monte Carlo*, she has had varied media experience other than photography. Her greatest success came with the *Biennale Internazionale Torino Fotografia 1987* and her two exhibitions, *Bahiart* and *Cercatori* (Seekers). Her image of Rome is neither loud nor brash, more a little dreamy and floating—for Rome has, deep inside, remained a small town, and you can tell that from the people in her pictures.

Schlitter   *Giancotti*

Morhart

More photographs contributed to the success of the book, from the Roman photographer **Flavio Bruno**, the American **Ping Amranand** and the German **Gerd Pfeifer**. Essential information was provided by the archives of the Vatican, the Italian government, the Garibaldi Society, the dance group Gaia Scienza and the cooperativa culturale blond. But the bulk of the material was provided by the Archiv fur Kunst und Geschichte in Berlin.

Special thanks for help, tea, advice and accommodation go to Luciano Bistulfi, Claudio Bernabucci, Elsa Byington, Vic and Clelia Lupis and Daniela de Freitas e Juju.

We mustn't forget to thank Helene Pede for her help. Without her vigorous and understanding support so many things would never have been done.

Nearly last but by no means least, we must mention **Heinz Vestner** from *Apa Publications*. He made his way to Rome to meet the editor Udo Gümpel in a pavement cafe and initiate him into the secrets of *Insight Guides*. For his reward he got piles and piles of manuscripts and photos on his desk.

In the publisher's office and at the printer's in Singapore who worked day and night to bring out this special book on Rome, the one the world has been waiting for.

Thanks to all of you.

—Apa Publications

TABLE OF CONTENTS

TABLE OF CONTENTS

All texts written by the Editor Udo Gümpel unless bylined.

Part Three

MAPS

OTHER INSIGHT GUIDES TITLES

COUNTRY/REGION

ASIA
Bali
Burma
Hong Kong
India
Indonesia
Korea
Malaysia
Nepal
Philippines
Rajasthan
Singapore
Sri Lanka
Taiwan
Thailand
Turkey

PACIFIC
Hawaii
New Zealand

NORTH AMERICA
Alaska
American Southwest
Northern California
Southern California
Florida
Mexico
New England
New York State
The Pacific Northwest
The Rockies
Texas

SOUTH AMERICA
Brazil
Argentina

CARIBBEAN
Bahamas
Barbados
Jamaica
Puerto Rico
Trinidad and Tobago

EUROPE
Channel Islands
France
Germany
Great Britain
Greece
Ireland
Italy
Portugal
Scotland
Spain

MIDDLE EAST
Egypt
Israel

AFRICA
Kenya

GRAND TOURS
Australia
California
Canada
Continental Europe
Crossing America
East Asia
South Asia

GREAT ADVENTURE
Indian Wildlife

CITYGUIDES
Bangkok
Berlin
Buenos Aires
Dublin
Istanbul
Lisbon
London
Paris
Rio de Janeiro
Rome
San Francisco
Venice
Vienna

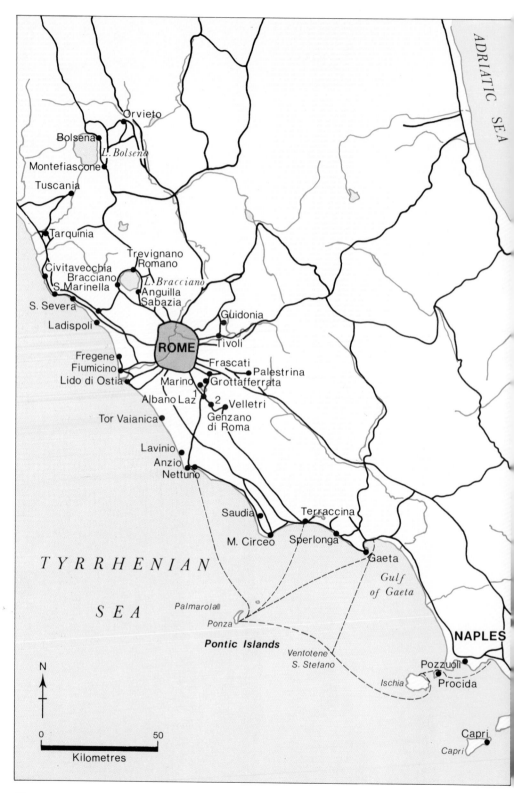

14

ROME, CAPITAL OF THE WORLD

A city that walks into the Job Centre and says that it wants to be capital of the world should really be declared insane right away. And yet, since its founding on April 21, 753 B.C., Rome has been making this claim. In fact, Rome's very existence is evidence in stone of the permanent conflict between its claim to rule the terrestrial globe, and the very different reality.

The astounding thing is that the world immediately accepted Rome's claim without argument. This is not to deny the long history of military resistance to Rome's rule in the Mediterranean, or the pig-headedness of German religious reformers who no longer wanted to submit to the dictates of Roman popes.

The Church: A New Power

The more people rebelled against Rome, the more they recognized its authority. The aim of every Praetorian commander was to rule on the Palatine. Every barbarian leader was obsessed by the idea of conquering Rome. But these revolts remained mere episodes, and with them, in spite of their military success, the Goths, Vandals, Franks and Langobards. They could not conquer Rome any more, because in the heart of the city a new power was emerging, which turned the legend of the capital of the world to its own uses: the church.

The popes had to replace the famed weapon power and golden palaces with spiritual authority, for militarily speaking the Vatican never rose above the level of a small central Italian state. But once they were successful in establishing the primacy of the Bishop of Rome over all others, they had also established themselves as legitimate successors of the Emperors. The only time the pope seriously attempted to interfere in European affairs, he was promptly paid back: the protestant mercenaries of Charles V looted the city for 40 days during the "Sacco di Roma" in 1527.

The wretchedness and greatness of this city are strongly bound up with the claim, never realized, to be the center of the world and eternal. This natural legitimacy of rule over all the world led every new master of Rome to put his mark on the city, in order to preserve his name for posterity.

To this end Nero—assuming that the stories about him are true, at least with regard to the lack of assistance in fighting the fire—allowed Rome to be destroyed by fire storms, in order to re-build it afterwards more beautiful than ever. To this end papal builders had streets laid out, bridges and churches built. To this end, after the unification of Italy, the Piedmontese rulers had their monument placed on the Capitol—a permanent reminder of their complete lack of civic understanding. The national hero Guiseppe Garibaldi tried twice to conquer Rome for Italy, but comforted himself that he was at least commemorated for posterity in the building of the Tiber walls, even if not as the liberator of the city from the papal yoke.

In order to lead Rome back to its ancient greatness, Mussolini depopulated half the Old City in the space of a few months to clear the routes for the great avenues, and to this end he had a whole new city built outside the gates of Rome.

As for the Romans themselves, a sense of greatness has mostly passed them by. Since the time of the rule of the Senate over the Plebs, the lower classes have been much more interested in obtaining the daily grain ration, a glass of wine and a roof over their heads, than in rejoicing in some phantom greatness. And every time that circumstances put an end to the rule of its conquerors and rulers (native or foreign, it made no difference) the city collapsed like a punctured balloon. For Rome has never possessed or needed economic self-sufficiency. As capital of the world, a city can claim a natural and understandable right to a de-

Preceding pages: on the Capitol—she-wolf suckling Romulus and Remus; Campo dei Fiori; Tiber bridge; St. Peter's; Piazza Navona; EUR district.

pendent existence. In ancient times the city was fed by fleets of grain ships from North Africa, Spain and Sicily.

As the body collapsed, the remaining rump could only survive on crumbs. At the beginning of the Middle Ages barely 30,000 people lived in the city. But then the church successfully re-imposed Rome's old and new role on the world. After that, money flowed into Rome's coffers once again, and pilgrims came.

The position of Rome didn't change even with the re-founding of the Italian state, for

the founding fathers deliberately planned a dependent role for Rome. Rome was to remain the purely intellectual head. The city was intended to administer, to lead, but not to produce anything—except ideology.

Even the modest growth of an independent industry in the widest sense in the Province of Rome has a background of dependence. This is where the "Cassa del mezzogiorno" begins, where generous financial aid to the underdeveloped regions in the south of Italy is distributed. On the map this northernmost corner of the "Casmez" regions stretches towards Rome like a hand

trying to grab the goodies.

The effect on the *populus romanus* of this permanent flow first of imperial grain supplies followed by charitable donations and by state subsidies (now lost) has been to make them politically indifferent, as long as there was food on the table: "O Francia o Spagna, basta che se'magna"—French or Spanish, who cares, as long as there's enough to eat. "Heroic" moments were remarkably rare. Today this lack of interest in what might be defined as "community politics" is known as *"menefreghismo"*, "I couldn't give a sh…"—one of the most used phrases in the Roman vocabulary.

Common Grievances

The visitor often encounters a rough unfriendliness which he is hard put to understand. The taxi driver is worried because he still has no official licence in hand, as the city committee that decides these matters won't be able to take up his case for a year and a half. The bus driver is upset because the communal bus company ATAC wants to put up the number of miles each bus should drive, but at the same time is doing nothing to protect the preferential public transport lanes, which are crammed full of private cars. The traffic police are threatening to strike, because they are the ones who have to put the closure of the Historic Centre into practice, but regularly get their negotiated wage increases paid out after a year's delay.

The car driver is annoyed at the fact that he alone is supposed to be responsible for the collapse of the traffic system, which has no car parks in the suburbs and insufficient buses and underground trains. The Roman-in-the-street is peeved, because twice a day he has to squeeze himself into a totally overcrowded underground train. Twenty years were needed to build Route A of the underground and the system closes at 11.30 p.m.

All Romans are troubled by the presence of young unemployed in their families—with youth unemployment running at 25 percent, every family has one. They are a drain on family finances, and the families worry that they would become criminals or drug addicts. The pushing and shoving old lady in the bus is worried because on the first of next month she faces another four-hour queue at the post office, because in Italy pensions are not sent through the post but can only be collected in person at the post office on certain days. The young couple necking outside McDonald's in the evening can't begin to think of their own flat, as the rents are impossibly high, and so remain living at home, until their parents can afford

edge of the Third World. It is still the most Christian city in the world, for the Popes have ruled here for a long time—but every Polish village wins hands down over Rome in piety.

Sometimes it seems as if Rome is now about to wake up from a long dream, in order, for the first time in history, to solve for itself the problems that native and foreign rulers have imposed on it, without waiting for salvation from a new conqueror.

People are put off by Rome, by its chaos, dirt and stench, by the yobs on mopeds who

a little flat through a Housing Association.

It is becoming obvious why the Romans are only just beginning to consider the problems of monuments destroyed by sulfur dioxide turning marble into limestone, vibration damage to buildings and acid rain.

Rome isn't the largest city in the world. The cities of the Third World can dispute that distinction without any rivalry from the metropolis on the Tiber, which is in the process of ending its own existence on the

Left, statue on the Ponte Sant' Angelo. Above, car thefts are a problem for many Romans.

snatch handbags off tourists, by the endless list of services that don't work. But we who don't live in Rome have often wanted to see the city as it never was or wanted to be; at least, for 2,500 years no-one has asked the city if it wanted to be "Holy", "Eternal", or "Capital of the World". This mixture of disgust and attraction for Rome, this "being a mother to all" as Fellini once called it, exists only inside our heads. The more we know of Rome, the more we find to criticize, but the more we love it. How could we be indifferent to a city when its name read backwards spells: ROMA=AMOR.

17

Wouldn't you have thought it? Like everything that has ever come into the hands of historians, the story of the founding of Rome has been the subject of dispute among different schools of thought. Some hold that the first settlements already existed over three thousand years ago, somewhere between the 12th and the 13th century B.C. Others hold that they did not take shape before the 8th century B.C.

The supposed *Roma quadrata* is believed to have been formed first of all by the union of three villages: *Germalus* on the Capitol, *Velia* near the Colosseum and *Palatual* in between. Three further villages on the Esquiline, namely *Oppius*, *Cispius* and *Fagutal* are supposed to have joined them. Together with the village *Querquetal*, these formed the Rome of the *Septimontine* period—not to be confused with "Rome of the seven hills", a later development. According to one school of thought, the founding fathers were exiled Greeks. According to others, they were local mountain tribes or nomadic Indo-Europeans from far, far away. They might even have been bandits from what is now central Italy. All these versions are possible, if not very romantic.

A Legendary Beginning

There is a beautiful legend of the founding of Rome—but unfortunately unimaginative modern historians have torn it to shreds. However, their spoilsport efforts haven't succeeded yet. The classical legend of *Romulus and Remus* is much more persistent than dull research reports about primitive huts of the 8th century B.C. between the Capitol and the Tiber, assumed mergers of the Latins of the Palatine hill with Sabines of the Quirinal and Viminal, or even of an alliance between all the inhabitants of the "Seven Hills" (Palatine, Capitol, Quirinal,

Viminal, Aventine, Esquiline and Caelian). Far more popular among the Romans is the story as told by the imperial poet Virgil in the Aeneid. As we can never know the truth for certain, we as guests of Rome had better stick to the more interesting version:

Aeneas was the son of the goddess Aphrodite and Anchises, King of Dardanos. When Troy was sacked and set on fire by Odysseus, Aeneas carried his crippled father out of the city. After an eventful journey he and a handful of survivors reached Sicily, left again, and came to North Africa. He felt quite at home there, not least because of the delightful Queen Dido, but a strident divine voice sent him on his way again. He returned to Sicily, but even there his divine travel courier refused to leave him alone. His women followers didn't think much of these voices and set fire to his sails (a kind of early Peace Movement). But nothing could stop the hero.

He traveled on, landing in Cumae, north of modern Naples. Here he met the resident prophetess, the Sybil, who gave a good prognosis for his further travels. And in fact a hundred or so miles further on he met more people who were friendly. They were from the Latin tribe and were looking for a suitor for the royal daughter. Aeneas volunteered, thus ensuring the succession for King Latinus, who promptly abdicated.

Now we are nearly there, at the place that is to be so important for the future history of the world. In the Alban Hills Julus, son of Aeneas, founded the city *Alba Longa*. Here life was obviously quite peaceful for a while. This changed later.

A power-mad descendant of Julus, Amulius, was not entitled to the throne, but still deposed his brother, the rightful King Munitor. He had Munitor's daughter Rhea dedicated as a priestess of Vesta. According to regulations, this involved 30 years of virginity and was intended to preclude any chance of a legitimate successor. But Amulius reckoned without the war god Mars. Mars wasn't bothered about the princess' vows of chastity, and the consequence was twins named Romulus and Remus. Of course the false King Amulius found out. He had the lapsed priestess put to death—as legal experts claim that the law of those times entitled him to do—and had her offspring set afloat in a bathtub on the Tiber. Understandably, the two babes squalled piteously. They were heard by the famous she-wolf on the bank, which dragged them ashore and suckled them (thus earning the grateful thanks of the souvenir industry to this day). Later the royal shepherd Faustulus found them and took

quite such fixed views on the subject and jumped over the ludicrous line—at which point his brother, lacking a sense of humor, murdered him. "So die all who leap over my walls" he is reputed to have cried on this occasion.

So Rome was founded. The storyteller gives a date corresponding to April 21, 753 B.C. The first act on city territory was one of murder, the beginning of a long series of wars and murders. These are always officially portrayed, following Romulus' example, as acts of self-defence or necessity.

them in. After more hair-raising adventures Remus ended up as a prisoner in his native city of Alba Longa. Here the origin of the two foundlings was clarified and they were honored. Still of one mind, they decided to found a city.

But the curse of power soon showed itself. Suddenly each of them wanted to rule. There was nothing else for it but to invoke the gods. Romulus, the more quick-witted of the two, saw twelve vultures, Remus only six. Romulus took this as a sign of his preferment and began immediately to mark out a city boundary in the dirt. Remus obviously didn't have

Next, the historical legend tells us about the mythical *Seven Kings*. The last one, Superbus of the house of Tarquin, was seen off around the year 510 or 500 B.C. However much of this might be true, the city certainly expanded remarkably. In the 6th century B.C. a sacred boundary was formally declared—the *Pomerium*—and Rome's power reached throughout Latium.

The basic reason for this expansion was that the Romans had come under the influ-

Above, Etruscan sarcophagus from the Villa Giulia.

ence of a more developed power—under the Etruscans. The latter possessed a highly developed iron industry—essential for making war—and owned copper, silver and lead mines. Their land grew 15 different kinds of wheat and had such a wealth of fish off the coasts that they put up watchtowers every few hundred yards for tuna fishing.

The Romans had their kings imposed on them for two centuries by the Etruscans, and they profited from the Etruscan example and took a good look at the technology of the strangers. They were so successful at this that they eventually got rid of their unloved teachers and rulers. Around the end of the 6th century B.C. the noble families were stripped of their power and Rome became a *res publica*.

A New Form of Republicanism

This was admittedly a long way from the state systems that we consider to be "republics". The great majority of the population were excluded from direct participation in politics, although many people had certain nominal rights and could even vote. There was no "one man, one vote"—votes were cast as block votes by clans, tribes or client associations. Slaves had no political and few civil rights. Many other people such as immigrants, freed slaves, subject and dependent peoples were excluded from the decision-making process.

All the same, the system worked for five centuries. A remarkably long time, considering that already in the 2nd century B.C. Rome ruled a multi-cultural state of over 20 million people spread around the Mediterranean. This was done using a form of administration and rule designed in the 5th and 6th centuries B.C. for a few tens of thousands of inhabitants. Two consuls, chosen every half year, wielded supreme political power. These were controlled by a Senate which was made up of representatives of the ancient nobility, former consuls, top civil servants and—from the 2nd and 3rd centuries B.C. on—representatives of the new upwardly mobile groups of society.

That the system survived for so long is undoubtedly due to the skills of the rulers of the time. Despite making rigorous use of their powers in most all conflicts, these remained flexible enough to integrate at least parts of the new social classes into the power structure.

After massive protests by the nouveau riche craftsmen and traders, mostly taking the form of their removal out of the city center on the Aventine, the old nobility allowed them access to more government posts. Out of necessity they also withdrew the prohibition on marriage between nobility and commoners, and guaranteed the lower classes their own representatives (*People's Tribunes*) with the right to veto the decisions of the Senate and the Consuls. In the end they even accepted that one of the consuls should be elected from the common people (*Plebeans*).

Of course this internal political flexibility only increased the political and economic strength abroad. The common people were only too pleased to take part in wars which brought in booty.

At the beginning of the republican era and up until about the 4th century B.C. Rome's wars were mainly fought to secure its living space. The Etruscans were still strong, and put on pressure from the north. In the southeast were the Samnites, not exactly a peaceful people, with a powerful desire for expansion. In the south, Greek colonies still withstood most of the attacks of the Italic peoples. The wars may have been purely defensive, but that didn't stop the Romans, quite as if by chance, occupying fertile lands, taking foodstuffs and goods as spoil and securing for themselves forward bases for quick raids into border country.

Let us leave the Romans their excuse that they had to defend themselves against envious, suspicious or just plain greedy neighbors. After the 3rd century B.C. at the latest this excuse was no longer valid. From this point on the Romans made war purely to further imperial interests, for the surrounding land all belonged to them. After the last Punic War, which ended in 147 B.C. with the total destruction of Carthage, they in practice controlled all Italy, as well as Sicily, Sardinia, Corsica, parts of Spain, modern Tunisia, Greece and Dalmatia.

Now pure greed took the place of calculated evening-out of spheres of influence. The Romans were unstoppable. In all parts of the empire they now went to war. The subjugation of neighboring peoples became a sort of initiation rite for up-and-coming politicians. In quick succession the generals extended the frontiers. By the middle of the last century B.C., around the time of Caesar,

tiny city of Rome in seven centuries. The maps were ordered by Benito Mussolini, dreaming of a resurgence of the Empire. What became of that dream is well known.

However imposing the Empire looked at its peak, expansion had ground to a halt. Gains in one place meant losses in another. The turning point was the battle in the Teutoburg Forest shortly after the birth of Christ, which ended with the loss of a piece of territory recently conquered by Rome. Much to the displeasure of many generals and captains of industry, the Emperor Au-

they had occupied Germany west of the Rhine, all of Spain, parts of Morocco, Libya, Egypt, Israel, Syria and parts of Asia. Shortly after the birth of Christ they added modern Bulgaria and the whole of Yugoslavia. A hundred years later they were in Britain and Albania, and had taken over the whole of Mesopotamia and further regions of North Africa.

If you go down the Via dei Fori Imperiali from the Piazza Venezia to the Colosseum you will find three maps carved in stone underneath the Basilica of Constantine. These show the gigantic expansion of the

gustus proclaimed that enough was enough. Saturation point had been reached.

His successors were less sensible. For the next three centuries the burden of military expenditure continued to grow, until finally the produce of more than two thirds of the Empire was going to the ever greedy armies. The spirit of conquest and aggression had made the spectacular blooming of Rome possible. At the same time it was the fundamental reason for its fall. The Romans continued merciless exploitation first of their own land, then of their neighbors', and finally of the whole known world, until nothing worked any more and people fled the Imperial City. Behind them they left a city which during Imperial times had blazed with more and more splendid buildings, particularly around the Imperial forums and the surrounding markets.

Even today the ruins bear eloquent witness. First of all the central area between the Capitol, Palatine, Caelian, Esquiline and Quirinal was built up. Here the swamps had once permitted no settlement. Drainage via the canal *Cloaca Maxima*—dedicated to the goddess Cloaca—had provided new room in

sense. We do have the lists of men fit for military service, which form the basis for working out the population figures. In the middle of the 3rd century B.C. there were already between 250,000 and 300,000 people living in the city, and the total population of the Empire was around 10 to 15 million. At the time of Augustus, around the birth of Christ, about a million Romans ruled an Empire of 60 to 80 million. About a third of the Romans were slaves—this figure can be established from the details given of slaves imported as booty. Another third

the city center. From the last century B.C. on the noble families and later the Emperors competed with each other to drive out the settlers and build splendid temples, palaces, theaters and other impressive buildings. These were paid for by taxes or by spoils won by the sword

We can only guess how many lived there, because there was no census in the modern

Left, Cicero appeals to the unity of Rome against the "public enemy" Catiline, fresco by Cesare Madma. Right, gladiators in combat before Nero and Agrippina.

were part-free persons of various grades. Of the remaining third of free people about 70 to 80 percent belonged to the lower middle class, small-scale craftsmen and traders. Like so many "free" people, they were totally impoverished. The wretched poverty of many is shown by the number of people who received the grain ration—a kind of ancient Social Welfare—at times this reached 200,000.

From the 5th century on the city itself expanded steadily at first, then very rapidly. The first city boundary for which we have evidence, the sacred *Pomerium*, could be measured by a line of some four miles (six km) drawn by a plough. This enclosed the one and a half square miles (three sq km) between the Palatine, Caelian, Quirinal and Esquiline hills. The so-called Servian Wall—built not as the name suggests by Servius Tullius in the 5th century B.C. but later, after serious attacks by the Gauls in 380 B.C.—was nearly six miles (four km) long.

A long period of internal security followed. Rome had no more enemies to fear and only needed to secure territorial borders.

In the 3rd century A.D. the capital had to be fortified again, following the German wars. The Aurelian Wall was built. The Aurelian Wall still stands today, apparently indestructible, but nonetheless merely a reminder of how useless was the attempt to try and postpone the fall of the Empire with this massive stonework. Modern Rome has long outgrown the 10-mile (19-km) edifice with its 380 watchtowers.

At the time when these walls were built the blooming of Rome already had a distinctly withered look. There had been no further wars of expansion—and no more rich spoils—since the 2nd century A.D. The great estates found it hard to obtain fresh supplies of slaves. One of the pillars of the Roman economy was looking decidedly shaky. The working life of slaves was short and was no longer quickly and economically replaced by raiding and booty. The Roman economy had developed no alternative means of production—quite the reverse. It was impossible to go back to using the resources of the immediate environment, as everything had been gobbled up—worse, the land had been made unusable for centuries to come. Attempts to re-cultivate the land had been made since the first centuries A.D., but they failed. Deforestation and planting with high-return vineyards and olive groves had led to the land drying out completely. The emperors pawned their possessions and ran up state debts, inflation came rushing in and the populace started panic buying. Crime figures rose enormously. Internal unrest showed the inability of the rulers to remain in control of the course of events. Towards the end of the 3rd century more than 50 emperors ruled in a space of only 70 years. Coups and counter-coups crippled the ruling classes in the same way as they drove workers and craftsmen out into the countryside.

Rome had grown great and mighty because its rulers could get the people behind them by parting with some of their rich spoils. *Panem et circenses*—bread and circuses—kept the people in a good mood and fed the expansionist spirit. But in the end there was nothing more to be shared out—neither bread nor circuses. At the start of the 4th century Constantine the Great moved the capital of the Empire far to the east, to modern Istanbul. This was the best place for administration of the Empire. The city of Rome was still great, but its monuments faded in memory and gradually crumbled physically, attacked by rain, wind and earthquake, till grass grew over the rubble.

Left, marble bust of Gaius Julius Caesar, 100 B.C.—44 B.C. Right, Gaius Octavianus 63 B.C.—A.D. 14 .

Girolamo Hewio
d 19 Maggio 85
[illegible signature]

HIC EST PP GREGORIVS
OLI EPS HOSTIENSIS
QVI HC̄ CŌ SECRAVIT ECCLESI

F POTIFICI SVML FVIT AÑO PICT SCDO FECIDŌM ꝟ IC PꝒ̄C̄E SVIO GVICTON

THE POPES AND THE REPUBLIC

In the A.D. 4th century chroniclers were still describing Rome as a "city of splendors". Reporting a visit by the Emperor Constantius II, they wrote "Whichever way the Emperor turned, he was dazzled by the great number of wonders…" But the rot had already set in some time ago. The Emperor was only visiting, his residence had been moved to *Roma nova*, modern Istanbul, much more convenient from a strategic and administrative point of view. Rome itself had for some time been on the periphery of the Empire, due to the massive conquests in the east. The whole known world had looked to Rome while the Roman Empire bloomed, but now only the facade remained of the old glories. The facade was still imposing, but politically nothing was left of the claim to be "center of the world".

A Classical Facade in Decline

Some two centuries or more later even the facade no longer existed. The city that had once housed millions had shrunk to a settlement of no more than 20,000. Among the ruined temples and impressive buildings scrub and bushes grew, meadows spread out and, increasingly, swamps returned.

Historians have been kept busy pointing out all sorts of possible reasons for the decay, from lead in the drinking water to a rapid change in climate to barbarian attacks. But none of these theories is of much use—even the attacks by barbarians (involving at most 100,000 people) would never have been able to endanger the Empire while it was intact. More convincing is the theory that the spiral of raiding, securing the spoils and more raiding simply broke down. A system of development that consists almost exclusively of the exploitation of other peoples in ever greater numbers must reach its limits

Left, Emperor Gaius Octavius Augustus, first Roman Emperor (63 B.C.—A.D. 14). Also known as Caesar Augustus, he was deified after death.

sometime. The organization of the gigantic Empire ground to a halt, and this was first noticed at the center. Already in the first century B.C. a widespread withdrawal to the country was in evidence. The emperors were followed by the upper classes, then by the middle classes, whose profits were getting smaller all the time, because the tax burden needed to pay for the military and the bureaucracy was getting ever greater. Finally the workers and slaves left and hid in the country.

The Western Empire, all that was left to Rome, finally collapsed with the death of the last Emperor Romulus Augustulus in A.D. 476. At the same time another power arose to fill the vacuum—the church. Not Christianity, as many history books claim, but the church as an institution, a tightly organized machine, with its own administration and an efficient executive power. The successors of Peter, with astonishing pragmatism, had, in the two and a half centuries of their existence, picked the brains of the once excellent administration of Rome and perfected many aspects of it. These ranged from a hierarchical structure with democratic elements, such as the election of bishops and popes, to the division of the church along the old lines of *dioceses*.

The last anti-clerical revolt died out in A.D. 363 with the death of the Emperor Julian the Apostate. An imperial declaration, the *Edict of Thessalonika*, made Christianity into a state religion in 380. This declaration was the start of the *Primacy of the Bishop of Rome* in the Catholic church. In the 4th century Emperor Constantine the Great incorporated an efficiently organized church into his system of government and strengthened it considerably. On the other hand this soon led to the state being an instrument of the church.

The church started to lay undisguised claim to temporal power as early as the reign of Pope Celestine (5th century). Gradually the popes organized their "new Rome" and began to make alliances with their strengthened neighbors to the north, the Merovingians and Franks. A visible result of the church's assumption of power was the increasing number of Christian sacred buildings in Rome. The four great basilicas—S. Paolo fuori le mura, S. Pietro, S. Giovanni in Laterano, and S. Maria Maggiore—were built between the 3rd and the 4th century. Shortly afterwards the series of seven "classical" major Roman churches was complete with the addition of S. Lorenzo, Santa Croce in Gerusalemme and S. Sebastiano.

But the popes were not only concerned as *Holy Roman Emperors of the German Nation*, and the popes opened up more freedom for the strengthened citizens. Hundreds of fortified towers built by power-seeking families sprang up in the city. Pope Leo IV took the opportunity offered by the Arab sack of St. Peters to surround the Vatican by building the *Muro Leonino*, while the supporters of civic independence continued to fight each other, divided into *Guelfi* (loyal to the Papacy) and *Ghibellini* (loyal to the Holy Roman Empire). The popes were usually on the "Italian" side, but could and did change

with sacred matters. The Castel Sant' Angelo, once a Mausoleum for the imperial family of Hadrian, gave them control of the access to Rome. It also guaranteed that they could keep an eye on the Roman people, who lived in the crowded area in the curve of the Tiber opposite the Castel Sant' Angelo. It was also a protection against attacks by the roaming armies of the times. In the 8th century the popes set up a Roman civic army, made up of Langobards, Saxons, Franks, and Byzantines, the *Exercitus*.

The continuing struggle between the northern rulers, even though they functioned sides quickly.

A hideous climax of the struggle and nadir of the Papacy was the macabre trial of his *Ghibelline* predecessor Formoso called by the *Guelf* Pope Stephen VI in 897. The corpse of the dead Pope Formoso was summoned to come in person before a tribunal of the Synod. He was dug up out of his grave, in which he had lain for eight months, and dressed in papal robes. In the council hall the corpse was placed on a table. Pope Stephen's counsel rose and accused the loathsome corpse. After the verdict of guilty the clothes were torn off the corpse and the three fingers of the right hand that the dead Pope had used for blessing were cut off. The body was then thrown into the Tiber. Fishermen later found it intact—according to legend—and after the death of his accuser, Pope Formoso was re-buried in St. Peter's with full honors.

Civil Rights

After a series of unsuccessful campaigns in the 14th century the popes ended up in Avignon, half as prisoners, for around 70 years. The most interesting political experi-

turies had been turning Rome into a battlefield with their blood feuds and had filled the city with hundreds of fortified towers. He began thorough reforms of the army and the legal and financial systems. At first he was frenetically hailed by the intellectuals of his time. But his demands for the immediate unification of Italy ran counter to the interests of the small state politics of the other cities, and he made the mistake of tacking to and fro in his alliances with the emperor, the pope and the cities.

Excommunicated by Pope Clement VI, he

ment of this time was the return to an autonomous civic constitution based on the ancient Republic and brought about by the demagogue Cola di Rienzo.

Rienzo had become familiar with papal circles first as Ambassador to the Court of Avignon, later as papal steward in Rome. In 1347 he declared Rome a republic. He drove out the great noble families, which for cen-

Left, the Emperor Constantine I, known as the "Great", after a 13th-century fresco. Above, siege of Rome by the Ostrogoth King Vitiges, in the 6th century A.D.

fled to the Prague of Emperor Charles IV, but was extradited to Avignon. In the meantime Innocent VI had become Holy Father, and he sent his uncomfortable guest back to Rome as a senator. However, open hostility awaited him on the banks of the Tiber. The intellectuals had turned away, and the people no longer understood his wheeling and dealing with the great powers. A few days after declaring the Republic for a second time he was murdered. These troubles were a signal to the popes that Rome would not liberate itself, so they prepared to return as masters of the city.

Francesa, the cars and impressions of the Baroque.

Medieval Rome seemed to its contemporaries to be a mixture of city and country. After the regulation search by papal mercenaries, the traveler would go through an arch in the Aurelian Wall only to end up in the countryside again. The mantle of Rome, dating from imperial times, was too big for the papal city. Only a small part of ancient Rome "entro le mura"—between the walls—was inhabited. The population was a mere 30,000, squeezed into the inhabited part in the bend of the Tiber opposite the Castel Sant' Angelo, a grandiose and phantasmal picture of alternating ancient ruins and grimy alleys.

The town was dominated not by the Romanesque campanile, so impressive nowadays, but by the fortified towers of noble families whose blood feuds split commoners and barons alike. Power lay in the hands of the old feudal families, in particular the Orsini and the Colonna. The nobility of the city lost their historical and spiritual legitimacy after the popes moved out in 1309. The "elite" of Rome sank to the level of cattle raiders and land thieves. Only if you keep this low point in mind can you really appreciate the subsequent resurgence.

A Glorious Resurgence

"Gregory XI returned to Rome on January 17th, 1377, in a solemn procession through the Gate of St. Paul. A crowd of dancers, dressed in white, leaped and clapped their hands before him. The Eternal City tried to polish up its miserable image as well as it could. Carpets lay on the badly paved streets, gates, doors and windows were decorated. The cheering populace on the rooftops threw a rain of flowers onto the

Left, Castel Sant' Angelo, former Mausoleum of the Emperor Hadrian, became a fort at the bend of the Tiber.

horses of the Holy Father, who had come at last to give the Papacy back to the city for ever—and take its freedom away for ever."
(F. Gregorovius)

Gregory died soon after, in 1378. The entry through the Porta S. Paolo can be seen in a relief on his tomb in the church S. Francesca Romana at the edge of the Forum. The Holy See floats in the clouds, and an angel flies through the air bearing the insignia of the Papacy, tiara and the keys of Peter, symbol of power over *urbi et orbi*, city and world. Nowadays, most Romans are familiar with the church as a place for weddings, or for a rather singular benediction: on March 9, St. Francesca's day, a huge number of cars line up between the church and the Colosseum to be blessed—St. Francesca is patron saint of car drivers.

But to go back to the Rome of the Middle Ages. The reality was of a wretched city of ill-smelling alleys with malaria in the diseased marshes. But there was also the *myth* that claimed Rome to be *caput mundi*, ruler of the world, "founded by Romulus, strengthened by Julius Caesar, expanded by Augustus and affirmed by our Saviour".

When they returned from exile in Avignon, the popes used this myth to raise their own standing after the humiliations imposed by the French kings. The squabbling nobility had realized that their own status was bound up with that of the popes. In a treaty with Gregory they withdrew all claims to their rights, without realizing that they had done so for ever. The city made over to the popes all bridges, gates, towers and fortifications—especially the Castel Sant' Angelo. One of the conditions for the pope's return had now been met—he was military commander of Rome. The other was the creation of his own state with Rome as its capital.

In theory, land for a papal state had existed since the Donation of Pepin in the 8th century—even if not from the forged *Donation of Constantine*, with which the popes liked to justify their papal lands. But even in the middle of the 14th century this area—comprising all of central Italy up as far as Florence, Siena and a few other enclaves—was a kind of "nomansland claimed by all sides" (Procacci).

It was a colorful mosaic of city states, lordships, monastic estates and independent communities in the mountains, of which the Republic of San Marino has survived to this day. The popes had to thank the diplomatic skills of Cardinal Gil d'Alberonz—he even tried military persuasion—that it became a state with its own tax revenues, making the

building site) or in the out-of-the-way Lateran Palace, seat of medieval popes, but in the center of Rome, right at the foot of the Capitol.

The Papal Capitol

A start had been made, and now that the Schism, the split in the western church (1378-1418 or 1449) was over, the Papacy could turn itself into an Italian superpower. "It moved into its most glorious epoch, a temporal and spiritual princedom, and its

popes independent once more of European powers. Now they not only ruled the souls of all Christians, but also the bodies and lives of their own subjects.

Now they intended the glory of imperial Rome to shine anew. Nicholas V ascended to the See of Peter in 1447. He was an ardent believer in imperial might. One of the greatest cultural reforms in history—later known as the *Renaissance*—was changing everything in the church, in politics and in society. Successors like Pope Paul II (1464-1471) tried to symbolize the rebirth of antiquity by residing neither in the secure Vatican (still a

darkest phase as a Christian priesthood." (Gregorovius)

The dualism of imperial and papal, the first division of power of the post-Christian era, might have become fragile. The "peril of the Turks" and the new opposition between nation-states and hereditary kingships had taken the wind out of the pope's sails. The last coronation of a German prince as emperor in Rome, held in 1452, was no more than an empty gesture. In the early 16th century the Medici Pope Clement VII wanted to be more than an extra on the political stage, but paid for his ambition with the occupation and sack of the city by mercenaries during the "Sacco di Roma" (1527).

An Artists' Enclave

"Under the rule of the Medici Popes, Rome, more than any other Italian city, turned into one great artist's studio", writes Procacci. In Leo's time the intellectual and artistic activity centered on Rome reached an intensity never known before. Ariosto published *Orlando Furioso* (1516), Raffael painted the *"School of Athens"* (1510), and

Reformation

The next century showed all the signs of an attempt to find a new role, as well as the dramatically worldly fleshing out of a spiritual vocation. All efforts at reform were resisted until it was too late. After Martin Luther's Reformation, western Christianity split into Protestants and Catholics. Also dramatic were the belated attempts at reform passed at the Council of Trent—reform through reaction. Reform movements of church and state were repressed; scientific

above all Michelangelo was drawn away from his native Tuscany again and again to Rome and the court of his Medici patrons, who wanted to bring him out of Florence "into Italy". But Raffael's death in 1520 meant the early loss of one of the stars of the artistic firmament. The pressures of reality turned the Renaissance style more and more towards Mannerism.

Left, view of Rome in the 18th century, painting by Caspa Vanvitelli. Above, St. Peter's in the 18th century by Giovanni B. Piranosi.

discoveries such as those of Galileo were suppressed and the discoverers sometimes destroyed, as was Giordano Bruno; books were placed "on the Index" and the Inquisition was renewed. However, some abuses were also removed, such as the sale of indulgences, which had been one of the starting points of the Reformation.

The new post-Tridentine self confidence of a church which believed that it had successfully countered all attacks was above all reflected in the new style of the times. Unity, power and strength are the external signs of the splendor of the Baroque age. The Pa-

STATUES AND PALÄCES

Michelangelo in Rome: Michelangelo Buonarroti was born in Caprese on March 6, 1475 and grew up in Florence. After an apprenticeship with the painter Ghirlandaio he was taken up at the court of that great patron of the arts, Lorenzo Medici "il Magnifico". The sculptor Bartoldo di Giovanni taught him the skill of working the white stuff of dreams. Throughout his life he was praised and damned by the popes, he intrigued, suffered and created. The bulk of his work can be seen in Rome. First, the *"Pietà"* in St. Peter's

he worked on the square by the Capitol, the upper story of the Palazzo Farnese and its cornice, the Porta Pia and the church of S. Maria degli Angeli within the Baths of Diocletian. After serving under 13 popes, Michelangelo died on Feb. 18, 1564 at the age of 88—"God's own child", who had shaped the face of Rome more than anyone who came after.

The Papal Capitol: The Capitol was the heart of Rome in ancient times. A thick layer of earth covered the rubble and ruins. Goats

(1496-1501). Four years later he contracted to build a gigantic tomb for his patron, Pope Julius II, which he was never to finish. After 40 years of work and endless disputes with the della Rovere family, three of the 40 planned statues were completed: *"Moses"*, *"Rachel"* and *"Leah"*, now in S. Pietro in Vincoli. From 1508 to 1512 he worked on the *"Creation"*, frescos on the ceiling of the Sistine Chapel, where he, from 1543 - 41, worked on the *"Last Judgment"*. Michelangelo, undisputably number one in papal Rome, was appointed architect of the new church of St. Peter in 1547. At the same time

grazed on the hill, giving it its nickname of Monte Caprino. The Forum Romanum was called Campo Vaccini, the cow pasture. This was the area chosen by Paul for his papal palace, the Palazzo Venezia. For the first time motifs from classical architecture were re-used. The Popes resided here before they moved to the Vatican. The Capitol is a fine example of the inclusion of classical art into city planning—Michelangelo's piazza with the statue of Marcus Aurelius, which was set up in 1538. It was taken for restoration in 1984 and will probably never be shown in the open air again because of pollution.

Palazzo Madama: Giovanni de Medici, later Pope Leo X (1513-1521), bought the Palazzo Madama in Rome when he was made cardinal. Here Giulio, later Pope Clement VII (1523-1534), another member of this illustrious family, also resided, as did Catherine of France. Giuliano, brother of Leo, married the Duchess of Savoy, an aunt of the King of France. In this way the banking family of the Medici combined papacy and royal power. Leo made the Palazzo Madama a center of the Roman Renais-

ment, has been meeting here since 1871, as can be seen from the guard of honor from the three armed forces posted at the gates.

Palazzo Barberini: Three architects worked on the family palace of Pope Urban VIII (1623-1644) on the Via delle Quattro Fontane: Maderna, Bernini and Borromini—the most important artists of the time, together with Cortona. The Palazzo Barberini is an expression of the political and economic strengthening of the papacy after the Council of Trent. It's a provincial

sance, although he never realized his idea of extending it as far as the Piazza Navona. At the same time he sponsored the restoration of the Roman university, and Clement began the work of building the church opposite, S. Luigi dei Franecesi. The Palazzo Madama takes its name from Madama Margherita of Habsburg, wife of Alessandro de Medici and a daughter of Charles V. It received its present facade during the Baroque era. The Senate, second house of the Italian parlia-

From left to right: Pope Sixtus; Pope Leo X; and magnificent fountain of the papal residence.

strengthening: Rome and the religious state are firmly in the hand of the Pontifex, and outside its borders he has (almost) no part to play. In the salon, Pietro de Cortona has possibly created *the* fresco of high Baroque times. The message of the "Triumph of Providence" is clear. No more do God the Father and Son stand in the center, but three bees, coat of arms of the Barberini. Today the Palazzo Barberini contains the Galleria d'Arte Antica, which concentrates on the years from early Renaissance to late Baroque—the time of greatness for the Popes in Rome.

lazzo Barberini is a classic example. During these years Rome was turned into a giant building site by popes hungry for glory.

A Building Craze

New roads broke through the twisting alleys of the old city, Renaissance facades were re-styled—S. Maria della Pace is an example—obelisks were used as symbols of power and dragged from one place in the city to another. This craze for building, which mostly took place at the expense of ancient

remains, exploited now as cheap quarries, was summed up in the popular slogan: "What the barbarians couldn't do, the Barberini did."

Between 1590 and 1650 the false impression of a unified, perfect world—long since torn apart in struggles between various nations and creeds—was given to the churches in the guise of mighty Baroque domes.

When Urban died in 1644, and, four years later, the Peace of distant Westfalia ended the Thirty Years War, calm returned to Europe. Urban's successors to the See of Peter gradually ran out of money and could

no longer finance great building programs. Very gradually an epoch died out. For the last time Rome had set the style for the whole world. It was not as a spiritual or temporal power, but as the "cultural" center of Europe that it became a model for the residences of absolute rulers.

In the 18th century even this claim collapsed. We can see the final "twitch" of building fever and papal nepotism, the old custom of popes giving their families a palace, in the Palazzo Braschi. It was built by Pius VI in 1792 for his nephew Luigi. The political center of gravity of Europe had moved north. The English and the Dutch ruled the seas, England underwent its Industrial Revolution, and in France the first citizen's revolution triumphed. London, Paris and Vienna blossomed, but Rome fell into a stupor, only awakened—apart from a brief interruption by Napoleon—by the Piedmontese troops of General Cadorna.

In the stretch of time between Jan. 17, 1337 and Sept. 20, 1870, the rulers of the Vatican shaped Rome "entro le mura" to such an extent that it is largely the city we see now. We are justified in referring to this period as "papal Rome".

Closing Lines

In 1796 Rome was of more importance as the destination of English lords and German bourgeois making the "Grand Tour" than as a center of any political or religious movement. In this year the German poet Goethe wrote to his friends Johann Gottfried and Caroline Herder:

"10th November, Rome. In the evening we came to the Colissee, when it was twilight; when one regards it, all else seems small. It is so great that one cannot hold the image in one's soul, one remembers it as being smaller, and when one returns, it seems greater yet again. Farewell. I could continue to write thus for ever. My paper is at an end, but I am not."

Above, Pope Innocent X. Right, the popes resided here.

UNITY AND MODERN TIMES

On Sept. 20, 1870, Rome and the remaining church state were surrounded by Italian troops. Right up till the end Pope Pius IX had refused to surrender the city. The gates were barricaded and each one was defended by papal mercenaries. The Piedmontese general Luigi Cadorna decided to have a breach shot through the old Roman walls of the Emperor Aurelian.

This was at the Porta Pia, and is still commemorated today by the Bersagliere monument. At 11 a.m. the liberators marched into the city without meeting further resistance.

This colorful and harmless fireworks display ended eleven centuries of temporal rule by the church. It also ended the anachronistic idyll of the pope ruling as absolutely as the Dalai Lama in his own religious state.

The rule wasn't always idyllic, as is shown by the memorial tablets at the entrance to the Piazza del Popolo. These commemorate the *carbonari*, patriots of the Italian national and democratic movement, executed in 1825 "without evidence and without defence", as the inscription on the building opposite the entrance to the church of Santa Maria del Popolo reads. The opera *Tosca* by Giovanni Puccini (1900) describes the suffering of the patriots incarcerated in the Castel Sant'Angelo.

Ignoring protests by the Vatican the new Italian state put up memorials to clerical intolerance, for instance on the Campo dei Fiori to Giordano Bruno, burnt at the stake during the Holy Year 1600 for his ideas. Like Galileo, he held that the sun was the center of the solar system and not the earth. Bruno did not recant and was burned. A memorial was also set up for Angelo Brunetti, known as *Ciceruacchio*, a leader of the Roman Republic of 1849. Both statues look accusingly towards the Vatican. The monument for Brunetti, seized by the Austrians while fleeing from the pope and executed on the spot, has the concise inscription: *To Ciceruacchio, from the people.*

At the start of the 19th century the French author Stendhal wrote "Papal administration is particularly hard to understand, as there has never been a more badly organized system." Living with inefficiency has been so familiar to the Romans for centuries that even today a sensible government hasn't much chance in Rome. Only rarely did the "Roman people" develop a sense of democracy, as for instance at the declaration of a *Roman republic* led by national heroes such as Guiseppe Mazzini and Guiseppe Garibaldi. After a few months, however, the revolution was crushed and the democratic leaders were exiled, imprisoned or executed. The pope re-imposed the old order with the help of French troops.

His reply to the 1849 Revolution was to announce, on Dec. 8, 1854, the doctrine of the Immaculate Conception. Not far from the Spanish Steps, in front of the "Ministry for the Propagation of the Faith" (*di propaganda fide*), a statue of Mary was placed on an ancient pillar. The pope places a wreath on it in an annual solemn ceremony on December 8.

The First Vatican Council was called in 1869. In spite of the doubts of contemporary theologians, the doctrine of papal infallibility in matters of faith was announced in July 1870. The more the clerical state crumbled, the more authoritarian the pope became in matters of faith. But neither Pius IX or his successor hit on the sensible idea, long overdue and supported even in clerical circles, of voluntarily giving up the claim to temporal authority. After Rome had been declared the capital of the new Italy the pope withdrew grumbling to the Vatican and considered himself a "prisoner" of Italy. He refused to come to agreement with the Piedmontese royal family, excommunicated them and

Preceding pages, one of the greatest masterpieces in the Sistine Chapel: Michelangelo's ceiling fresco (1508-12). Left, Guiseppe Verdi, the mentor and the leading Italian composer of 19th-century Italy who provided the principal form of public entertainment of the century.

forbade participation in politics to all the faithful.

A concordat of church and state ending the old dispute was only reached in 1929, under the Fascists, of all people. As a sign of reconciliation the Via della Concilazione was built. Old and picturesque streets were torn down to make room for the masses of pilgrims and tourists to walk up to St. Peter's Square, as they can still be seen doing daily.

When Rome became capital of a young nation in 1871 it had about 200,000 inhabitants, of whom about a third were beggars.

achieved almost nothing positive.

The new Italy had inherited a heavy burden in the form of the run-down city. However, instead of well-planned development, they often came up with nothing but destruction, corruption and nationalist rhetoric. An example is the Altare della Patria, a monument that took from 1885 to 1911 to build, swallowed enormous sums of money and destroyed half the Capitol. The nation wanted to take over the Roman Capitol with this monument. It was intended to overshadow everything ever built by the Ro-

There were craftsmen, but no industry. Flood water several feet deep regularly flowed from the Tiber into the Old City after every heavy rainfall. This extent of the flooding can still be seen in the high water marks on the facade of the church of Santa Maria Sopra Minerva. The surrounding countryside was mostly barren, made extremely unsafe by bandits and infested with malaria. The money of the papal government had been spent on the luxurious lifestyle of the cardinals and on great religious occasions, but not on the social infrastructure. In the last hundred years the popes had

mans, the emperors and the popes. But it remains a sorry intruder which has nothing in common with the universal claims of the Roman Empire of the church. The size, the proportions, even the color of the limestone from Brescia doesn't fit the Roman style.

A long series of macabre and sinister acts of nationalist history were celebrated here: the entombment of the Unknown Soldier from World War I, at whose tomb guards-of-honor from all regiments still stand; the march of the women who sacrificed the gold of their wedding rings to pay for World War II; and, also macabre, the cheering of tens of thousands at the founding of a new empire after the African conquests in 1936. A sinister act was the bombing on Dec. 11, 1969 of the "Altar of the Fatherland", planned by Neofascists to coincide with the attack on the Banca dell' Agricoltura on the Piazza Fontana in Milan. The Fascist bomb in Milan killed 16 people, but the attack in Rome claimed no lives—only material damage was done.

If this monument is taken to represent the character of the ruling classes of the "New Italy", the verdict could only be damning. It

1910), was to be the third great mass of stone beside St. Peter's and the Castel Sant' Angelo. But after a mere hundred years the new building shows cracks, the foundations are steadily sinking, the edges of the roof are falling off and the entrances are barred. Its contemporaries already judged it harshly "It seems to us, rather than a palace of justice, to be the seat of a tyrant in some northern Babylon." (Ugo Fleres, 1911)

The feverish building activity between 1870 and 1914 was often interrupted by crises. Among its positive achievements

is a giant gravestone under which the democratic and republican ideals of the Italian *Risorgimento* (resurrection) and the 1849 Revolution lie buried. The "New Italy" mostly built ministries and barracks in Rome, but also a Palace of Justice which, according to the opinion of the time (1889 to

was the regulation of the Tiber, sponsored by Garibaldi. Its banks were straightened and ran between massive quays, copied from those in Paris. Today Garibaldi's equestrian statue looks out from the Gianicolo—site of the battles of 1849—across the bend of the Tiber.

Another successful addition dating from the founding years is the quarter of Prati, built after 1880. A residential quarter for civil servants was built on meadows to the north of Castel Sant'Angelo. The civil servants were to be loyal to the new state, and the streets and boulevards were planned so

Left, Giuseppe Garibaldi defending the Roman Republic against the French on June 30, 1849. Garibaldi was known in his day as a great revolutionary and one of the most skilful guerrilla generals of the time. Above, memorial to King Vittorio Emanuele II.

that they gave no point of contact with the Vatican and pushed it, in planning terms, to the periphery. Other newly built up areas, especially around the Piazza Barberini and the Via Veneto, were built in the gardens of villas and parks, for instance in the park of the Villa Ludovisi. These were supposed to be among the finest gardens in the world and were irretrievably destroyed.

The building boom wasn't only good for speculators, it brought a new class into being—the builders. Anarchist and socialist ideas circulated among them, and up until 20 years ago builders and railway workers were the mainstay of the Roman workers' movement. Industrial workers have no historical roots in Rome. Already in 1871 the decision was taken to allow no heavy industry in Rome—not for aesthetic, but for security reasons. Fear of 1871 Paris Commune was in the bones of the new rulers, and the new capital was to be "worker-free". The builders were carefully watched and had no residence permits. Most were commuters or lived in illegal barracks on site or at the brickworks. So Rome remained a deeply conservative city. Until after World War II nobility and land were what mattered.

The middle classes were formed of academics and civil servants, and the Plebs were banished, as they had been a thousand years before, to the alleys and the backyards of the palaces, while shanty towns reminiscent of the Third World grew around the periphery. "This capital," wrote Alberto Moravia, "had no society that would have been able to represent the whole nation." However, landowners, civil servants and Plebs did have a common factor in their lifestyle—to survive without too much effort.

"March on Rome"

The *March on Rome* in 1922 brought Fascism to power, supposedly heralding a new era but doing nothing to change the character of this city. In the first speech he made after the march on Rome, Mussolini declared, "I could have transformed this gray hall into an armed camp of Blackshirts,

a bivouac for corpses. I could have nailed up the doors of Parliament." And Rome was supposed to resume its role as *caput mundi*, center of a new empire. All that is left of that dream are the huge gaps Mussolini had hewn in the Old City, according to his views: "All merely picturesque things are to be swept away and must make room for the dignity, the hygiene, the beauty of the capital...It is necessary to reconcile the demands of ancient and of modern Rome...The new Italian and his attitudes are formed in the bracing climate of the capital." Rome was to be the cultural and political center of a "Latin bloc of states, encompassing the Iberian peninsula and stretching across to Latin America". Pope Pius, a man of similar cultural stance, echoed "Rome is the new Zion and all peoples that live in the Roman faith are Romans." Mussolini countered with "The cross follows the eagle's flight."

Most of the planned buildings of this time—the modern churches of Pius XII, the Fascist public buildings—were realized and completed after World War II. Symbolic of the continuity between Fascist and post-war Christian Democrat Rome are the "tablets of history" in the Foro Italico which show the stages of the "Fascist Revolution".

The first tablet begins with Italy's entry into the war on May 23, 1915, the last one inscribed by the Fascists celebrates the founding of the empire on May 9, 1936. Thereafter things become much more peaceful: overthrow of the Fascists July 23, 1943, referendum in favor of the Republic July 2, 1946, declaration of the Constitution January 1948. In front of the Forum, opposite the bridge of the Duca d'Aosta—built in 1938/ 39 as the "hero's bridge"—there stands an obelisk with the still clearly legible inscription *Mussolini Dux*. Hardly anyone pays any attention to it today. "Eternal Rome" has its own method of teaching history.

Right, Benito Mussolini holding one of his speeches from the balcony of the Palazzo Venezia. Mussolini, leader of the "Blackshirts", the Italian Fascists, was the authoritarian head of the Italian state for more than 20 years.

Illustrious visitors come looking for history, but first they have to take a deep breath before trying to link up the Roman reality they find with imagined ancient greatness. There is a long list of complaints about the way in which the Romans treat the remains of their own history.

Majoran, one of the West Roman Emperors, accused his contemporaries of obtaining the necessary material to build new houses by tearing down "magnificent old buildings". Pope Pius II shuddered at the crime committed by those Romans who burned marble monuments to obtain lime. Even popular slogans joked at the expense of Urban VIII: "What the barbarians couldn't do, the Barberini did."

The poet Goethe complained "What the barbarians left standing, contemporary architects have destroyed." Ferdinand Gregorovius raised his voice in a thunderous outcry, as the Piedmontese re-modeled the papal city. "The Italians are destroying Rome" was his verdict. And Alberto Moravia classified four-fifths of the city as "a disaster area of civic architecture".

And yet all these sharp-tongued critics stayed in Rome for months and years, lived here, and wouldn't have dreamed of moving out of the city. What draws people to this city, and what keeps them here? Maybe it is the wish to excavate just a little more, to discover an aspect of Rome that no-one has seen before. Perhaps it's the first moment in front of a building whose foundation walls are formed by a Roman temple, with a first story built on in the early Middle Ages, a second story stuck on during the Renaissance, a third in Baroque times and a modern roof garden built in the 1960s.

For this is the aspect Rome shows us: one layer on top of the other, a city standing on the shoulders of its predecessors. Here nothing is made history, all the stones stay in circulation. This is the particularly exciting

thing about Rome. As in a dissection of tissue, all these layers can be clearly seen but are inseparably bound up with one another. You can dissect from top to bottom, as in the Senatorial Palace; the bottom layers, for instance in San Clemente; layers running into each as at the Theatre of Marcellus, or lying side by side—next to the portico of the Emperor Augustus' sister, the kosher butcher sells his Rabbi-approved chicken drumsticks and through the hideous new housing estate runs an old water supply pipe, still in use.

Visible aspects of ancient Roman belief are the *madonelle*, little statues of the Madonna on corners and buildings. They are to protect the houses, and lit up the streets in the times before electric light.

A Visible Past

The past, telling the story of Rome's development, is scattered over the modern face of Rome. Only the myth remains of those ancient huts on the Palatine, but the essential feature of Italian life—the piazza—was created by republican Rome. These beginnings left us with a square between the Comitium, the actual Forum, the place of the people. Around its edges traders sold meat at first, and then later precious silver.

Caesar's Rome saw the beginning of a practice that changed the face of Rome again and again. A Commission for the improvement of the city began its work; this was highly necessary, for the face of Rome was nowhere near as splendid as its imperial role demanded. "How strange that everywhere we were invited in Rome, we ate off the same silver plates," reported the Carthaginian Ambassador a hundred years before Caesar's time. But soon Rome could show off its wealth. At the Games, Caesar had 640 gladiators appear in silver armor. Rome had to wait till Caesar's time for the Senate to agree to the building of the first theater, the Theater of Pompey. It was very nearly standing room only, because seats in the theater might have

Preceding page: in the Forum Boarium. Left, exhibition scaffolding in the EUR district.

tempted the Romans to sweet idleness.

The Julian Basilica was the proper solution to the needs of a city which now had more than a million inhabitants. The new piazza, surrounded by a double row of buildings, had little shops along one side. They were divided into mezzanine floors and had embossed rounded arches, models for Renaissance architecture. The new city plan combined glory for the Julian *gens* with usefulness for the people.

The Emperor Augustus boasted that he had found Rome made of brick and left it

Rome was heavily built up. The *insulae* or apartment blocks rose up so high that after the fire a decree of Nero's limited their height to 60 feet (20 meters). After the fire, which destroyed the whole city center, a vigorous argument began between the lovers of old historic Rome, who wanted the dim picturesque alleys retained, and Nero the innovator, who wanted broad avenues and low buildings. Nero forbade the use of wooden ceilings and insisted on the provision of water buckets in houses. A basic feature of Roman history was built by the

made of marble, and managed to restore temples as well. This project was made possible by the discovery of marble in the Appenine Hills. Under Augustus the urbanization of the Campus Martius began. The sundial was built, and its central obelisk can now be seen in front of the parliament building. Rome's division into "Rioni" had its origins here too. The city was intended to develop in the shape of a six-pointed star, supposedly suggested by a comet that Augustus had seen as a young man. The marble remnants of ancient times that we find in today's buildings mostly date from this time.

Flavians, who destroyed Nero's Golden House (it covered 346 acres/140 hectares) and built the Colosseum. Enforced clearance now had a historical precedent. Domitian's legacy to Rome was the Stadium, a Hellenistic building that underlies the Piazza Navona.

Reconstruction of Rome

Trajan's master builder would have deserved a place among the most modern architects. While building the Forum, Apollodorus of Damascus (active early 2nd century A.D.) still followed the Greek-Roman Mediterranean style, but in Trajan's Market he designed completely new interiors. Row upon row of windows and domes made an unprecedented amount of interior light available, and were precursors of the Romance and Gothic styles.

A thousand years had now passed since Rome was founded, and another thousand were to pass before the city had another facelift. In 1447, under Nicholas V, a start was made on the Renaissance and Baroque aspects of Rome. Nicholas began a program

Sixtus IV had the first bridge over the Tiber for more than 1,000 years built. Alexander VI, the Borgia Pope, fortified the Castel Sant' Angelo and started work on the Palazzo della Cancelleria. His successor was Julius II, whose personal architect Bramante—satirized as Maestro Ruinante—worked on the new St. Peter's. Michelangelo re-designed the Capitol. Leo X had the Via Ripetta built, in order to link up the family palace of the Medici with the Porto di Ripetta. Another Medici, Clement VII, had the Via del Babuino built and thus

for the rebuilding of many of Rome's architectural wonders, including St. Peter's Church, and became the patron of many artists, artisans, Humanists, and literary scholars. The process ended in 1590 with Sixtus V. Nicholas decided to leave the Lateran palace, and the seat of papal power shifted to the Vatican. He laid the foundations for the facade of papal Rome, though this was completed by his successor.

Left, a statue on the Ponte Sant' Angelo being restored. Above, flea market with the "new" antiquities along the Acqua Felia' acqueduct.

created the "trinity" of streets at the Piazza del Popolo.

The Early Street System

Sixtus V perfected all previous efforts. His main innovation was that he thought more of improving road communications for pilgrim traffic and less of hospices. A network of streets was drawn up linking all the city gates. It is still the definitive street system of the Old City. The Via Felice connected the Porta del Popolo in the north with S. Maria Maggiore and S. Croce in Gerusalemme. With the existing streets it formed a system with four nodal points, at which obelisks were erected: Piazza del Popolo, S. Maria Maggiore, S. Giovanni and S. Pietro. Sixtus' short period of office prevented the demolition of the Colosseum, which blocked his direct route from the Lateran palace to St. Peter's. The visitors in the Holy Year of 1600 saw an image of an ordered world, only spoiled by the numerous thieves, as contemporaries complained.

The next "improvements committee" was brought to Rome by the French army. The

architect Joseph Valadier re-designed the Piazza del Popolo and built the terrace on the Pincio—but then came Waterloo. But signs of modern times moved into Rome even before the Piedmontese: in 1856 the railway line from Rome to Frascati was opened, and the decision was taken to build the Stazione Termini where they stand today.

After unification came the next measures for improvement (1881), with visible results in the Tiber walls and the network of main roads through the papal city that angered Gregorovius so much. The "Piedmontese Quarter" followed, the ministries built

around the Piazza Vittorio Emanuele, and, just before the next great demolition, the Coppedé Quarter. Mussolini cut through medieval Rome, with the well-known results of the Via dei Fori Imperiali, the Foro Italico and the EUR. His time is also responsible for the beginning of those four-fifths of architectural disaster areas of which Moravia complained.

However, the actual creator of this concrete high-rise aspect of Rome was Salvatore Rebecchini, Mayor of Rome from 1947 to 1956. If the mercenaries of Charles V were responsible for the first "Sacco di Roma", and the speculators of the young Italian nation for the second, Rebecchini created a third. Speculators would give the city a green meadow, which the city then opened up by providing power and water. Speculators, church foundations and holy orders then cashed in on the fortyfold rise in price of the neighboring pieces of land.

Planning permission was given to film starlets and diplomats to build along the Via Appia. Indeed, Rebecchini's first stumbling block didn't come till the attempt to build the Hilton in the green belt of the Monte Mario. However, Rome has continued to expand at such a rate since 1961 that the Agro Romano has now disappeared inside the Reccordo Annulare. Six hundred thousand people moved into developments which had never been planned by any commission and the number of Borgate, known as "Suburbi", rose from six to 26. Not even the communist administration from 1976 to 1985 could master the perverse system of "clearing" and then sanctioning illegally built Borgate.

The project "Roma Capitale" is supposed to clear all this up by the year 2000. The ministries are leaving the Old City, the Underground is being extended and illegal building is to be stopped. Then the long-awaited Archaeological Park, unifying the ancient city center, will be a pedestrian oasis among old ruins. That at least is the plan.

Above, in the Foro Italico, the district planned by Mussolini and opened for the Olympic Games. Right, palms and orange trees in the city center.

RHYTHMS OF CITY LIFE

Life in this city is much more unhurried than the first impression of noise and confusion leads you to believe.

The visitor first discovers this when his train arrives at the Stazione Termini and he looks around desperately for a porter. The porter would come, but among the travelers he's just spotted the nephew of the sister of his neighbor Jolanda. It's far more important to him at the moment to hear the latest news of Zio Pepe. After all, everyone knows that he, a member of the Porter's Co-operative at the station, has never neglected his duty.

The different sense of time, the real basic rhythm of Rome, comes over the visitor on his first visit to a bank. In the last few years the queue, even in Italy, has replaced the previously customary jumble of people, but this queue is being pleasantly entertained by a certain Marta, who is exchanging news of her far-reaching network of contacts with the cashier.

Romans view authority with a deep-seated mistrust, and try to overcome this by taking officials into the family, so to speak. Either they are already blood relations (a cousin three times removed counts here), or they come from the same village, or they are former colleagues. Everyone is always looking for contacts. In the end a sure thing is discovered, the queue jerks forward, and dazed North European and American tourists wake up again.

Noise and a superficial bustle are among the mechanisms that protect the Romans against high expectations and crowding. The inhabitants of this city are highly allergic to both. This has something to do with the fact that even nowadays most of Rome's population wasn't born in the city. Rome is only just beginning to come together as a city. The great majority of people in the city come from the southern part of Italy, from the mountainous areas of the Abruzzi and Calabria.

Preceding pages, Christmas Eve in Rome. Left, coachman.

The people from those areas have brought their lifestyle with them—an uncomplicated and familiar daily routine. Their first contact with Rome must have been traumatic. The result is their continuing nostalgia for village life. In Rome a vast number of micro-rhythms has developed—the whole city never moves in unison. These rhythms are layered, like the waves made by stones thrown into the water. They can flatten out or intensify one another.

Those who feel at home in Rome have their fingers on the pulse of the city. They know the right time and place to join in—or to make their escape by the back door. Of course the impartial observers themselves don't leave the rhythms unaltered. They make their own, quite powerful ones too: around four million tourists visit the town every year.

Times of the Day and Year

Many places in Rome only come alive at certain very definite times. Anyone who turns up at the wrong time will find nothing but emptiness, dirt and ruins. Only the cafés give the false impression of a pulsating metropolis (Rome in reality is nothing of the sort). These are hardly like the leisurely establishments in Vienna. These "Café-Tramezzini" are coffee and sandwich bars, with a mirrored decor reminiscent of American bars of the 1950s.

Here is the heart of Roman life, in these few square yards between the high counters. There are no chairs (if there are, it shows that some tourists' meeting place is in the vicinity). But everyone goes to the café—the facade restorer (one of the up-and-coming businesses in Rome), the "Onorevole" (Right Honorable) and the MP to the Café in the Galerie Colonna, the employee of the American Embassy to the Café Doney, the author and would-be film director to the Café Canova, the unemployed to the Café on the Magliana. It doesn't matter who, where or when: everyone goes to the café, at all times of the day and year and ten three-minute visits are preferred to one lasting half an hour.

Coffee Talk

In these coffee bars the Roman night is at its longest. Before going to work at 7 a.m., during the morning break, shortly after the morning break, after *pranzo* (lunch) at 2 p.m., before going home, before going to dinner at nine p.m., after the theater at 11.30 p.m., after a friend's party at 1.30, after

café and a *cornetto* (croissant).

The markets are a part of Roman life and change their prices with the time of day and their color with the time of year. Early in the morning, and that really means at 6 a.m., the food markets offer produce that has just come fresh from the wholesale markets. Even the newest housing estates have their local market, often nothing but an empty space between rows of houses. The later in the day, the lower the prices, especially for meat and fish, which are unrefrigerated. Around noon, when the stalls close, the

going to the disco at 2.30—although by this time it is getting difficult to find an open coffee bar.

Café is drunk standing up. It is twenty times thicker than any "Espresso" sold in other countries. Because not even all Italians can bear such a concentrated shot of caffeine, it's often diluted: *café macchiato*, or *café lungo*, a slightly diluted coffee. Or *café latte*, with a little more milk. The next one down is *capuccino*, but this isn't drunk till second breakfast. For most of this century, an unbreakable tradition has decreed that the first "breakfast" shall consist of nothing but

remaining goods are sold, and the stallholders become more and more hectic. This is the hour of the illegal immigrants from African and Arab countries.

The Afternoon Snooze

At the approach of midday, when the banks close, the rhythm of city life slows down and takes a short nap during the obligatory *pranzo* (lunch). Shortly beforehand tens of thousands of government employees stream homewards, because their departments shut at two. The city suffers a short rush-hour as everyone goes home. Some go back to work at 4.30 p.m. Others stay at home or start their second jobs. Private companies sometimes attempt to introduce all-day working, but this only works in winter. As soon as the temperature rises above 30 degrees—this can already happen in May—the siesta is sacred. Now people stroll through the empty streets, go to the restaurant, gossip, sunbathe in the Villa Borghese or on the Pincio. The city rests.

Slowly life gets moving again, and from the opening of the shops till they close at 8

Vespa is locked away in the garage. On winter evenings people go out mostly to the theater or cinema, or to visit relatives. *Cena*—dinner—is eaten copiously on winter evenings.

But from May to October, people leave the house in order to be outside in the piazza—although "piazza" is a relative term. Most of Rome's squares have degenerated into car parks and have no features that could invite anyone to linger. Almost all squares are impossible, and the same applies to the streets, which have also been taken over

p.m. the city meets at the Via del Corso. A dark-haired serpent winds its way through the quarter, but the crowds don't necessarily mean that any shopping gets done.

It may seem odd, given the average winter temperatures in Rome, but the seasons have their own quite distinct rhythms. In the winter the Romans hide away. Although the temperature is 19 degrees or more, the streets are full of women in fur coats, and the

completely by the internal combustion engine. So people meet in the few remaining "piazze" which have restricted traffic, at open-air summer events, or for the weekend in June or July, just before the great exodus of the *Feriae Augusti* on the August 15, at say a beach near the city, near Ponza or Argentario.

The Roman Summer

Summer is the great gap in the rhythm of Roman life. The university year, which shapes the lives of 120,000 students, ends in

Left, Bar Navona, a meeting-place at all hours. Above, the Roman love of gesture. Following page, "unofficial" bookie at work.

June. The theater season ends in May, the discos close down and schools go on holiday from the end of June to the beginning of October. The factories, offices and shops take a summer break lasting for the whole of August, and every year the state has to draw up emergency plans to supply that part of the population which stays behind. About half the population stay, but withdraw to the shade of their houses.

The Red "Zampano", Renato Nicolini, was the inventor of the *Estate Romana*, the Roman Summer. The forgotten places of

Rome were re-discovered and a new summer life began. In the Circus Maximus there was a cinema with a giant screen, in the Foro Italico people danced into the night. After the communist "Giunta" (city government) had ended, the Christian Democrats wanted to end the *effimero*, this short-term political spectacle. Money was supposed to flow back into the museums, and the Senator for Culture actually made the suggestion that culture should be carried into the suburbs by setting up sculptures. But the custom couldn't be eradicated. Now new places are full of summer life, such as the Orto Botan-

ico (the Botanical Gardens). Instead of medieval squares, foreign academies offer space for activity—the French Villa Medici and the German Villa Massimo.

Rome's nights are short even in summer. The few bars that are open close at midnight, a few coffee bars and gelaterie stay open longer. The myth of Roman nightlife is obviously indestructible—this is of course the fault of 1950s films like *Vacance Roma* and *La Dolce Vita*. Their images convey the idea of a pulsating metropolis that never actually existed—there may have been hints of it once upon a time in the Via Veneto. On summer evenings, when the *pontina*, the south wind, provides a fresh breeze, life moves out of the capital to the coastal resorts. These June weekends are a foretaste of August, when the city almost comes to a standstill. There are many Romans who like this time of year best—it gives them a chance to get their streets and squares back for themselves, without hectic crowds.

Everyone who lives here is quite unable to understand why foreign tourists seem to hold the fixed idea that the city is particularly exciting at Easter time. By middle of April the weather is still quite unstable and it rains frequently. You can see the pope better on Mondovisione, especially as the blessing *urbi et orbi* is as effective via the television as under an umbrella.

October, the second most popular time to visit, is also a puzzle. The visitors arrive in the city at the same time as the Romans return and have to put up with the latters' irritable end-of-holiday mood. October is the time to travel in the surrounding countryside, enjoying the wine festivals, swimming in the still-warm Mediterranean, which the Romans have long since left, and not for filling up the city. On top of this summer's departure announces itself in Rome with heavy rainfall—in October. Afterwards the weather settles again, and 24 degrees in the December midday sun are almost the rule. But perhaps tourists should continue to come when they always have done: perhaps the Romans might like to spend December among themselves.

63

THE VATICAN—STATE WITHIN A CITY

You have to keep up appearances. Within 110 acres, less than a third of the area of Monaco, the "Bishop of Rome, Vicar of Christ, Successor to the Apostles, Head of the Catholic Church and Servant of God" is still "Sovereign of the State of the Vatican"—to list only a few of the pope's titles.

Once the papal state was quite a considerable piece of land; it stretched from the Adriatic to the Tyrrhenian Sea and, shortly before its conquest by the Piedmontese, had a population of more than three million.

The pope's army today consists only of a corps of Swiss guards. These protect him and the 200 others (among them 30 women) who live within the walls. All the other employees of the Vatican, lay or clergy, are commuters. Every morning they travel in, and every evening they travel out.

Self-Sufficiency

The Vatican has almost everything a city needs. It has a railway station, which the Wojtyla Pope does not like much (he has used this mode of transportation only once, to visit Italian railway workers); a helicopter pad, the pope's favorite means of transport; a post office, which wins hands down over the Italian one in efficiency; a TV and radio station which broadcasts around the world in over 30 languages; a bank, which has brought the Vatican some embarrassment; a hospital, a few refectories, a drug store and petrol stations.

In 380 the Primacy of the Bishop of Rome over his colleagues had been recognized officially—except in the eastern churches. Since then Rome has been the "Holy City" for Catholic Christianity, numbering some 850 million souls at present. But since the treaty of 1985 with the Italian state, Rome is no longer "holy". This claim, never realized, was still in the old treaty of 1929, a concession of Mussolini's. The sentence in the treaty did nothing to change the profane city: no anti-papal memorial was removed because of it, Giordano Bruno continued his

warning, and Giuseppe Garibaldi on his monument continued to ride against the Vatican.

Pope Pius was happy to put up with this, as he was now released from the uncomfortable, if self-inflicted role of "prisoner in the Vatican" played by the popes since 1870. And in any case the payment of a billion lire compensation—at the time an enormous sum—sweetened his attitude to heretical monuments considerably.

The reborn state of the Vatican immediately swept into the mainstream of politics. The pope could be forgiven his pact with Mussolini, as it could be seen as a normalizing of relations, but people took the silence of his successor Pius XII in the face of Hitler's crimes very badly. The rush of the "Holy Spirit" over the church wasn't felt again until Pope John XXIII. The Second

Preceding pages: viewing the sacred columns; view of St. Peter's from Castel Sant' Angelo; Vatican postboxes are blue; and St. Peter. Above, Via della Conciliazione.

Vatican Council opened the church to the world. No counter-tendencies could hold up change any longer. The words spoken by the Roncalli Pope to the Council seemed to be aimed at the Prefect of the Congregation for the Doctrine of the Faith: "There are people who see in our modern times nothing but neglected duty and ruin. It seems necessary to us to distance ourselves from these prophets of disaster, who see new dangers in everything."

Pope John Paul II no doubt is aware of this development also. He has brought home from his travels in the Third World the knowledge that his enthusiastic followers live there and not in the uninterested communist countries. The encyclical *Sollectudo res socialis* with its call to the church to rid itself of the wealth on its altars has come late, but still in time to win the battle for souls.

Since the Vatican came into existence people have talked and argued about its

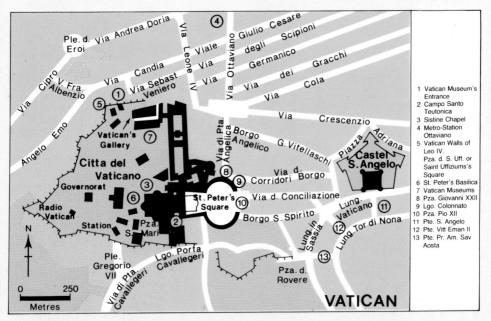

1 Vatican Museum's Entrance
2 Campo Santo Teutonica
3 Sistine Chapel
4 Metro-Station Ottaviano
5 Vatican Walls of Leo IV. Pza. d. S. Uff. or Saint Uffiziums's Square
6 St. Peter's Basilica
7 Vatican Museums
8 Pza. Giovanni XXII
9 Lgo. Colonnato
10 Pza. Pio XII
11 Pte. S. Angelo
12 Pte. Vitt Eman II
13 Pte. Pr. Am. Sav Aosta

The hard line of the orthodox probably has something to do with the fact that the Roman clergy feels that Rome is losing its grip on its central role in Catholic Christianity. Already nowadays most Catholics live in Latin America and Africa. Rome as a center for faithful pilgrims is pushed into the background, for who among the faithful in the Third World can afford to travel to Rome? This is not the least of reasons why Cardinal Ratzinger fights so bitterly against liberation theology. He is fighting for the spiritual precedence of the Roman clergy over the poor church of the Third World.

wealth, starting with the sale of indulgences right through to the days of the Vatican bank IOR, but the Holy See has never given out an official balance sheet. Apart from the original gift of Mussolini, almost the only certain figures are the 241 million dollars compensation paid out as its share in the bankruptcy of the Ambrosio Bank. It's known that Pius XII slept with a cash box under his bed, and that the Roncalli Pope left it all to his employees. When the Italian state wanted the Vatican to pay income tax, Paul VI moved fortunes abroad. With these transactions he unfortunately fell into the hands of the bankrupts and conmen Michele Sindona and Roberto Calvi, who drew the Vatican Bank *Istituto per le Opere di Religione* (Institute for Religious Works) into deep water. The damage to the church's image also brought financial damage, as the faithful donated less.

The revenues of the church come from four sources: the administration of sums of money, IOR and Peter's Pence, donated in the churches of the world on June 29. Frequent papal travels and synods have increased expenditure, and in the 1980s the

ums are a must on every visit to Rome. The different museums take up the greater part of the 1,400 rooms in the Vatican. You can see works by Raffael, Titian, Leonardo da Vinci, Bellini and Caravaggio. The Vatican museums also have what is probably the greatest collection of ancient finds in the world. It comprises Egyptian pieces, finds from Etruscan tombs, the famous Laocoon sculpture, plus a library of more than half a million manuscripts.

The crowning glory, however, is the Sistine Chapel (erected 1473-81 by Pope

Vatican has been closing each year with huge deficits. However, most bishops outside Rome seem to be only willing to help once the murky waters of Vatican finance have been cleared. Up till then, the sale of post cards, stamps and entrance fees to Vatican museums will remain the sources of revenue.

Touring Vatican Grounds

Despite a system which insists that you see every museum department even if you only want to see one hall, the Vatican muse-

Sixtus IV), which can now be seen in a partially restored state. The chapel is famous for its Renaissance frescos and as the meeting place of the Sacred College of Cardinals. The sidewall frescoes were painted from 1481 to 1483; those on the north wall depict events from the life of Christ. Masterpieces of the chapel include Michelangelo's ceiling fresco and *"The Last Judgment"* fresco on the west wall behind the altar. Dirt, poor restoration and smoke from torches had darkened the frescos. Whole generations of art historians have written deep interpretations of the dark colors, till the Vatican restorers brought the truth back into the light of day. The work, which is expected to go on till 1992, is being paid for by the Japanese TV, which received in exchange the exclusive world rights to pictures.

The Vatican gardens are not open to the ordinary visitor, but you can join one of the few guided tours instead. Previous popes often relaxed by walking in the gardens, too, but now this is limited to the route from the papal palace to the helicopter landing pad, and the trip is mostly made by car.

Open to all, on the other hand, is the

Emperor Constantine had an early Christian Church built over it, and Pope Julius II had it rebuilt in 1506 and it was finally completed in 1615 under Paul V. The work was often interrupted by lack of funds and poor organization, but in 1626 the church was consecrated. The church has functioned as a chief pilgrimage center in Europe and also as the scene of papal ceremonies and of the Vatican ecumenical councils.

The first plans were by Donato Bramante. The dome and the design of the Greek cross shape are by Michelangelo, who worked on

greatest church in the world, St. Peter's. This really impressive basilica of St. Peter—611 feet (186 meters) long, 462 feet (140 meters) wide and 393 feet (120 meters) high inside—has room for 60,000 believers. At the Easter and Christmas Mass it is often so crowded that the faithful arrive hours beforehand. Legend has it that the tomb of St. Peter lies under the bronze canopy. The

Left, Pope John Paul II holds an address. Right, pilgrims in St. Peter's Square; crowds like this are commonplace especially during Easter and Christmas.

it for 16 years without pay, "for the love of God and piety". Both are modeled on the Basilica of Maxentius and the Pantheon, but could not match their size. Carlo Maderno designed the facade as a Latin cross, with the nave of Michelangelo's design lengthened.

The inside of the church is resplendent with works of Renaissance and Baroque art, from Michelangelo's "Pietà" (1499) to the bronze canopy over the main altar by Gian Bernini, for which the material came from the Pantheon. Also, the statue of St. Longinus can be found in the crossing, and the bronze cathedral of St. Peter in the apse. In the grottos of the church are the tombs of the popes. The dome offers a wonderful view of Rome.

The Vatican State

At the head of church administration is the pope, and at his side is the state secretariat. Secretary of State (1988) is Cardinal Agostino Casaroli, who is at the same time Prefect of the Council for Public Affairs, which is busily involved in relations between church and state. The Prefecture for

Congregation for Beatification is headed by an Italian.

The pope also keeps a firm hand on the reins by the requirement for all 4,000 Catholic bishops throughout the world to travel to Rome to report to the pope, a trip *ad limina Apostolorum*, to the "threshold of the Apostles", every five years.

About 4,000 members of the Catholic clergy living in Rome are not priests in the Catholic churches but are attached to the Vatican and its various organizations and offices outside the walls. There are many

Economic Affairs administers the funds, and the Vatican Court judges cases, although the final decision is reserved for the pope.

Purely clerical matters are dealt with by the 10 Congregations, with a cardinal at the head of each. The "Congregation for the Doctrine of the Faith" is the first and definitely the most important, for it guards the purity of Catholic doctrine. The chairman is Cardinal Ratzinger. In earlier years this was the "Holy Office", in other words the Inquisition. Once leading a Congregation was a right reserved for Italians. Now only the

more nuns outside than inside the Vatican—they number almost 20,000. A special point of church law ensures that the pope can only be elected by Roman Cardinals, so all cardinals in Rome are members of a non-existent parish, a titular church. Only those under 80 are entitled to vote when the pope is elected by the College of Cardinals. Bishops have to retire at 75.

Church marriages are divorced by the tribunal "Sacra Rota". However, marriages can be divorced at diocese level, but only according to Catholic teaching, that is, if they have never been consummated. For this reason the pope severely criticized the nearly 40,000 annulments made by dioceses in the United States in 1987 alone, mostly on grounds of "physical inability". In the same year in Italy 871 marriages were officially dissolved by the church.

The Election of the Pope

The election of a pope is a process as fascinating as it is unusual. Shortly after the passing bells of the Vatican have fallen silent, the College of Cardinals meets in con-

whereby a commission is formed and its recommendation accepted.

All popes in modern history have been elected by the second method. Although most conclaves do their duty with appropriate speed (Pope John Paul II was elected after two days, his predecessor John Paul I after only one), there have been times when external help was needed. In 1216 Prince Matteo Orsini forced the conclave to meet in the presence of the deceased Innocent III. Gregory X left instructions that after five days the cardinals were to be put on a diet of

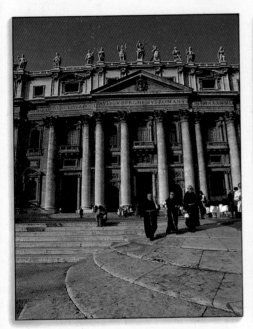

clave. It comprises 120 bishops and archbishops chosen by the pope. The electors are locked in. They are not allowed to leave the Sistine Chapel until a successor to St. Peter has been found. The election can proceed in three ways: one is by acclamation, in which divine providence causes all the cardinals to call out one name. The second is by a majority decision, in which votes are cast four times a day until one candidate has a majority of two-thirds. The third is a compromise,

bread and water.

After every vote the voting slips are burned. The smoke from the small chimney of the chapel is the only sign the outside world sees of the progress of the election: if there is no result, black smoke appears; if there has been a result, white smoke can be seen (a chemical is added to the fire). The leader of the College announces *Habeamus Papam*, and shortly afterwards the newly elected pontiff appears in one of the three sets of papal robes (small, medium and large) held in readiness. The coronation takes place next day in St. Peter's.

Left, the facade of the biggest church in the world. Above, the Swiss Guard on parade.

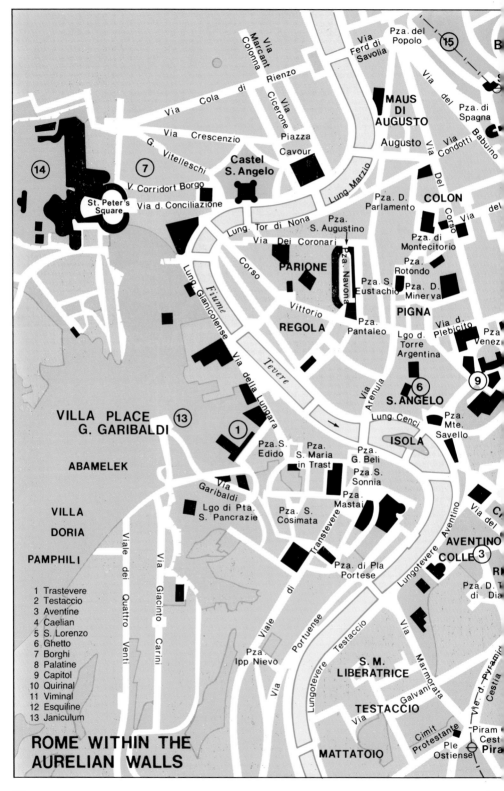

ROME WITHIN THE
AURELIAN WALLS

1 Trastevere
2 Testaccio
3 Aventine
4 Caelian
5 S. Lorenzo
6 Ghetto
7 Borghi
8 Palatine
9 Capitol
10 Quirinal
11 Viminal
12 Esquiline
13 Janiculum

VILLA PLACE
G. GARIBALDI

ABAMELEK

VILLA

DORIA

PAMPHILI

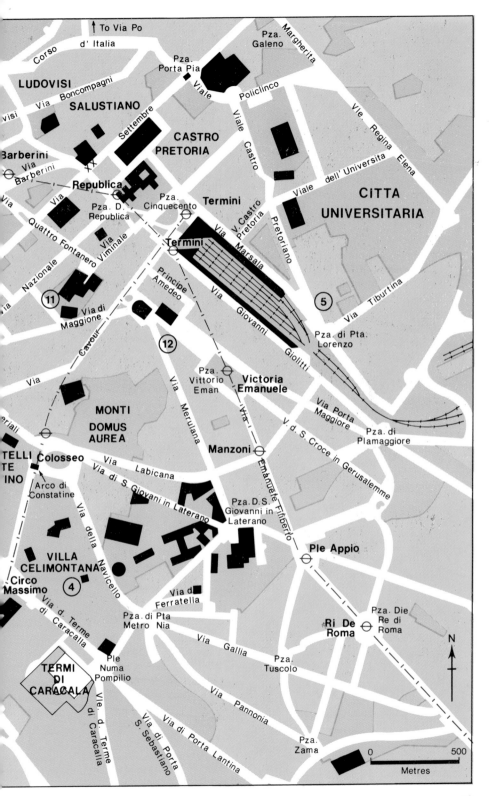

QUARTERS, STREETS AND SQUARES

Rioni; Quartieri; Borgate—Roman Italian has three terms for three different types of housing. These are much further apart from one another than they appear to be in miles. There are social, political and historical divisions in the way people live in Rome. For instance, the population of the 22 Rioni *entro le mura* in Rome, that is, inside the Aurelian Walls, think that they alone are the true Romans. Outside the walls, but running into the Rioni to form a single sea of houses, are the *Quartieri*. People have lived here since the 1930s, shortly before and indeed during the building of the Borgate. The most recent building boom for this three-class system of Roman society came with the social housing programs of the 1970s. These got rid of the slums—but at the price of the tower blocks.

The incredible complexity and color of Roman life is still best experienced in the squares and, to a much lesser extent, on the streets—the streets are almost finished as a place for meeting people because of the volume of traffic (1.4 million cars). Although in today's Rome, television is increasingly replacing real entertainment, strolling across the piazza remains an inalienable part of Roman life. The *Borgatari*, the inhabitants of the Borgate, also spend their evenings strolling up and down the "Corso"—outside the walls there are few places to meet.

The variety is immense—from the small-scale Piazza Santa Maria in Trastevere to the mass meeting place of the Campo dei Fiori; from the office worker's resting place in the Piazza Mincio to the beautiful Piazza del Popolo; from the secretive Piazza di Testaccio to the impressive Piazza di Spagna; from the meeting place for Romans in the Piazza Venezia to the meeting places for tourists in the Piazza by the

Pantheon, the Fontana di Trevi or the Piazza Navona. Some places have local names, different from the official ones: the Romans continue to call the Piazza della Repubblica the Piazza Esedra, and the Piazza Buenes Aires is known as the Piazza Quadrata.

Rome's streets and squares often tell the tale of some ruler—a pope or a cardinal—who wanted to build it as an eternal monument to himself. In no time at all such people would flatten whole quarters of the city without a thought; ancient gardens would be covered in concrete, streets that had grown to make an organic whole torn apart. Rome has suffered it all patiently and patiently borne the damage. But always something new has grown out of the wounds. The end result was usually different from the one the builders intended. Rome has taken even these strange places into its possession. This city is alive, and nothing is conserved.

Preceding pages, taking a nap after the Audience. Left, market in the Campo dei Fiori. Right, view of the fountains in the P. Navona.

The Centro Storico

"Historical center" probably makes the visitor think first of the classical sites of ancient Rome, like the Forum, the Colosseum, imperial fortifications. But the Italians consider it to include the lived-in and commercially used parts of the old city. Remains of ancient times are mentioned in building and place names ("Colosseum", "Fori") or included under the heading *zona archaeologica* or *cavi*, excavations. So the "historical center" is the area which was inhabited throughout the Middle Ages, when the population was only a few tens of thousands, right up to modern times—the inner bank of the great bend of the Tiber, roughly covering the area between the Via del Corso and the river.

This region roughly covers the area of the ancient Roman field of Mars, the *campo martio*, the training ground dedicated to Mars, the god of war, for the cohorts of the generals. It lay outside the *Pomerium*, the sacred city boundary, because up until early imperial times no armed man was allowed inside it. Here returning generals discussed with the Senate the size and form of their Triumphs—usually in front of the nearby Temple of Apollo, of which three particularly beautiful pillars survive.

In imperial times the city had already spread far beyond the old walls. Given the increasing shortage of building space around the central fora, even public buildings were being moved "out of town". In Caesar's time the super-rich were already building their great complexes out on the Field of Mars, such as Pompey's imposing theater, which also served as a parliament. Later there was no more room even for the showpieces

Reproduction antiques for sale.

of the rulers in the center. The oldest surviving temples in Rome at the **Largo Argentino**, dating from between the 4th and the 2nd century B.C., were incorporated into the Theatre of Pompey in 55 B.C. You can still see traces of the complex at the Campo dei Fiori in the way the street follows the curve of the spectators' seats. The Piazza Navona was built into the **Stadium of Domitian**, which had space for 30,000 spectators in A.D. 86.

The **Pantheon**, "temple of all the gods", was begun in 27 B.C. by the statesman Marcus Agrippa and later completely re-built by Hadrian (117-138 A.D.) and is today the best preserved of all Roman buildings. Its front porch of Corinthian columns supports a gabled roof with triangular pediment and beneath the porch are huge bronze doors of 24 feet high, the earliest known large examples of this type. Within the space is roofed by a 142-foot- (43-meter) wide dome, and is designed so that a sphere can be described within it, making it a symbol of beauty and harmony. The floor and the lower part of the wall decoration are part of the ancient interior. Statues of gods stood in the niches. The splendid bronze vaulting in the anteroom was used by Pope Urban VIII in 1620 to be melted down for cannon for the Castel Sant'Angelo and the tabernacle of Bernini in St. Peter's.

The **Mausoleum of Augustus**, A.D. 31, is today a charmless brick ruin. It belonged to a generously proportioned new park with cypress groves in honor of the Emperor, in which the **Ara Pacis**, the "altar of peace" dating from 9 B.C. and a gigantic sundial were placed. The Ara Pacis was moved by Mussolini and shows, among other things, Augustus and his family in procession.

Another circular tomb is the **Mausoleum of Hadrian**, today **Castel Sant' Angelo**. The tomb, built in A.D. 139, was connected to the Field of Mars by the **Pons Aelius**, today the Ponte Sant' Angelo. The first storey is 292 by 292 feet (89 meters) and 49 feet (15 meters) high. On it stood a circular building, 69 feet (21 meters) high and 210 feet (64 meters) in diameter. On the outside it was clad in marble, on top stood a figure of a four-horse chariot with the Emperor. The numerous funeral statues were used in A.D. 537 as missiles against the besieging Goths. The **Theater of Marcellus**, dedicated 13 or 11 B.C., held 20,000 spectators and was used for plays, but in the Middle Ages it was a fortress. To the south on the Forum Holitorium, the vegetable market of Rome, stand the **temples of Juno, Spes and Janus**, dating from republican times, into which the church of **S. Nicola in Carcere** has been built. In the **Forum Holitorium**, the cattle market, you can still find the **Temple of Portunus**, the harbor god, dating from the 2nd century B.C., and the so-called

Mounted carabinieri in front of the Pantheon.

Temple of Vesta, which was probably dedicated to Hercules Victor and, dating from 120 B.C., was Rome's first marble temple.

In the Middle Ages, when Rome had grown small, the remaining people thronged this area—the bend of the Tiber eased defence and the falling ruins provided building material for repairing houses—but especially for the building of many churches and papal buildings. The family of Pope Urban VIII, whose worldly name was Barberini, removed so much bronze from the ceiling of the Pantheon for the main altar of St. Peter's, that the Romans sneered "What the barbarians left, the Barberini have stolen," a loose translation of *Quod non fecerunt Barbari, fecerunt Barberini.*

In fact almost every medieval building in the "Historic Quarter" is a result of clerical building. With a few exceptions, (Pantheon, area of Domitian's Stadium, Column of Marcus Aurelius, Mausoleum of Augustus) antiquity was buried under modern buildings. Hardly any of the ancient remains we see today still stand in their historic places, for instance the obelisk on the Piazza del Popolo or the Ara Pacis, the altar of peace of Augustus with its autobiography in stone—this was moved from the Via del Corso to the bank of the Tiber.

But the historic center has more to offer than numerous churches and Renaissance palaces. It is a tangle of streets and alleys, in which the infrastructure of the old craft guilds, which has grown over the last three or four centuries, still survives. Whole quarters are full of the *botteghe* of the same trade. You will not miss the printing presses, some still hand-operated, between the Via del Plebiscito and the Pantheon. Cabinet makers congregate in the area of **Via di S. Maria dell' Anima**. Further towards the piazza, up

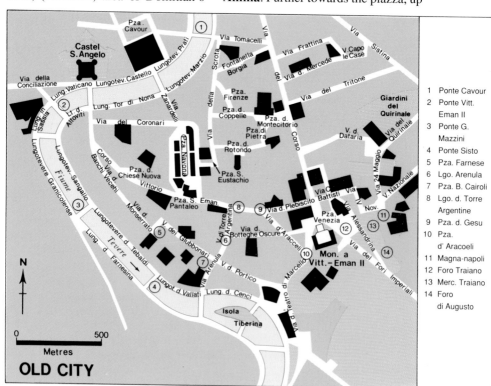

1 Ponte Cavour
2 Ponte Vitt. Eman II
3 Ponte G. Mazzini
4 Ponte Sisto
5 Pza. Farnese
6 Lgo. Arenula
7 Pza. B. Cairoli
8 Lgo. d. Torre Argentine
9 Pza. d. Gesu
10 Pza. d' Aracoeli
11 Magna-napoli
12 Foro Traiano
13 Merc. Traiano
14 Foro di Augusto

OLD CITY

to the **Via Tomacelli**, there are many second-hand book shops. Don't forget to look upwards as well—many facades have old guild signs or pieces of ancient marble built into them.

When looking at the churches—there are more than a dozen around here—don't just follow the guidebook, but take a good look around. For instance, if you go to the church **Santa Maria della Pace**, you will of course be delighted by Raffael's *"Sybils"* and the *"Four Prophets"* of his pupils. The banker Chigi was paying for the work. He was horrified by Raffael's bill and asked Michelangelo for an evaluation. The latter valued each of the heads at 100 *scudi*. The financier was horrified: "If he wants me to pay for the clothes as well, I'll be ruined!"

But you should also take a walk round the octagonal building—unfortunately it is hemmed in by buildings on all sides. But you should read the inscription at the rear by an 18th-century Roman judge, threatening dire penalties for polluting the environment.

To get to know the historic center it is best to move in a spiral which combines history and modern life. For instance: from the Piazza Venezia along the Via del Plebiscito to the **Piazza del Gesu** with its Jesuit church of the same name, now party headquarters for the Christian Democrats. Turn left to the **Via delle Botteghe Oscure**, where the communists reside, and then right and immediately left again into **Via Gaetani**, passing the memorial plaque to the murdered President Aldo Moro, whose car stood here in 1978.

Go on in this direction to the Via del Teatro di Marcello, passing the ruins of the Temple of Apollo and, once past the theater, up to the Tiber promenade. From here turn right in the direction of the Synagogue, which was the target of a terrorist attack 10 years ago, and under which lies Diocletian's Stadium. If you don't go into the old Ghetto or to

the Tiber island, you will come to the **Via Arenula**, where the first thing you see is the Ministry of Justice. Better to avoid this street and take the next one right, Via Pelinari leading to the Piazza Farnese. There Renaissance buildings stand so close together—this continues into the Via Giulia—that you stop in front of almost every house: **Palazzo Falconieri**, **church of S. Eligio degli Orefici**, **Oratorium S. Luca del Gonfalone**, **Palazzo Sacchetti**...At the end of the street of S. Giovanni dei Fiorentini turn off right, go right a short way towards Piazza Tassoni and then sharp left. This is the first banking quarter in modern history. The attractive building of the **Banco di San Spirito** survives, which the Vatican, faced with bankruptcy, hastily sold off to the Roman government. This brings us to the tangle of alleys with hundreds of *botteghe*, so close together that you could almost miss the churches in between.

THE GHETTO

The name **Ghetto** was given to the medieval quarter of **S. Angelo,** one of the classical 14 Rioni, but not until the height of the Counter-Reformation. Pope Paul IV intended to keep the Christian faith pure with his decree of 1555 and ordered the Jews, who had up till then lived mostly in Trastevere, to move to the other side of the Tiber. About 8,000 Jews were forced into an area of less than five acres (two hectares).

Thereupon he forced them to sell all their goods and follow no other trade than buying and selling old clothes and household gear. Further, he commanded that men and women should wear a yellow hat, so as to be distinguishable from Christians," Maximilien Misson reported 50 years later.

Not until the bourgeois revolutions, in which many Jews took part, was the Ghetto opened, for a short time during Jacobin times in 1799, and permanently in 1849, when the Ghetto walls were torn down.

The Jews

Nonetheless the Jewish community in Rome has remained remarkably faithful to this quarter and even today the population (about 1,000) is almost entirely Jewish. The Jewish community in Rome consists of about 20,000 people, a third of all the Jews in Italy.

The church of **Tempietto del Carmelo**, on the **Via della Reginella**, is now a mere historical reminder of the enforced catechism. Here and in two other churches on the edge of the Ghetto, Jews were ordered to attend penitential sermons. If you didn't turn up, you had to pay a fine. If you went to

The kosher butcher at the Porticus of Octavia.

sleep, you were prodded with some force by a Swiss Guard. During the wave of anti-papal feeling that swept Italy at the time of unification the Synagogue was consecrated, in 1904. Architecturally speaking, it's too tall, but that was deliberate—the anticlerical citizens wanted it to be visible from the Vatican.

The Ghetto was also the place where mass deportation of Jews to German concentration camps took place on Oct. 16, 1943. The German officer Kappler—later infamous for the massacre in the caves of the **Ardeatine**—ordered the Jews of Rome to pay a ransom of 110 pounds (50 kg) of gold each. With the help of many priests, this sum was delivered, but the Wehrmacht still surrounded the Ghetto and deported all the Jews they could find. As the search-and-arrest units moved in, the remaining 4,000 Jews who didn't live in the Ghetto were hidden by neighbors, priests and friends as quickly as possible, an act which could bring the death penalty on the rescuers.

This active solidarity of the Roman populace with other peoples has ancient roots. In A.D. 70 the Emperor Titus destroyed Jerusalem, but the Jews in Rome could live relatively free from fear. Even Fascism in Italy was not anti-semitic at first. There were no extermination camps here, and many of the early Fascists were Jews themselves. The deportations only started when Italy had broken with Hitler in 1943 and was occupied by German troops.

On April 13, 1986, in the Synagogue in the Ghetto, the historic meeting of Pope John Paul II and Rabbi Elio Toaff took place. It was the first time since Peter's day that a Bishop of Rome had prayed in a Jewish synagogue and the Catholic church had distanced itself from the wicked doctrine of the "perfidious Jew".

Busy life in the Ghetto.

ISOLA TIBERINA AND TRASTEVERE

Asclepius, Greek god of healing, found a home when he came to Rome in 261 B.C., and it has remained his to the present day—the **Tiber Island**, **Isola Tiberina**. According to legend, a ship was wrecked in the Tiber, which really has a racing current at this spot. The serpent of the bearded god sprang onto the shore to found a hospital.

Whether it was so, or whether the isle was formed by the sacks of grain thrown into the river as a revolt against the Tarquinian kings is still not known. It is at any rate certain that a hospital has been run here since the Middle Ages by the *Fatebenefratelli,* which means "do good, brothers!", a slogan used by the monks when begging for money for the sick.

With a fine Roman sense of continuity the German Emperor Otto III had a church of St. Bartholomew built over the old shrine of Asclepius.

On the way to Trastevere, look below. The two bridges to the island are among the oldest ancient structures still in use in Rome.

The **Ponte Fabricio** was built, as the inscription shows, in 62 B.C. by the civil engineer L. Fabricius and the **Ponte Cestio** was built in 42 B.C. by L. Cestius, during Caesar's stay in Spain. To the left are the remains of the first stone bridge in Rome built in 142 B.C., known as the "Ponte Rotto".

On the other side, in a sort of splendid isolation lies Trastevere. Through self-imposed distance **Trastevere**—"trans Tiberium"—has kept its character over thousands of years. In ancient times this once Etruscan shore was mainly settled by sailors, foreigners and people passing through. *Noantri*, "us others", is an expression of the self-confidence of the *Trasteverini*, who see theirs as the most

Roman of all Roman quarters, without being truly Roman. Its best aspects lie in its size and secrecy, in narrow alleys and dark corners.

From the Ponte Cestio your way leads straight to the **Chiesa di S. Benedetto in Pisculina**, which isn't quite as big as S. Pietro, but has the oldest bell in the city, dating from the 10th century.

Not far away is the church of **St. Cecilia**, who was beheaded for her conversion at the court of Marcus Aurelius, after vain attempts to suffocate her in the caldarium. In 1599 her tomb was opened and she was found crouching, her head struck off, but uncorrupted. A sculpture by Maderno on the altar portrays the saint.

Something Old, Something New

Like every old quarter of Rome, Trastevere had to make sacrifices to the city's pretensions to be a capital after 1870.

Here you have to cross the broad swathe of the **Viale di Trastevere**, once dedicated to the king, and then "to labor". In the **Piazza G.G. Belli** on the banks of the Tiber the Roman people have put up a monument to one of their poets, the one with the initials SPQR as *Soli Preti Qui Regnano* ("only priests rule here").

The other poet of the people, Trilussa, has his monument at the "mostra", the showpiece, of the foundation at the Ponte Sisto. From here he looks out towards the water of the aqueduct of Pope Paul V, which pours down from the Gianicolo.

Your way to Trilussa leads you through the **Via Lungaretti**, where just behind the church of **S. Agata** a marble plaque refers to an episode in the struggle for liberation from papal rule of the *Garibaldini*. A brave woman from Trastevere, Tavani Arquati, was

eft, the
hurch of S.
laria in
rastevere.

arrested here when, on Oct. 25, 1867 she and others were posting bills announcing the revolution. At the same time Garibaldi moved to Rome, but was thrown back by the French troops defending the pope. The Gianicolo was also the scene of the battles to defend the Roman Republic in 1849.

A New Cause for Concern

Nowadays Trastevere mainly has to defend itself against the gradual exodus of its long-standing inhabitants—craftsmen, small tradesmen, poor Italians and foreigners, as well as the Jewish families that have lived here for two thousand years. Today it can happen that a flat with a monthly rent equivalent to 50 is snapped up tomorrow for a sale price of 100,000. Wealthy Italians and foreigners are slowly but steadily changing the character of life in the quarter, and there is less and less room for the old Trasteverini. However, Trastevere has kept its peculiarities, even if the old trattorias and osterias are giving way to pizzerias and restaurants. Near the "classic" place to meet, **Piazza di S. Maria in Trastevere**, nightlife is developing rapidly. New clubs and bars are constantly opening, slowly but steadily, as is the way of people around here. What is left is the hope that so many bars and places of amusement will lower the value of the area for rich people because of the increased noise level. In this way the special character of the quarter, not to be confused with any prettified "ethnic" poverty, will be saved.

If you want to see a bit of greenery after so many narrow little corners, go to the **Orto Botanico**. Just to the left of the city gate Via delle Lungara you will find the Botanical Gardens, at the foot of the Gianicolo, with a wonderful view of Rome.

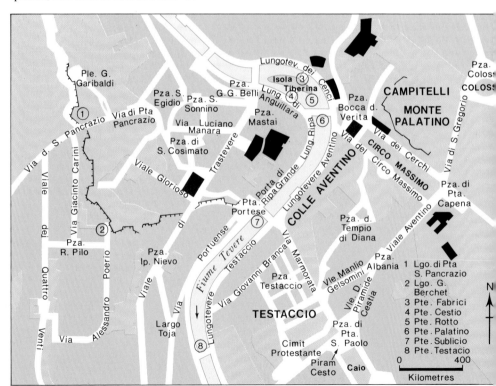

THE BORGO

The part of the city known as **Borgo** could rightly be called genuinely Catholic. From earliest Christian times right up till today two cornerstones of Catholic greatness overshadow life in the quarter. The Borgo stretches along the Tiber as far as the military fortress of the popes, **Castel Sant'Angelo**, built as a mausoleum for Hadrian. To the east it is bounded by the greatest church of the Catholic world, **St. Peter's**.

In this place the imperial court once entertained themselves in Caligula's garden. The Christians built inns, chapels and hospices for the pilgrims to St. Peter's tomb. These buildings, intended to accommodate pilgrims, were known as *scholae* and one of them, the "Schola Saxorum", was a Saxon foundation known since the 7th century. Now the **Ospedale e Chiesa di San Spirito in Sassia**, it gave the Germanic name "burg" to the area, which developed into **Borgo di San Spirito**.

If you want to imagine the Borgo as it was for over a thousand years, up to about 1950, take a walk through the narrow alleys along the edge of the **Corridore**. This imposing ruined wall can be seen for some distance. It forms a direct corridor from the Vatican to the Castel Sant'Angelo with its promise of protection, and is part of the fortifications built by Leo IV in 846.

The Borgo really blossomed after the end of the Great Schism and the following Jubilee Years celebrated by the Popes Nicholas V in 1450, Sixtus IV in 1475 and Alexander VI in 1500. Pilgrims squeezed into the Borgo, bought devotional items and brought new money into the city. About half of the 5,000 or so inhabitants at that time were in Holy Orders. Sixtus V expanded the Borgo to include the area around Castel

his "indulgence" is on sale in the Borgo for 500 lire.

Sant'Angelo, and the standard of living in the quarter rose with every Jubilee Year. In 1605 Pope Paul V founded the *Banco di San Spirito* with revenues from the hospice **San Spirito in Sassia**. The basic capital was guaranteed by the property owned by the hospice.

The inhabitants of the Borgo had considerable autonomy. Anyone who got into difficulties with the temporal powers on the other side of the Tiber could, if he moved to the Borgo, claim sanctuary from the law. After the liberation of Rome in 1870 the Borgo-dwellers had to make a clear statement in favor of joining the new Italian state. Even the patriots were convinced that the Borgo would definitely prefer to be part of a future religious state.

The Lateran Treaty of 1929 between Italy and the Vatican ushered in the end of the classical Borgo. The recognition by Pius XI, so necessary to Mussolini, was thought to be worth some radical demolition work. The reconciliation between church and state, "Conciliazione", was celebrated in 1936 by hacking a wide gash through the narrow little alleys, the **Via della Conciliazione**, officially opened in 1950.

This road robs the pilgrim of today the overwhelming impression made by St. Peter's Square on earlier generations of pilgrims. Coming out of the network of dark alleys, they suddenly found themselves in the square, bathed in light. Now everything can be seen from a distance, there's no surprise. To recapture the earlier impression, go towards St. Peter's Square from the side street Borgo Sant' Angelo. Then you will understand the raptures of earlier descriptions. Historical continuity, that trademark of Rome, is nonetheless still provided by the never-ceasing flow of visitors, and by the many "followers" of the religious life. That's what keeps the Borgo alive even today.

Cool refreshments in the city center.

TESTACCIO

It is unlikely that you will end up here by chance, so we recommend a special visit to this historic working class area. You will be rewarded if you take the trouble to travel towards "Lido-Ostia", get off at the **Metro station Piramide** on Line B. First, you will see the well preserved tomb of the Roman officer Gaius Cestius (A.D. 12)—he was inspired by the pyramids while serving in Egypt—which later, during the rush job of building the Aurelian Wall, was simply bricked in as well to save time. Then you go past the so-called **English Cemetery**, also known as the "non-Catholic cemetery", where the Italian Communist Party founder Antonio Gramsci, the two English poets James Shelley and John Keats and the son of the German poet Goethe are buried.

Here, by the **Porta S. Paolo**, the ancient **Porta Ostense**, Roman partisans and regular Italian troops fought their first battles against the occupying German army on Sept. 9, 1943.

Around 1890 builders working on the new capital came to live in Testaccio. The Piedmontese rulers had to let them into the city, for after all they had helped to build the new Rome. This quarter, which looks so uniform, was nevertheless—like so much of Rome—not planned, but is the result of private building initiatives on land that belong to the working people even in ancient times.

In the Middle Ages the area was still known as "Prati del Popolo Romano", ("meadows of the Roman people"). It was an infamous malaria-ridden swamp, and then it was built up with rectangular tenements according to what was fashionable at the time. But

A new cellar bar in Testaccio.

the buildings are not as bad as they look. The courtyards usually have an elegant exit and the flats are lighter than they appear to be from the outside.

Work has been going on in Testaccio since ancient times. Walk down the **Via Marmorata** and you will be reminded at once of the booming trade in marble which made Rome's palaces famous. Here the fine imported marble from the Roman Empire was unloaded, and the marble guilds were based here right up until modern historical times, when they worked marble from the ancient ruins. A "census of pillars" at the beginning of the last century found that there were still more than 8,000 marble pillars scattered throughout the whole of Rome.

Turn left into the Via Galvani and you will immediately see the **Monte Testaccio**, a hill 115 feet (35 meters) high, built of shards of amphorae, remains of 600 years of the Roman wine

and oil trade. Most of them came from Spain. The name "Monte dei cocci" (hill of shards) of the ancient *Teste-amphorae* gave the quarter its name.

The way up leads off from the corner of the **Via Zabaglia** and the climb is steep, but definitely recommended. You will have a view of the whole Tiber valley, from the working class areas of the Magliana up to the west to the Aventine and over towards the Villa Borghese, and further to the Monte Mario, easily recognized by the RAI TV mast. On the banks of the Tiber you will see the landing place of Roman trading ships, now the **Piazza Emporin**, which brought the amphorae to the warehouses of the **Porticus Aemilia** (A.D. 190). The harbor of those days was built in 193 B.C., when the first Roman harbor at the Forum Boarium proved to be too small. The warehouse, Porticus Aemilia, adjoined the harbor markets. These warehouses must have been enormous, for there were 294 pillars just holding up the roof. There are important remains to be seen in the streets **Via Branca, Rubattino** and **Florico.**

Also noticeable is the tall symbol of Testaccio, the gasometer. Since the changeover to underground gas it is no longer in use. It was one of the successes of the left-wing "Blocco Popolare" (people's block) government, which assured Rome an independent supply of energy.

At the rear the "Monte dei Cocci" falls steeply towards the "Matta-taoio"—the slaughterhouse. From its opening in 1891, when the cattle market and shambles were moved here from the Piazza del Popolo, till the move to a highly modern "meat center" out of town (1975), this was the main source of revenue for Testaccio. Now the huge complex is mostly empty. It is used by the "cavallari", the horse and cart drivers of Rome, and sometimes as a cultural center.

Left, the old gasometer, not in use anymore.

AROUND THE STATION

Knocked out—that's probably the right phrase to describe your state when you step on Roman soil for the first time at the Termini station. Absolutely everything around you tends to exceed anything you previously imagined. This applies to your sense of wonder, but also to your disorientation. The incredible noise begins at the platform, but then there's the graceful ticket hall (one of the few successful pieces of post-war architecture, pleasantly lightening the Fascist giantism that otherwise pervades the station). Then the forecourt—one of the biggest piazze in Rome, a good 1,312 feet (400 meters) square. And yet the size doesn't really make an impression. Grandiose urban planning has stuck the biggest bus station in the city just in front of it, so obvious that even the Romans can't get used to it.

If you do find the square empty—early in the morning or on Sundays—or patiently wait for a gap in the crowd of buses, you will get a new and fascinating impression. Through the trees on the Piazza dei Cinquecento glow the red bricks of the oldest and ancient baths. Their Italian name also gave the name to the station. The **Baths** (termini) **of Diocletian** date from the 3rd century. Today they house a marvelous archaeological museum. Sensitized by this view, you will see another piece of ancient Rome to the right of the station—part of the **Servian Wall** from the 4th century B.C. There are more in the basement of the station.

Impressions of the people only filter through gradually—the queues in front of the ticket offices, the shouting men and gesticulating women in the telephone boxes, the children skipping about and the many dark-skinned people who are noticeable in this part of Rome.

Italy is one of the most popular countries for immigrants because it is easy to get in. At present there are at least a million "secret" guests in the country, about 300,000 in Rome alone.

Start a walk around the station by crossing the forecourt in the direction of the museum—this experiment alone will give you an undreamed of insight into the mentality of local car drivers, who, in spite of all their honking, actually respect pedestrians, even away from traffic lights and zebra crossings. To the left of the baths is the **Piazza della Repubblica**, which is marked on many maps and on the announcements for demonstrations—which almost all start here—with its old name, **Piazza Esedra**. The first thing you will see is the Fountain of the Naiads, dating from the turn of the century. There was a scandal when it was unveiled, because

95

of the allegedly obscene postures of the nymphs.

Elegant shops once lay under the colonnades, but now they are full of sex cinemas. The **Via Nazionale** leads down to the **Piazza Venezia**, uphill you come to the **Via XX Settembre**, which on the left leads to the **Quirinal Palace**, once seat of the popes, today of the state president; to the right it ends at the **Porta Pia,** where Italian troops broke into the city on Sept. 20, 1870.

Opposite are the Baths and to the right the unassuming church of **S. Maria degli Angeli.** Step into it, and you will be knocked out again, for no-one would ever have expected so huge a church (nearly 328 feet or 100 meter long). Michelangelo designed it in the shape of a Greek cross. The porch is modeled after the Pantheon.

To carry on your journey around the station, you have to turn into the Via Cernaia. Crossing the Via Palestro you come to the Viale Castro Pretorio, on the edge of the university quarter, bursting at the seams with 100,000 students. Turn right in the Via Castro Pretorio and you will enter a tangle of little streets, in which, along with some obstinate Romans, live the foreigners that you see by day around the station or the nearby official departments. This area is on the threshold of becoming a racial ghetto, even though many of the "illegals", faced by Roman unemployment, give up and move out to the country in southern Italy.

But at some time they will all come back to the "Stazione Termini"—either because the police move them into the southern Italian ports, from where they are deported to North Africa, or because they have made it and can now travel, but perhaps also because they have gone right down in the world and are queuing for one of the 300 beds in the Caritas hostel for the homeless.

In front of the Verano cemetery in the quarter of San Lorenzo.

SAN LORENZO

Few maps mark **San Lorenzo** as a separate quarter of the city. In this area, however, a part of Rome—modern but already becoming historic—has held its own astonishingly well, if only against the expansion of its more aggressive neighbors. The area takes its name from the **Basilica San Lorenzo fuori le mura**, one of the seven "classical" churches of the early Roman Christians. It lies squeezed in between the University area, which worms its way in from the north, the railway station, which is separated from San Lorenzo by the Aurelian Wall, the industrial area and the motorway of Prenestina and the cemetery of **Verano**, which starts right next to the church. After admiring the beautiful frescos in the church porch or the building's original architecture—a 4th-century church

has been amalgamated with a later one, built in the 13th century, which faces the opposite way—and visiting the **Catacombs** of **Santa Chiara**, you might have had enough of sacred architecture. But don't miss the cemetery next door. There are few other places where the social hierarchy is so demonstrably adhered to, even after death. The pompous tombs of the wealthy and the high-ranking clerics line the boulevard-like main paths. Further back you go down the social scale to the lower classes, and yet each grave struggles to emulate the "great", even if only on a small scale.

Cross the splendid flower market in front of the cemetery entrance, and go into the "real" San Lorenzo. To your left, behind the **Piazza Verano**, part of the area is at work. The undertakers and monumental masons are all to be found in the low houses, two storeys high at most, which are typical of the quarter. If

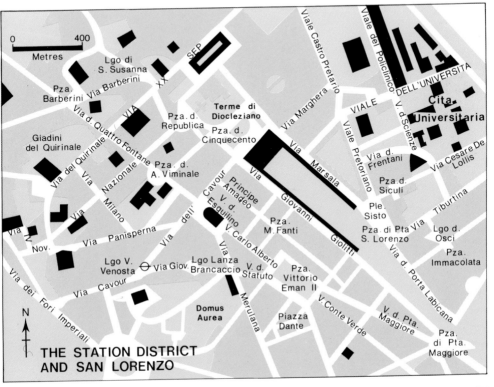

THE STATION DISTRICT AND SAN LORENZO

you go on to follow the **Via Tiburtina** towards the station and turn off into any side street, you will find plenty of examples of this type of house, even if they are often run down and in danger of demolition. These little houses were built in the last century. While other recently built areas—for instance in **Testaccio** to the south or the area beyond **Trastavere** to the west—have been extensively altered by Rome's various stages of development, and show the scars of redevelopment, San Lorenzo has remained almost untouched until the last decades. Change only arrived with the explosive expansion of the University 20 years ago, and now even here houses are being torn down and multi-storied buildings and student hostels are being built.

The sharpest contrast between "old" and "new" San Lorenzo can be seen if you follow the Via Tiburtina towards the station. Here and there you'll find occasional impoverished, but once splendid two-storied houses. In the Via Marucini or the Via Ramni, for instance, you can find houses of nouveau riche families in decorative and often well restored style. In the Piazza dei Siculi and along the Via Peligni you can find more, and here even today you can see posters telling the story of the area's struggle for more places for people to meet. Go back to the Via Tiburtina and turn right, and you will come back to the Aurelian Wall. To your right, northwards, the wall literally "comes alive". Flats have been built into the towers and into part of the wall.

If you want to go to the station, you should go through the **Porta San Lorenzo**. This gate is perhaps a sign of the future for this once typical part of Rome. It looks as if a giant truck or crane has roared through. Only the two side pillars are left, the rest has simply been swept away.

Flower stall in San Lorenzo.

THE EUR-QUARTER

The acronym "EUR" is pronounced as it is written—but pronounced in Italian, E-UR, so foreigners often don't know what it means. The "Esposizione Universale Roma", the World Exhibition, was intended for 1942, for the 20th anniversary of the *March on Rome*. Work had begun in 1937 on architect Marcello Piacentini's plans, but was interrupted by the war. After the war the EUR area looked like a bomb site, although Rome had not suffered any bombing. At this time the region between the Aurelian Wall and the EUR was still undeveloped. The **Via Cristoforo Columbo** ran through empty fields. After the war they carried on building—at first, for simplicity's sake, following the old plans.

The idea of a town in the countryside,

with a new interpretation of the old Italian use of space, is mingled in Piacentinis' plans with a monumental grandeur and a repetitive motif: square pillars, square ground plans, square roofs, softened only by the six stories of arcades on the **Palazzo della Civiltà** at the end of the **Via della Civiltà**. The buildings radiate a cold beauty that is all the more effective because in the Baroque Rome of the popes nothing is rarer than a straight line. After the war the EUR quarter was the only part of Rome in which skyscrapers were built. There was a consensus that such buildings would be incompatible with the style of the city center. Now the EUR wasn't any longer doing its intended job of increasing Mussolini's fame, it became a status symbol for the state-owned oil company ENI, for *Alitalia* and other companies which were supposed to spread pride in the Italian "economic miracle".

ttempts at modernity in e EUR uarter.

The offices and ministries took their employees out to EUR with them. The city made a tired attempt at a unified plan for the rising new buildings, but gave up when everything was thrown into confusion by the 1960 Olympic Games. These presented the EUR with a sports hall which is now enthroned up on the **Piazzale dello Sport**. It holds about 20,000 spectators and is used for musical, trade union and political events on a large scale. The Olympic buildings, recognizable by the then fashionable glass facades, were built along the lake (intended to please the eye, not for swimming) in the hollow between the two EUR hills.

The viewing platform, known as the **Fungo** (mushroom), gives the best view. The next building boom came at the end of the 1960s. The style is recognizable by the tangle of steel girders across the facades. More departments and Party offices moved in—followed by civil servants and well-off Romans. The result is that the area now has more politicians, diplomats and industrialists living in its flats than any other part of Rome—and it also has the highest number of thefts and break-ins.

Nonetheless the EUR has some genuine attractions—in the form of four museums, hideous on the outside, but full of priceless riches within. The **Museo Preistorico ed Etnografico** has many objects from prehistoric cultures from Africa, Asia, America and Australia, and also a separate department for finds from Latium. Then there is the **Museo delle Arti e Tradizioni Popolari** with its display of crafts and documents relating to folklore. There is also the **Museo del Alto Medioevo**, a collection of finds from the Middle Ages—and finally the **Museo della Civiltà Romana**. Here you will find a collection of documents and discoveries, partly originals, partly facsimiles,

The "square" Coliseum, built in Mussolini's time.

which cover just about everything that historians have ever learned about Rome and its history, from its beginnings up to the collapse in the 5th century. You can admire the model of Rome at the time of Constantine the Great, covering an area of 1900 sq yards (1600 sq meters), that was donated by Fiat. If you have to drag your children out on guided tours outside the gates of Rome, you can keep them in a good mood by promising to visit the fun fair which is on your right on the return trip from the EUR.

The architectural equivalent of the EUR in the north of Rome is on the Tiber, not far from the Ponte Milvio, at the end of the city stretch of the Via Flaminia. Once it was the Foro Mussolini, now it's called the **Foro Italico**. The Duce had an obelisk placed there with the inscription *Mussolini Dux*. His other legacies were unfinished—a marble stadium, an Institute of Sport,

swimming baths and the plans of the architect Enrico Del Debbio for the Sports Stadium with room for 100,000 spectators, which was only completed by the new state for the Olympic Games. The best use of these buildings was made during the events of the *Estate Romana*, when the rhythms of Brazilian sambas made even the stiffly-posed marble figures look friendly.

During the terrorist years the democratic state turned the Gymnasium into a super-safe courthouse for trying members of the Red Brigade. Near here is the **Farnesina**, the foreign ministry, which began life as the "palace of the Party". High rooms, long corridors, hall-like waiting rooms all become involuntary reminders of Charlie Chaplin in *The Great Dictator*. It looks so much like a film set that only one person could possibly reside here—the cunning old fox of Italian politics, Foreign Minister Giulio Andreotti.

ew uildings in e Tor de enci istrict.

THE BORGATE

The countryside around Rome is a classic example of how quickly a landscape that has grown up over thousands of years can be destroyed.

The famous *Agro Romano* was a wide landscape of hills and fields stretching out from the gates into the city. It was crossed by the consuls' ancient roads and inhabited by sheep, farmers and herdsmen. Nowadays it has practically disappeared. If you look down from the nearby Alban Hills towards the plain of the Tiber, you will see a single sea of houses below. And now it's time to squash one widely held misconception. It certainly wasn't all the fault of the Fascists and their ideas of moving people out of the city and into the satellite towns known as **Borgate**. The present situation is due to the combined efforts of the city fathers over three epochs.

The idea of building self-enclosed estates on the suburban edge of Rome first appeared in the town development plans of the "Red" people's bloc under Ernesto Nathan in 1907. Since 1870 Rome had been the goal of a steady stream of immigrants, especially from the south and from the Abruzzi. In 1922 there were about 800,000 inhabitants. Just before World War II the number had risen to 1.3 million, and after the war it was 1.8 million.

The immigration problem was made considerably worse by Mussolini, also known as "His Majesty the Sledgehammer", who demolished old housing to build grand streets. He saw Rome as needing two things: "living space and greatness". After his first attempts with detached houses he began the building of the classical Borgate of Prenestino, Pietralata and San Basilio. These were

Traders set up shop by the old aqueducts.

so depressing in form and building material that **Pietralata**, **Triburtino** and **Quarticciolo** soon became symbols of wretchedness. Here lived poor immigrants from the south and from the mountains, casual workers of a lumpen proletariat that, particularly between 1950 and 1976, made a girdle of slums all around Rome.

Pier Paolo Pasolini, prophet of these rootless people, came to Pietralata as a small-time teacher in 1950. Here he found his *ragazzi di vita*, "in houses like mountain ranges...empty or full of flapping laundry, quiet or filled with the chatter of women and the crying of children." The Christian Democrat city government did nothing to help, and Rome spread like an oil spill into the Agro Romano.

In 1976, after the election of the communist mayor Carlo Giulio Argan, whose votes largely came from the slum areas, Rome's great slum clear-ance program started. The Borgate were given lighting, power, mains water and bus routes. This was followed by the building of the exemplary new towns such as **Tor bella Monaca** and **Tor de Cenci**. These, in spite of their architectural modernity and sensible planning, have still developed the problems of all such districts everywhere in the world—vandalism and drug abuse.

The illusions have flown, and the loss of votes in these areas was the main reason for the communists' electoral defeat in 1985. All the problems of Rome—for example unemployment—hit the Borgate twice as hard. The climate of the "loss of political illusions" resulted in a loss of solidarity and a struggle of the poor against the poorest. In 1988 tens of thousands of *Borgatari* blockaded the roads out of Rome in a protest against the settlement of a few thousand gypsies.

Pensioners playing Boccia in the Tuscolana District.

STRIKES: A POPULAR CUSTOM

It is impossible not to have heard of strikes in Italy, and just as impossible not to have been affected by one. The impression of chaos given by strikes in public transport can easily lead the foreign visitor to the false conclusion that the country is sinking into anarchy. But the traveler has simply had the bad luck to end up in the only remaining "strike-active" area of Italian employment. Since their defeat at Fiat in 1980 the metal workers have kept quiet and have accepted redundancies without any notable resistance.

Factory Strikes

Strikes in factories are never noticed by most people, especially travelers from a foreign country—either because they do not affect them (unless they particularly wanted the strike-bound make of a car custom built) or because they do not understand the language. On top of that, widespread strikes are rare in Italy. Only individual workers or groups of employees within a factory usually strike.

As far as trains, buses and planes go, the situation is more complicated. Here unions which have only a few hundred members are calling strikes. The three official big, politically orientated unions—the CGIL, a member of a communist-socialist organization; the CISL (formed in 1950 after the merger of two trade union parties—the LCGIL and FIL), Christian Democrat; and the UIL, liberal-socialist, have little say. The standard is set by the "autonomous" unions, which are more a matter of class, as well as the fascist CISAL groups, and in recent years also CO-BAS (*comitati di base*).

The end of a strike.

In Italy's transport sector, trouble has been brewing for years. Modernization plus planned privatization of the railroads make for unrest, and an inflexible administration adds to it. On top of this the regulation of strikes exists in a legal vacuum in Italy. The Italian constitution guarantees the right to strike "within the framework of the law". The irony of it is—there is no such framework.

Every union in Italy is free to call a strike, whenever and wherever it wants, with or without asking its members, however many they may be. Ballots are unknown. Arbitration involves a mere voluntary declaration of purpose and had no power in law until 1988. The unions are free to use their right to strike, but the employers are just as free to fire active trade unionists and hold lock-outs.

The government of Italy has, after all, given the unions an example. Conflicts among the coalition parties are solved by announcing a crisis—this is only the beginning of solving the crisis and not its traumatic end.

Strikes: An Italian Ritual

Strikes are an Italian way of drawing attention—*"Hey, I've got a problem, let's talk about it"* is how they perceive strikes. Someone feels ignored, or disadvantaged compared to another profession—strike first, discussion later. The employers think along the same lines: "If the workers don't strike, I can't offer what I would have offered anyway." *The ritual* has to be observed. We observers, standing outside these local disputes, can only help ourselves in two ways. One, we can look in the papers, which regularly list strikes under the heading *sciopiero* (strikes), and two, arm ourselves with *pazienza*, patience.

emonstra-
on by
ensioners in
ome.

PIAZZA VENEZIA

All roads lead to Rome, and all roads in Rome lead to the **Piazza Venezia**. From here you can follow the Via del Corso to the Piazza del Popolo, go to the Vatican via the Corso Vittorio Emanuele, to the station by way of the Via Nazionale, to the Fora along the Via dei Fori Imperiali, and to southern Rome, passing the Capitol, along the Via del Teatro Marcello, across the Via Luigi Petroselli to the Circus Maximus and the Viale Aventino.

Before the demolition of many old parts of the city this square, the origin of all roads in Rome, was merely an extended side bay in the Via del Corso, and for many modern Romans it remains just that. *Sotto il Balcone*, under the balcony, is one of the most popular meeting places in Rome. The "Balcone" is the little balcony of the **Palazzo Venezia**, from which Mussolini impressed his militaristic triumphs on the Italians.

A Traffic Junction

Rome's piazze can be intimate, loud, *popolare*, dreamy, splendid or quiet— but the Piazza Venezia is nothing but a traffic junction. It isn't a piazza in the Roman sense. People come here and drive on, but never stay.

A long stay here is not advisable, because of the high air pollution levels—just take a look at the house walls on the **Via del Plebiscito**, near the bus stop. The new laws to keep traffic prohibitions won't change that. Rome's car drivers know where they can quickly get a *permesso*, a "special licence". In the "totally" prohibited areas of the Centro Storico, at least 45,000 VIP Romans are allowed to drive their own cars. If they all did it at once, traffic chaos would be unavoidable.

It is still worth your while to stop in the place, at least for a moment. For in this place you can admire the magic of the Roman traffic policeman, who from his little podium conducts the streams of vehicles, like a Karajan of the cars. Recent measurements have proved noise levels of 75 to 85 decibels.

Planning a New Capital

Three million Romans are still suffering today because of the laws to beautify Rome, made in 1881 for the new capital. Anyone who wants to move from one part of the outskirts to another is forced by the arrangement of roads to come via the Piazza Venezia. It is almost impossible to imagine what it must have looked like here just under a hundred years ago, before this "enormous white cancerous tumor", as the poet Gabriele D'Annunzio called it, was built. Instead of the monument known as *macchina da scrivere*, typewriter, the houses of medieval Rome stood row upon row, the Via dei Fori Imperiali didn't exist. A view of the Colosseum could be seen from roof gardens, and a little street snaked its way along the heavily built up Capitol, pulsing with life.

Nowadays 800,000 Romans squeeze their cars past every day, even if they don't want to go to the Centro Storico, but just from Pietralata to the Aurelia Nuova. But up till now the tangential street network of Rome is a rump of short race tracks in the "semi-periphery" near the Aurelian Wall. The Piazza Venezia is still waiting to be promoted from a traffic junction to the rank of Roman piazza. From here the visitor has to take the weighty decision which way to go when sightseeing. We recommend that you take a drink in one of the bars in the side streets off the Via del Corso, it's cheaper and the service is usually friendlier.

VIA DEL CORSO

This Corso is an unusual street. In ancient times it was "the" street to be seen and to shop in, just as it is today. Yet only in one spot is there any reminder of classical times: at the **Piazza Colonna**, where the column of Marcus Aurelius still stands. Its base, however, is 15 feet (five meters) under today's street level. A hundred feet high and decorated with reliefs of the Emperor's German and Sarmatian campaigns, it is now topped by a statue of St. Paul. The obelisk at the **Piazza del Popolo**, stolen by Augustus from Egypt, once stood in the Circus Maximus as a turning post for chariot races.

Past the **Porta del Popolo** the Corso runs into the **Via Flaminia**, which leads straight on to the **Ponte Milvio**, where Constantine the Great was converted to Christianity. The Corso's present appearance dates from the 15th century. Up till then the area between the modern department store **Rinascente** and the Piazza del Popolo was merely a stretch of ancient ruins, meadows and swamps. The old central street only returned to its past glory when the popes came back as rulers of Rome after the "Exile in Avignon" and made the Piazza Venezia into their first seat of power. However, almost all the existing buildings have been built in the last three centuries, except for the churches of **S. Marcello**, **Santa Maria in Via Lata**, **San Carlo**, **S. Giacomo** and **Gesù e Maria**. Symbolic of this hour of birth of Roman capitalism is the almost oppressive number of large banks in the Corso.

Even if you only walk down the street to look at the shops, you still feel hemmed in by the mighty palazzi, built much too close together and too high.

The end of the Via del Corso: Piazzale Flaminia.

This should not stop you from stepping into one or other of the banks. Suddenly you are in quite another world—Baroque inner courtyards with ancient statues, beautifully restored frescos and reliefs, fountains. Most doorkeepers will let you in "just to browse" without grumbling.

On the right-hand side—and partly on the left—the Corso from the Piazza Venezia to the Piazza del Popolo is a solid row of shop windows. This development only came about in the last century. One hundred and fifty years ago only two *botteghe* were known. But only certain types of shop are found here. No craftsmen, no food shops—instead the area offers everything you could want for *svago* (leisure) and fashion. In spite of the impression of expense, you can still find a bargain here, because the great number of shops has increased competition. Not that this makes the Corso in any way cheap.

Nonetheless, every Saturday an enormous crowd of suburban Romans makes its way along the Corso, as there are so few places to meet "out of town".

Unfortunately the changeover to a plain shopping street has swept away a tradition that delighted all visitors to Rome. The poet Goethe, who lived in Corso number 19, could still write about it. The popes had moved the "corsi" (races, hence the street name) from the Via Giulia to their new grand street. Starting point for the youth races was the modern **Galleria Colonna**, the men ran from the Via delle Vita, buffaloes and donkeys from S. Giacomo and riderless horses from the Piazza del Popolo.

Today the MPs and ministers race to Parliament or to the seat of government, the **Palazzo Chigi**—and so does the army of those who have, in some miraculous fashion, obtained a special permit to drive in a pedestrian zone.

he Via del orso is the in" shopping street.

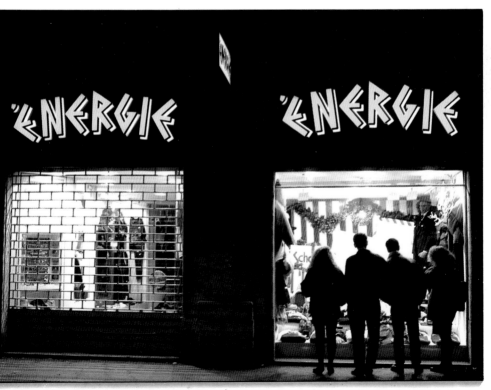

VIA NAZIONALE
TO THE STATION

The road is a mile (1.6 km) long and was originally planned as a straight line connecting the **Piazza della Repubblica** (**Piazza Esedra**) near the station with the monument to Vittorio Emanuele, the **Altare della Patria**, on the Capitol. Shortly before reaching its goal, however, it bends to form an angular "S", and this stretch was given another name—Via Cesare Battisti. This street is a true memorial to the desperate efforts, in the days after unification, to give the capital a cosmopolitan appearance. The imperial fora demonstrated the splendors of antiquity, the center and the opposite bank of the Tiber spoke of the might of the popes—but the kingdom of Italy, thrown together by the adventurer Garibaldi and north Italian capital, had no suitable accommodation either for its workers or its rulers. In those times Rome was a mere provincial town composed of classical ruins and fading clerical glories.

The new rulers exhausted themselves in a few monuments. Even the building of a few useful streets was left to speculators such as the former papal War Minister, Monsignore Francesco Saverio De Merode. He bought all sorts of houses between the old Baths of Diocletian and the Forum, tore most of them down and sold the building space to other speculators, who built offices and apartment blocks. The Via Nazionale is a prime example of these changes to the city. The heavy symbolism of the time incorporated in this connection between a historic area and the station has now disappeared under the patina left by the attacks of exhaust fumes.

If you want to look at the street in more detail, start at the bottom, near the **In front of the Quirinal seat of the state president.**

Piazza Venezia. This way you will get a much more direct impression of the changes in the function of the "Nazionale" as you move from the old city towards the station. In the lower part of the street you can still find impressive buildings such as the **Banca d'Italia** and the **Galeria nazionale d'Arte**. Further up there are shops and hotels. But aside from the change in use, an upward glance at the palace-like facades will give an incomparable insight into the character of the previous century, with its desperate, ridiculous-looking attempts to give the mostly five-storied and uniform Palazzi a "historical aspect". They are absolutely crawling with romantic, decorative roof ridges, stern classical or Renaissance style imitations, even straightforward copies of Gothic elements, such as the Anglican church **St. Paul within the Walls**, built in 1880, on the corner of the Via Napoli.

The street is lacking in impressive buildings. Important government departments such as the War and Finance Ministries preferred the hills, such as the Quirinal, visible from the lower junction with the Via XX Septembre. The banks preferred the Via del Corso. So, along with the National Gallery, only the National Bank came here. The building turned out so grim that even the palm trees bend away from it in alarm. They are now being pulled back with thick ropes. Because of building faults, the gallery is in a permanent state of restoration. Two theaters, the "Elisio" and the "Teatro nazionale dramatico" attempt to entice the Muses. With great difficulty **San Vitale**, once a three-nave basilica built in 402, has survived in the basement of this street. Here even Monsignore De Merode took pity, because Pope Sixtus had already amputated the two side naves on another occasion—they got in his way.

ᵢe fountain
f the
aiads, P.
epubblica,
front of
e Baths of
iocletian.

VIA DEI FORI IMPERIALI

Down 930 yards (850 meters) of race track, before they end up in the grasp of the "Vigili Urbani"—such is the fate faced by the Roman motorists on this shortest racetrack found in the world. Early in the morning, at 7.30, a solid traffic jam blocks the points where the **Via Labicana** runs into the **Via dei Fori Imperiali**. Here Nero had an artificial lake built and the Flavians returned the tyrant's palace to the people in the form of the amphitheater. Now thumbs down has given way to feet down—on the accelerator.

At least car drivers can have fun on the 88-yard-wide road. Visitors to Rome are usually somewhat puzzled. So this is supposed to be Rome's number one prestige avenue—although there isn't a single street in Rome which doesn't have at least a tobacconist, a bar or an alimentary shop—except this one.

After dark, except for lost tourists, the street belongs to the "ladies" lighting their cigarettes at the **Domus Aurea** and a few flashers at bus stops. The *Duce*, ruler of Italy's thousand-year empire from 1922 to 1943, wanted it this way—and this is how it came to be.

Seen beside a number of other things which Rome has unwillingly inherited from him, this street really is a masterpiece. In a single year (1932) bulldozers flattened one of the oldest medieval quarters of the city in order to hack out the route of the street, known by its earlier name of **Via dell'Impero**. About 5,500 flats belong to the people living in the quarter, who proudly called themselves *Monticiani*, were destroyed. Some 366,200 cubic yards (280,000 cubic meters) of earth were removed, plus 65,400 cubic yards (50,000 cubic meters) of tufa, old walls, imperial palaces, temples, arches, ninfei (buildings from the 3rd century

B.C.)—all without exception fell victim to the sledgehammer.

A story about Mussolini shows up the colossal idiocy of contemporary architects. On the edge of the Colosseum he saw an unassuming pile of stones. It was in the way of his vision of a ruler-straight street, so he simply ordered it removed. No-one dared to tell the D*uce* that this was the **Meta Sudans**, an ancient spring, which had survived the ages until 1932, but then became a victim of ignorance.

"It would have been easy, while building the street, to excavate those parts of the Fora of Julius Caesar and of Trajan still lying underground and to direct the road over them as a bridge, but the Dictator, concerned only for his next demonstration of power, was in a hurry..." This was how Ludwig Curtius, at that time director of the **German Archaeological Institute** in Rome, reported the "massacre".

The best actor in Rome, in the Piazza Venezia.

The *Duce's* plan was for an Archaeological Park stretching from the Forum to the Via Appia Antica and containing the heart of ancient Rome.

The Archaeological Park was intended to combine the excavations of the Forum Romanum with the area around the Baths of Caracalla and the valley between the Via Latina and the Via Appia Antica into one park to the greater glory of the Fascist Empire. Get rid of Mussolini's high-falutin ideas and you are left with the modern-sounding idea of a pedestrian park around the monuments, giving them back for the Romans to use without having to wall them up in special buildings first. But like everything which the *Duce* undertook, it was only done half-heartedly and badly. Soon nothing moved in the Monti quarter except crowbars. After the war the left-wing city government headed by the Professor of Art, Giulio Ciarlo Argan revived the project of an Archaeological Park in 1976. In this plan the Via dei Fori Imperiali—narrowed—was to make a bridge over the excavations.

But city planners argued that such a huge arterial road in a network of small city streets was a plain invitation to increase the volume of traffic. The timid attempts to excavate the road can be found to the right of the entrance to the Forum Romanum. They are the car parks surrounded by metal fences. Since the Christian Democrats have returned to the Capitol, all work has stopped. However, every April 25 there is an annual row: on the day of the Liberation of Italy the military regularly want to hold a parade. With equal regularity archaeologists and pacifists unite and protest. A compromise is reached every time: the tanks have to stay at home and only infantry can march—but with a light tread, without disturbing the monuments.

man
use
llection in
e Foro
ario.

CORSO VITTORIO EMANUELE II

The Corso Vittorio Emanuele II is one of the most historically important streets in Rome. Since the closure of the Via del Corso, however, a chaotic traffic system has turned it into a constantly blocked main arterial road. Every day the united traffic jams of the east to west and now also the redirected northwest to south flow squeeze their way through. In ancient times what is now the **Corso Vittorio Emanuele II** ran from the Largo Argentina to the Tiber bridge by the Castel Sant'Angelo.

The most impressive building on the street was the **Theatre of Pompey**—a gigantic complex which stretched from the temples of the Largo Argentina to the Piazza Sant'Andrea della Valle. The Church of St. Andrew, built here in 1608, has the second largest dome after St. Peter's, but despite its huge size it doesn't cover even a quarter of the space taken up by the earlier theater. After the fire in the old Curia in the Forum the Senate met here, and it was here that Julius Caesar was murdered on March 15, 44 B.C. Remains of the theater can be seen in the cellar of the restaurant **Da Pancrazio** in the **Piazza del Biscione**, and more are buried under later buildings.

For the street kept up its importance for traffic. In the papal Middle Ages it was held to be the most important and therefore the best guarded street. It was after all part of the route from St. Peter's to the Lateran. The pope had to be able to walk down this route in procession without fear of danger. The street was first called *Via Papae*, but after the final move of the popes to St. Peter's it was also known as Via Sacra. In Renaissance times the quarter was the center of extensive building by papal and

Domes near the Piazza Venezia.

noble families. It was also the top address for the very wealthy: Charles V for instance lived in the **Palazzo Caffarelli**, partly designed by Raffael, the palace was later also known as **Vidoni** and Mussolini made it the headquarters of his party.

After the founding of the Italian monarchy in 1870 the new rulers tried to make all sorts of changes to turn the street into one of their grand avenues. The result was the usual destruction of the once well-balanced architecture of the squares. Even so a number of important buildings survived the alterations, but these are now beginning to suffer from the effects of traffic.

Still in fairly good condition is the **Little Farnesina** in the **Piazza San Pantaleo**, an interesting building with its displaced stories, home to a collection of sculptures named after Senator Barracco. There is also the **Cancelleria** at the square of the same name, built in the 15th century, where you should take a look not only at the church of **San Lorenzo** but at the three-part inner courtyard. On the other side of the street is the **Palazzo Braschi**, which looks 16th-century but was actually built 200 years later for Pius VI. Today it contains the **Museo di Roma**, which displays modern art, portraits of the popes and a compartment of the special train used by Pope Pius IX. Lastly there is the **Chiesa Nuova**, designed by Filippo Neri in the 16th century.

From here the street originally turned to the right, to the bridge by Castel Sant'Angelo. Now you cross the Tiber by the **Ponte Vittorio** and come from the side, not straight on, into the **Via della Conciliazione**. This was built by Mussolini and Pius XII 50 years ago, straight through the quarters of the "Borghi", as a "street of reconciliation" after the re-creation of the clerical state abolished by the unification of Italy.

vement list in the rso ttorio nanuele II.

VIA VENETO

Sip a daiquiri in the Café de Paris, then have a meal in the Excelsior...this street, at first called simply Via Veneto, only received the name **Via Vittorio Veneto** after the victory over the Austrians in World War I.

Moving slightly uphill between plane trees it was and is the symbol of *la dolce vita*. Though the modern aspect of the street doesn't exactly make you think of fast living in the quarter, with the double rows of parked cars, the grim marines outside the American Embassy and the heavily armed carabinieri at the corner of the Via Bissolati next to the Lufthansa offices.

It's true that the times of *la dolce vita* with Anita Ekberg have long gone. She herself lives in retirement in the Castelli Romani, and the intellectuals have

chosen the **Piazza del Popolo** to meet. Today the only international flair is due to the stewardesses and pilots from the nearby airline offices who are using up their coupons here. The fashion designers remain true to the Via Veneto, however, and hold their *Super-Sfilata* fashion show in the Excelsior.

Old Roots in the Gardens

The Via Veneto is certainly not the only place in Rome to remain true to its origins for nearly 2,000 years. Between the Piazza Barberini and the Porta Pinciana things have old roots. In this place lay the **Gardens of Sallust**.

A nouveau riche war profiteer and contemporary of Caesar, Gaius Sallustius called himself a historian and had made enormous fortunes out of the countless campaigns between 40 and 30 B.C. His narratives of Rome in the 1st century B.C. influenced other historians and may be credited with the development of the monograph. Around his residence he created a garden palace and the gardens, named after him, were immediately recognized as one of the wonders of the world. Their beauty could not be long hidden from the emperors, who quickly laid their hands on them. Vespasian and Titus preferred this area to the damp Palatine. Nerva died here and Aurelian had the gardens enclosed by his wall.

The best-preserved part of the gardens themselves is a ruin in the **Piazza Sallustio**. In the previous century the splendor of the gardens drew pilgrims to them. They boasted underground fountains, pools and mosaic floors. Now they lie 46 feet (14 meters) under modern street level. The rubble of frequent house collapses in Rome and the building activity of the last century have buried the remains.

Christians honor their martyrs, tortured here, in the gardens. Archaeological finds from the gardens can be seen in **Shop in the Via Veneto.**

the **Museo Nazionale delle Terme**. Among the finds from the Via Veneto is the obelisk at the **Piazza della Trinità dei Monti**, which lies at the upper end of the Spanish Steps.

The splendor and colorful life of the gardens only came to an end with the invasion of the Goths under Alaric, who stormed the Holy City by the nearby **Porta Salaria** in 410. In the Middle Ages the family of Ludovisi-Boncompagni continued the lively tradition of this place, with 74 acres (30 hectares) of vineyards and garden festivals.

Gardens for Sale

The uninhibited property boom of the 80s of the previous century put an end to this marvel. The *Società Generale Immobiliare*, backed mainly by German and French capital, suggested a sale to the princes of Ludovisi. They accepted the swap for ready cash and the villa was split up. It lay around the modern streets of Boncompagni-Ludovisi. Remains of the villa can still be seen only in the gardens of the **Swiss Cultural Institute** the **Casino dell' Aurora Ludovisi**, which can be visited on request.

The other part of the garden spared by developers is inaccessible—the back of the present American Embassy. Prince di Piombino Ludovisi had this gigantic building built as a substitute for the sold garden. But his money ran out and he had to sell to the Savoy royal family. They accommodated the queen mother here, and it bears her name to this day.

If, after so much speculation and grandeur, you feel like a macabre diversion, look at the bones of 4,000 Capuchin monks in the church **S. Maria della Concezione** at the end of the street. You could hardly believe it, but here bones and skulls are used as a kind of interior decoration.

oman
shion
how in the
rand Hotel
xcelsior.

VIA GIULIA

An oasis of peace between the traffic-crammed Lungovetere and the equally badly off Corso Vittorio Emanuele II—that's the **Via Giulia**. A fate which its founder probably hadn't foreseen. On the contrary, he wanted it to be an imperial road, testifying to the recently gained greatness of the Apostolic Church. But like so many things in Rome that were built to glorify someone or something, the course of history cut this plan back to human size.

Officially, Pope Julius II had this street in the *Renovatio Romae* named Via Giulia in honor of Rome's ancient greatness and claimed that he was using Julius Caesar's name. But none of his contemporaries had much doubt that he named it above all for himself: Julius II's Italian name was also Giulio. Bramante began work in 1508, with the intention of making it the center of papal Rome.

The street was part of a papal plan for the city that stretched from the bridge **Ponte Sisto IV** to the Vatican. All the land was firmly in the hands of the *della Rovere* family. Sixtus IV was Julius' uncle. The Via Giulia connected the harbor **Ripa Grande** with the Vatican, and it was to be an "imperial" road. The parallel **Via dei Banchi Vecchi** was to take on the commercial role and appropriately, at its end by the **Ponte S. Angelo**, lay the papal mint, leased by the German Fugger family. They minted a special new coin, the Julius dollar, for the pope. He hoped to break the power of the Florentine bankers by this means and make his papal state economically independent.

The centerpiece of the new street was to be the Tribunal Palace, and Bramante began work on it. But the death of the pope turned everything upside down. The old Roman nobility had not taken well to the dispossessions that preceded the building of the street and allied themselves with the Florentines, who were hungry for revenge. One of the latter, from the banking family of Medici, succeeded to the Holy See as Pope Leo X.

The building of the Tribunal Palace had only got as far as the foundations, and these can now be seen between the **Vicolo del Cefalo** and the **Via del Gonfalone**. In the best adapt-and-make-do tradition of Rome, the Roman nobility simply had houses and churches built on the giant basalt blocks. The planned main entrance of the Tribunal was rapidly made into a street and is now the **Via dei Bresciani**. The Via Giulia soon became a good address for patrician Roman families, who are still here today with their palazzi, spacious flats, and antique shops. It is one of the ironies of history that this anti-Florentine street had the patron church of the

On the road—on foot.

Florentines, **S. Giovanni dei Firentini**, stuck on its northern end. It was built according to plans by Sangallo the Younger, Michelangelo and Maderna.

The open space halfway up is the work—fortunately unfinished—of Mussolini. It was to be a road up to the **Gianicolo**. Here, with a view of the Tiber to the right, is the "New Prison", **carceri nuovi**. With this building Pope Innocent X put an end to the torture chambers of the Savella family, who were up till then the papal gaolers. Prisoners were kept in single cells, like the personal prisoners of the pope in the Castel Sant' Angelo.

Palazzo Farnese

The Palazzo Farnese, symbol of victory of the Roman noble families over the strangers (all non-Romans), lies with its back to the Via Giulia. After 100 years of foreign popes, Cardinal Alessandro Farnese had this third papal palace built from 1517-1589. The Palazzo Venezia became a papal residence, and the Palazzo della Cancelleria was seat of the papal law court, but in the Palazzo Farnese Pope Paul III celebrated nothing but the dignity and power of his family. Three hundred and six (!) families moved with the Farnese-Sforza into the palace and the surrounding houses. The Colonna, the Caetani, The Orsini all added their family palaces. Packed close together, they took possession of Rome once more.

Roman history displays a fine sense of continuity. Who else could occupy the Palazzo Farnese, with its splendid Renaissance facade and the frescos by Annibale Carraci but the country with the greatest need of "grandeur"? It is now the French Embassy, and on Bastille Day a great party is traditionally held at the Piazza Farnese.

iew of the
ia Giulia.

VIA CRISTOFORO COLOMBO

Another of those roads with which the Fascists tried to change the face of Rome, and particularly to revive ideas of the glorious times of city and Empire, the avenue **Via Cristoforo Colombo** was supposed to lead out from the Porte Ardeatina, linking the ancient city center with the EUR center planned for the World Exhibition of 1942. Then it was to follow the shortest route out of the city to the sea, where the waters between Gibraltar and Syria, as is well known, once all belonged to Rome.

Like so many of Mussolini's projects, it was never completed. Work on the road started, but was only finished after the war, and the road still has no real function. This is partly because a parallel road, the **Via del Mare**, leads to the sea, and only a few miles further on the motorway to the airport of Fiumicino, also by the sea, was built.

The Via Cristoforo Colombo runs at first through the outer buildings of 60s Rome, passing the ill-planned and unattractive exhibition area **Fiera di Roma**, where small traveling circuses are the main attraction, then over valleys and hills along the new buildings of the **FAO** on to the EUR. It goes round the **Palazzo dello Sport** and then crosses the wide Via del Oceano. Now you have to be careful: the broad, straight continuation is the **Via Pontina**, leading to the bathing areas of the former Pontine Marshes.

The parallel exit on the right is the continuation of the Cristoforo Colombo. After a few hundred yards the road recovers and now has four lanes. About 13 ruler-straight miles (20 km) are only broken by traffic lights, where wide roads cross in open country, remains of the once planned and now ridiculous network of roads. Then

the road ends in a kind of ski jump, which leads to a swimming pool named "Kursaal".

To the right and left the road is bordered by the pine woods, the **Pineta**, famed and infamous. Famed for mushrooms, which can be found there, and infamous, because it is rumored to be the burial ground of the Roman *Mala*, the underworld.

Further on, about half-way along, you can see new housing estates, keeping a respectful distance from the road. These are two-story houses with all sorts of architectural idiosyncrasies which display the lifestyle of *Roma bene*. The well-off have recently started to move out here because the area is quiet except for airport noise—and there's not much of that due to the strikes. Also there are no exhaust fumes.

To the right, by the sea, you can see **Ostia** in the distance. This is the "new" Ostia, of the beach houses and holiday hotels, mostly in decline since bathing was prohibited in 1986 because of water pollution. This hasn't thinned the crowds on the beaches in summer, but the wealthy build their summer apartments a bit further south, in **San Felice Circeo** and **Terracina**.

After a few miles of beach road you can recognize, behind the former promenade-palazzi to your right, something like a city center. It's a purely functional center, with no urban structure and chaotic streets, which often end in the dirt by the railway tracks. It has a big piazza and houses that look more like cliff caves than homes. This is where most of the 5,000 Poles seeking asylum live. If you drive into the tangle of streets, we can guarantee that you won't find your way out again for the next half hour. The best thing is to go back to the beach and take the single exit road towards Rome (it is well signed). It also leads past all the turn-offs to **Ostia Antica** or to the airport.

Right, Via del Mare, the end of the Via Cristoforo Colombo.

PIAZZA DI SPAGNA

The *piazza*, the square, is the essential feature of Italian urban culture. In Florence and Sienna it is the bourgeois parlor in front of the Town Hall. In Milan and Venice it is the central place in front of the cathedral. In any case it's the town's focal point. Rome is different, it no longer has a single focal point. In ancient times there was *the* Forum, court of law and market in one, in which the most important religious ceremonies were held, in which people gathered to make themselves heard on political matters or to cheer a victorious general. But grass had long grown over the ancient places, *the* Forum had become a cow pasture and Rome was only a provincial town when the Eternal City split into a collection of city quarters, each of which had its own center.

There was no need for an impressive central place. Here and there markets were held, and the huge churches were enough for any official functions. This changed during the Renaissance, but most of all in Baroque times, when giant showplaces were designed—for plays, for ceremonies and popular festivals. A thousand-year-old Sleeping Beauty. Rome woke once more and breathed new life into the squares with their fountains and obelisks: Piazza Navona, Piazza S. Pietro, Piazza del Popolo, Piazza di Spagna, Piazza S. Ignazio and Piazza del Campidoglio, just to name the "great" ones.

Rome, subsequently capital of the kingdom, Fascist state and finally democratic republic of Italy made new and different places for itself, or it re-used the old places in a new way; Mussolini turned the dignified Piazza Venezia into a forum for his propaganda appearances. If you go to a Roman piazza today, you will always feel something of the presence of history, as if it looked back with eyes sometimes large and sometimes small, sometimes sad and sometimes laughing, on the past when Rome's squares were the destination of many large and small demonstrations. Columns of people came from all over Italy, according to old traditions, to let their voices be heard. Take a look back, but without post-modernist rose-tinted lenses, and see the vigorous life of a southern European metropolis.

Many Roman squares, if they haven't degenerated into car parks, are still places for the trendy to be seen, places for tourists to rest, places for children to play—or simply places in the sun for everyone.

Today many visitors arrive at **Piazza di Spagna** (the "Spanish Square") in one of two ways. Either they come from the Metro station up a long escalator, on foot through a long tunnel and then turn left. Or, strengthened by Coke, salad or

hamburgers after leaving the most beautiful and stylish McDonalds in the world (unfortunately, apart from the salad bar, the food is the same as everywhere else in the world), they then turn right. These two entrances are a sign of the speed with which the square adapts to modern life, for both are new. The Metro entrance dates from 1979, the entrance to the right of McDonalds from 1986.

The self-confident Piazza di Spagna is the crown of the Baroque quarter to the right of the Via del Corso with its shopping streets, cafés and restaurants. The Spanish title of the square dates from the 17th century, when the Ambassador of the Catholic country had his residence here (the Embassy is still here today). The Piazza di Spagna, where the best of addresses is found in the best part of Rome, was fought over for years by France and Spain. The Spanish sat in their Embassy in the square and laid claim to this spot in the heart of the Eternal City for themselves, while the French sat in Trinita del Monte and based their claims on their protection of the Pope. The opposition of the two Embassies often ended in bloody struggles, which were only brought to an end by Pope Innocent XV.

The design of the Steps themselves, built in 1726 according to plans by Alessandro Specchi and Francesco de Sanctis, was for decades a matter for dispute among the parties. In the original designs statues along the edge were to increase the fame of France and the Sun King. Fortunately, that particular design was not taken up.

Now only the French national church, **S. Trinità dei Monti**, on the hill of the Pincio, sings the praises of France. The obelisk, completing the upward view, has only been there since 1789. At the feet of the church the water of the ancient aqueduct *Aqua Vergine* **The Spanish Steps.**

pours into the no less famous **Barcaccia Fountain** by Pietro Bernini, father of Gian Lorenzo Bernini. The fountain had to be built deep into the paving, as the low water pressure did not permit a high fountain.

Anyone can stand here and speculate what symbolism is contained in fountain and steps. At any rate, apart from the early morning hours, no visitor will ever be alone in this pedestrian oasis. Hundreds, on Sunday afternoons, sit on the famous steps, mingle with all those who have come to see or be seen. In wonder they watch the crowds. If, when in Rome, you want to see all its possible colors, you should come here several times a day. The light changes just as the people do—from the office employee taking a break to the Borgate-dwellers in the late afternoon to the casual strollers of the evening. Here you'll always see whatever happens to be the latest thing. Silently watching the

crowds are several palm trees, a Column of Mary and the **Palazzo di Propaganda Fide**. The 1854 Column of Mary symbolizes the doctrine of the Immaculate Conception, which marks a high point in the cult of Mary. It was Pius IX's answer to the bourgeois revolution of 1848. The Palazzo di Propaganda Fide has been the missionary center of the Catholic Church since 1622, or, a more worldly term, its Ministry of Propaganda. Also part of the X-shaped piazza are two bank branches, an American Express agency (here you can cash Eurocheques even on a Saturday morning!) the Keats-Shelley Museum, two newspaper kiosks, lots of boutiques and a small memorial plaque for socialists killed in the anti-Fascist resistance.

Fashion—fashions—McDonalds: the Piazza di Spagna offers you a glimpse back into modern times as it wears the Janus face of history.

Loving couples in front of the Church of S. Trinità dei Monti.

FONTANA DI TREVI

This place, which was made famous in the 50s by Anita Ekberg's plunge, is now firmly in the hands of the tourists. But if you dare to put even one foot into the water, when your feet are steaming after hours of walking around on red-hot asphalt, a whistle blast from the city police, Vigili Urbani, will put a stop to such blasphemous behavior. A 1987 order from the Assessor for Tourism insists that people respect the "dignity and cleanliness of the city of Rome". According to the Assessor, that includes covering the top half of the body and keeping your feet out of public fountains. Why cars in the ancient center—around the Fontana di Trevi as well—aren't an insult to the dignity of Rome, never mind a danger to its existence, the Assessor unfortunately didn't tell us.

Wine for Water

The first fountain at the end of the restored aqueduct was built by Pope Nicholas V in 1453, using the money from a tax on wine. The populace sneered: "He took our wine to give us water." This fountain, described by Charles de Brosses in the 18th century as looking like a "dilapidated village well" was the first papal *mostra*, showpiece, of the ancient Aqua Virgo and stood at the **Piazza dei Croceferi**. It was enormously important for the Rome of that time, because, for the first time since the barbarians had destroyed the water supplies, it brought fresh water back into the city.

The ancient water supply was built by Agrippa for his baths near the Pantheon. Its name goes back to the story that a maiden found the spring. The fountain, moved to its new position, got

its present appearance, after a competition among 16 artists, in the early 18th century. It was to be the last great patronage of the arts under papal rule, and the play of waters was intended once more to bring glory to its patron.

The fountain was dedicated to the ocean and Nicola Salvi devised the form. The German author and sharp observer Dieter Brinkman describes it as a "crazy idea" to put so huge a fountain in a square that is much too small. It is a gigantic piece of kitsch, and seems only to have been created for the film *La dolce vita*—perhaps they forgot to take it down after the shooting, suggests Brinkman.

Even so, it is hardly possible to resist the fascination of this constant gurgling and foaming, and the smallness of the piazza makes the show into a theatrical performance, with the crowding tourists as involuntary actors. Ancient legends are tied to the customs of throwing

Fontana di Trevi.

money into the fountain. The ancient Romans threw money in certain imperial fountains to propitiate Jupiter. The Christians took over the custom and threw coins onto Peter's tomb, till the old custom of throwing coins into fountains returned and people threw money in order to return to Rome. Every year coins to the value of hundreds of thousands of lire are thrown into the fountain. In a film made in the 1950s, the Italian comedian Toto sold the right to clear the fountain to American tourists—who couldn't have taken it up, as the right belonged to the city of Rome. It still does—every few months the coins are cleared. The annual catch is some hundreds of tons of coins.

The second place passed through by tourists on the obligatory Trevi-Navona route is the Piazza della Rotonda, better known as the **Pantheon**. This temple to all the gods, built by the son-in-law of the Emperor Augustus, was made into a church in 609, which preserved at least the basic building from being torn down. The Pantheon—44 feet (13.4 meters) above sea level—is the lowest point in Rome and used to be regularly flooded. How much the rubble has raised Rome over the centuries can be seen by the ditch around the Pantheon. In ancient times you climbed up to the Pantheon, not down. The dome of the Pantheon was the model for an endless number of copies, from St. Peter's in the Vatican to the White House in Washington. But even Michelangelo couldn't exceed the diameter of the Pantheon, its dome is five feet (1.4 meters) bigger.

In front of the Pantheon three bars and a hamburger shop have opened, making the piazza a popular meeting place. We recommend the speciality of the Café Tazza d'Oro, Granita di Café, frozen and ground up coffee with cream.

owds ound the untain.

PIAZZA NAVONA

This is the place that every visitor to Rome must go and see, otherwise no-one will believe that he's been to Rome. Everyone has read about it in the guidebooks—it is on the site of the Emperor Domitian's ancient race course, the aspect we see today was the work of the Baroque popes, its name refers to its ship-like form and comes from *nave*. The Piazza Navona is simply *the* place where the Eternal City meets.

The Piazza Navona is indeed worth seeing. It is one of the few places in Rome where a pedestrian zone is really observed—possibly because there is simply no way any road could be built through here. But most of the other information, as is so often the case, simply isn't true. For instance, Domitian's stadium does lie under the piazza,

but today's square simply isn't identical with the building of that time, although parts of the seats can be found in the foundations of houses at the side. Domitian's successors messed around a good deal with the stadium—when the Colosseum was damaged by fire on one occasion, an amphitheater was built into the stadium, and later it was modernized by the Emperor Septimus Severus. After the fall of Rome there were no more races. The population dragged the stones away as building material for their houses, the popes took the marble for the churches. You can still get an impression of the stadium's appearance when "intact" by looking from the **Piazza San Pasquino** into the basement of the INA-building.

In its original condition, the stadium was 177 feet (54 meters) wide, 906 feet (276 meters) long, and the seats reached a height of 110 feet (33.5 meters). Chroniclers describe athletic competitions and horse races. The bad practice of dragging away parts of the stadium was incidentally started by a certain Emperor Constantine II, who carried off works of art and decorative portions to his new residence in Constantinople. Nonetheless the stadium is still supposed to have been fully usable at the time of invasion by the Goths, in the A.D. 5th century.

There isn't much left of the original papal glories, either—only the church of **S. Agnese in Agone** (where the saint is supposed to have stood naked in the stocks) and, beside it on the left, the **Palazzo Pamphili**, designed by the same architect Rainaldi in the middle of the 17th century.

To the other church, **Madonna del Sacra Cuore**, he added little Baroque arches and figures to the Renaissance facade. These have gone now, but the result is hardly an exact restoration. Of the **Bernini Fountains** only the central Fountain of the Four Rivers is by the master himself. It shows the symbols of

Detail of the Fountain of the Moor, P. Navona

the Ganges, the Danube, the Rio de la Plata and—blindfolded because of its undiscovered springs at the time—the Nile. The **Fountain of the Moor** at the southern end of the Piazza is by one of his pupils. The **Fountain of Neptune** with its fish-horses was originally just a large basin. The sculptures were placed in the 19th century for symmetrical reasons—oddly enough, for nothing else surrounding this symmetrical centerpiece is symmetrical at all.

The two churches, for instance, are neither placed at the two ends nor in the middle of the two sides, there are no balanced, opposing palazzi, and even the two bars only appear to correspond—they are in fact not aligned.

The meeting place remains. The Piazza always was one—and up until a century ago it was a fairly well organized one, too. At weekends the Piazza, unpaved at that time, was sometimes flooded and horses and traps raced through it. There were also all sorts of races, of human beings and animals. Among the latter were not only horses, but also donkeys and buffaloes.

Even today the Piazza is still full of people—especially salesmen of all nationalities. They sell African jewelry, paintings and candyfloss. Romans, however, have become rare in the Piazza Navona. They only come here for special reasons—for instance when small political parties or pressure groups hold meetings. Or between Christmas and Epiphany, *befana*. Then for two weeks the square looks as it did in earlier times—a gigantic market, in which you can buy anything from trousers to books. "An ark, filled with everything you need to live" wrote the poet Giuseppe Belli in those times.

But *navona* still doesn't come from *nave*. It's merely a contraction of the name of the church "Agnese in Agone": in Agone, 'n Agone, Navone, Navona.

untain of
e Four
vers, in
nt of S.
nese in
one.

CAMPO DEI FIORI

For foreigners in Rome and also for many a nostalgic Roman this is the most secular, for some even the most heretical of Roman squares. It is as old as Rome itself, but has never been dedicated to any cult and is to this day free of churches. Right in the middle, a symbol of its separateness, is the statue of Giordano Bruno, who was burned at the stake in 1600. Everything around is picturesquely dilapidated and yet full of life. This is how you would imagine Rome to be when you were fed up with the ancient and the pompous.

But how did the **Campo dei Fiori** come by its name—was it once, at the height of Rome's glory, a meadow? Or did a noble Roman lady named Flora leave it her name? Or is it a result of the underlying Roman tendency towards anarchy to call the place of execution by this name?

The fact is that it was used as an execution ground by the popes until well into modern history. Its present aspect dates from the time of Pope Sixtus IV, at the end of the 15th century, part of the general re-shaping of the quarter during Renaissance times. The Piazza was never splendid. The lords of Rome saved their glories for the impressive palazzi such as the Farnese, for the Via Sacra (now Corso Vittorio) and the Via Giulia.

The Campo is kept alive day by day by the perfectly balanced infrastructure—it has everything from the butcher and baker to clothes shops and a cinema—and the daily food market, which up till midday draws in buyers, idlers and tourists. As soon as the market is gone, the pensioners come and children play football. In the evenings, strangers in particular are overcome by

Typical osteria in the Campo dei Fiori.

the feeling of "wordliness", able to imagine themselves as sitting among the rebellious and being part of the tendency to revolution that the Romans are supposed to harbor. The monument to Giordano Bruno intensifies the sinister atmosphere. Bruno and the eight other "heretics" (from Erasmus via Wyclif and Hus to Campanella) whose names are carved on the monument really deserve a better memorial. In fact it wasn't until 1887—after the "liberation from the pope"—that they got one at all. On every anniversary of his death the free thinkers' association "Giordano Bruno" lays a wreath here.

"17. febraio 1600. A hore di notte due…at 2 a.m. the condemned man Bruno, Giordano…an unrepentant heretic, was surrendered to us. Two fellow brothers of Holy St. Dominic…explaining holy doctrine to him with great feeling, showed him the error of his ways…his brain and intellect were lost in his cursed obstinacy, full of a thousand errors and self-satisfaction…he was led to the Campo dei Fiori, there stripped naked and burned alive at the stake, accompanied by the Litany of our Compagnia, adhering to his obstinacy to the last moment, and in it ending his miserable and unfortunate life." This is from the report of the Compagnia of monks on the man who was guilty of saying that the earth moves round the sun and not the other way around.

Unfortunately another monument had to be moved to make way for the statue. It was a 17th-century fountain, lovingly called "Terrine" by those living around the Campo dei Fiori. That now stands in the **Piazza della Chiesa Nuova** and on the edge of the basin you can find one of the neatest sayings of papal Rome: "Ama Dio e non fallire— Fa del bene e lascia dire" ("Love God and don't fail, do good and make sure people talk about it").

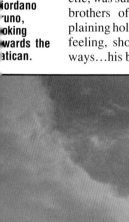

atue of
Giordano
Bruno,
looking
towards the
Vatican.

LARGO ARGENTINA

The Largo Argentina is actually called the "Largo di Torre Argentina" and is one of the most curious crossroads in the city. You run into people all the time, but you never meet there. This is because, driving the obligatory route round the city center, you are forced to come this way. At the bottleneck of the Corso Vittorio everyone squeezes past everyone else. Also no less than seven roads lead into the Largo—and it's a stop for a dozen bus routes.

The architecture around isn't very fascinating, either—palazzi of varying heights, none of them particularly attractive, banks, insurance companies. Only the **Teatro Argentina** could radiate some atmosphere, if only the dilapidated facade would allow you to make out the details. Inside, however, the

theater, built in 1730, is in fairly good condition and claims, as the *teatro stabile*, to be the center of events in Rome. However, there are a few big events to celebrate nowadays, and the theatrical library next door is a better bet.

Even the "Torre" on the corner of the Corso Vittorio, built in the northern style, isn't particularly impressive. It once belonged to the papal Master of Ceremonies Johannes Burckhard from Strasbourg (Latinized *Argentarium*— hence the name of the square). The actual attractions of the Largo lie elsewhere—you might say, deeper.

In the middle of the square, archaeologists have excavated four temples dating from republican times, probably from the 3rd or the 4th century B.C. Street level in ancient times was a good 26 feet (eight meters) below today's, so that the temples look as if they've been pushed down into the cellars of Rome. The temples, three square and one round, had been so thoroughly buried that we don't even know to which gods they were consecrated. They are therefore known as Temples A, B, C, and D (starting from the bus stop).

They were excavated in the 1920s, during another attempt to sort out the traffic arrangements in the square. In the middle there still lay the remains of a medieval marble works, which collected broken marble from ancient buildings and re-worked it for new uses. There was a short confrontation— traffic island or open-air museum—and this time, culture won. The temple complex was dug out down to original street level. You can see quite clearly how the Romans always raised their temples high above the people with many steps. At times when excavation was halted people called the site the Forum of Cats, because there were so many of them about. It's worth going down, if not for culture's sake, then for the sake of the peace and quiet under the noisy square.

The State Theater in the Largo Argentina.

PIAZZA S. GIOVANNI IN LATERANO

Here communists, believers in witchcraft and bazaar traders meet, overlooked by the mighty facade of the Lateran Basilica, whose apostle figures can be seen from Frascati. The African Pope Melchiadis received this stretch of land, which once belonged to Nero, as a gift from the Emperor Constantine.

The "mother of all churches", the first Christian basilica in Rome, has stood here since 313. It was the main church of Christendom, *locus legitimus*, up until the removal to Avignon. Afterwards the popes moved to the Vatican. The medieval church was richly decorated with marble and had a red-gold color, which gave it the nickname "the gilded basilica".

In earlier years the immense collection of relics was particularly treasured:

the heads of the Apostles Peter and Paul, a piece of the wooden table of the *Last Supper*, and the blood of Jesus, collected by the legionary Longinus. Here the equestrian statue of Marcus Aurelius, thought to be of Constantine, stood. The central portal is the original door of the Roman curia of the Forum, and the obelisk, 102 feet (31 meters) high, is the tallest and oldest in Rome. It praises the Pharaoh Tutmoses III and once stood at the Circus Maximus.

After the removal to the Vatican heathen customs took over the square. The eating of snails on St. John's Night, June 24, is considered a celebration of witchcraft. Here the communist leader Enrico Berlinguer lay in state in front of two million people. In the **Via Sannio** there is a second-hand clothes market, and an almost oriental bazaar under the city gate **Porta Asinaria**. Art lovers can see good exhibitions in the gallery in **Santa Scala**.

Piazza San Giovanni in Laterano.

THREE SQUARES IN TRASTEVERE

So the King asked on the last occasion: "How's your health?" "Oh, Majesty," said he, "I suffer from rheumatism! It's a torture!" The King said: "It's the season!" This moved the council meeting deeply and made an impression far and wide.

—Trilussa

The poet Carlo Alberto Salustri, known as Trilussa, was popular because of his satirical wit. He died in 1950, and even after his death he seems to go on addressing the people in the square that bears his name. His statue is bending forward slightly, and his hand is stretched out in a gesture, as if every evening he wants to talk to the old folks who still know him, and, winking mischievously, to accompany the younger ones at the start of a night out.

You can start a stroll through the squares of Trastevere in the **Bar Trilussa**, which has a cold buffet, or later on in the little mirrored bar in the **Piazza San Giovanni della Malva**. Your way will pass by the already famous theater for unattached troupes, the **Teatro in Trastevere**, down to the lower end of the **Via Garibaldi**. This was the way taken in the Middle Ages by the pilgrim crowds to the Vatican, before they turned right through the **Porta Settimiana**, a gate built by the Emperor Septimus Severus.

A True Trasteverino

The **Botanical Gardens** are delightful. You can find them immediately to the left behind the gate, but the true Trasteverini know this route for quite another reason. It runs straight to the old Roman prison, the **Regina Coeli**, the

The Sistine Bridge across the Tiber.

Queen of Heaven. The euphemistic name was taken over from the previous occupants, Carmelite nuns. If you want to be a true Trasteverino, it is said, you have to go down the steps to the dungeons at least once—to "make your mark", as the folk song says.

But to return to the squares of Trastevere—the area around the Piazza Trilussa is mainly full of new clubs, little bars, and the black-clad arty set, but the **Piazza Santa Maria** in Trastevere is the only real center of things. This is a square that stays alive round the clock. This is where the "quarter" walks past, rich and poor, both with dignity. Some rush from work, to the shadow of the oldest church in Rome dedicated to the Madonna, to gulp down a *bitter analcolico*; others just stop for a chat. The church is supposed to have been founded by St. Calixtus I (pope from 217/8 to 222). Its present appearance dates from the 12th century, and the mosaic is 13th-century.

The square is really beautiful only on Sunday morning, when Trastevere is waking up. Sleepily people buy the morning paper, drink capuccino and swap gossip. In the morning the square is beautiful because, despite all stone obstacles, the feeble enforcement of the prohibition on traffic means that it still turns into a car park by evening.

By contrast, the third square in Trastevere is never at its most lively on a Sunday, but on weekday mornings. In **Piazza San Cosimato** there is a food market. Every evening it turns into a turbulent passage for the night-lifers on their way to the bars around the square, but never becomes a meeting place. The Galeotti restaurant, with excellent Roman cuisine; the best fish restaurant in Rome, Alberto Ciarla; a spaghetti house; the Meta Theater and Brazilian folk music are only some of the possible sources of entertainment.

The "Bar Trilussa" in Trastevere.

PIAZZA VITTORIO EMANUELE II

Rome is usually famed for continuity, but since it was built, this square has probably undergone the most fundamental changes of any in the city. Its builders were the victors of united Italy. Having moved their ministries to Rome, they were looking for suitable accommodation for their civil servants. Moving from Turin to Florence, they had now reached the Tiber. The Romans had a good reason for immediately christening the area around this square the *quartiere piemontese*.

This right-angled square really was a "square", and yet both it and the strictly right-angled streets along the station were only a copy of the street plan of Turin. But here history teaches us to respect the individual character of Roman squares—this one, intended as a home for bureaucrats—ended as the most chaotic market in Rome. Foodstuffs of varying quality—prices and quality go down steadily from the **Via Carlo Alberto** to the **Via Principe Eugenio**—clothes, shoes and everything else can be bought here. The prices here set the limits for many other markets in Rome.

For years now the area around the market, among the now much dilapidated former palazzi of the Piedmontese, has become an Arab-African Casbah. Most of the illegal immigrants have made a market of their own here, in competition with the Romans. After the latest house collapse experts inspected the barely 100-year-old buildings and proclaimed most of them unfit for human habitation. The inhabitants often pay ridiculously low rents for huge flats, and are now afraid of the onset of gentrification, which could cost them the roofs over their heads.

Market in the "Piedmontese quarter" on the Piazza Vittorio Emanuele II.

THE PORTA PORTESE MARKET

Everyone's talking about the biggest flea market in Europe, the Roman **Porta Portese** in the Trastevere quarter. The inhabitants of this district are thoroughly sick of this regular Sunday "casino" (Italian for chaos, mess and sloppiness). These particular Romans can never dream of a lie-in.

The market has more than 4,000 stalls, and only 10 percent at most have a proper licence. Early in the morning the stallkeepers start to fight for the best places. The market stretches from Porta Portese itself to **Viale Trastevere**—easy to get to from there. Everything is on offer: antiques, flowers, spare parts for cars, used shirts and trousers, foodstuff, dairy products, comics, china and other household wares.

The city gate, the Porta Portese itself, has not been here all that long. Pope Urban VIII had an ancient city gate of Trajan moved to this place, half a mile (one km) nearer to the inhabited city, in 1643. Shortly after the gate was moved, the Swedish Queen Christina, converted to Catholicism, had herself driven through the gate in a coach specially designed by Bernini. She did not want to walk into Rome, perhaps for superstitious reasons, for the pope had ordered a Jewish cemetery in this place to be leveled.

This is the most popular market in Rome, even if the prices—particularly for antiques—have taken a sharp upturn in recent years. Plans to move it mostly consider shifting at least part of it to the river bank. However, if you know the speed with which decisions are taken in the Capitol, you will be pleased to know that you can safely continue to look for the Porta Portese market at the Porta Portese.

.urope's
.iggest flea
narket:
'orta
'ortese in
'rastevere.

PIAZZA MINCIO— COPPEDÈ

Italy's controversial poet and symbol of the 1920s, Gabriele D'Annunzio, called it "a genuine disgrace and an insult to Rome". He was speaking of the most curious square in Rome, the **Piazza Mincio**.

You can get to this curious collection of houses, built in a "fantasy style" that is neither Liberty's nor Deco, but simply Coppedè, by following the route from the German Embassy in the Via Po up to the Piazza Buenos Aires. If you can't find the Piazza Buenos Aires, ask for the Piazza Quadrata. This is the local name for the square, as the people living here, contemptuous of the official name, have a better memory for the shape the square makes with the Viale Regina Margherita. By day office employees and diplomats from the quarter fill the square. They promenade in their two-hour lunch break, eat in one of the good Chinese restaurants in the area or rest by the fountain. The builders of this quarter and the "fairy house", easily recognizable in the square, were a housing association who wanted to give the less well-off a chance to buy their own flats at a fixed rate of interest.

Coppedè's Creation

Creator of the square and its impressive **Toad Fountain** was the Florentine architect Gino Coppedè. His buildings were the last notable architecture of pre-Mussolini Rome. After them the massive blocks arrived, and the Byzantine-medieval grotesque style vanished. It was supported by the nouveau riche class, who wanted fairy-tale castles with flowing facades. Coppedè intended this square to show harmony between the individual details of each house and the great tradition of Florentine craftsmanship. In this

square, and other "fairy-tale palaces" scattered about the city (for instance the last house designed by Coppedè, **Via Veneto no. 7**), the Roman middle class left a memorial to its dream of individualism, which was however rapidly pushed aside by the pseudo-collectivism of the Blackshirts.

It's only a short step from the Piazza Mincio to two of the most beautiful parks in Rome. The **Villa Trolonia**, begun in 1748 by a nephew of Clement XI, can be seen about 110 yards (100 meters) down on the right-hand side of the Viale Regina Margherita. To get to the **Villa Ada Savoia** you need to go in the opposite direction. When you reach the Via Salaria, turn right and after about 220 yards you will see the entrance to this park, once the property of the Royal Family. In the house of the Villa Ada Savoia Mussolini was arrested, after he had been stripped of power on July 25, 1943.

Rome's strangest piazza.

PIAZZA DEL MATTATOIO

Here, in the Mattatoio Bar in the piazza of the same name in the quarter of **Testaccio**, the union of pleasure and work goes back a long way. According to tradition, the wine amphorae were cooled on the Monte dei Cocci before being decanted. In the Middle Ages the wine festival processions of the *ottobrate* marched through the streets every October, and at Carnival time the uninhibited *Giochi di Testaccio*, the Games of Testaccio, were famous. These games were held from the 12th to the 16th century and began with a procession with the Pope borne at the head. A bear (symbol of the devil) and a stallion (symbol of lust) were slaughtered. Then 13 bulls fought two pigs dressed in red velvet, and finally all the animals were killed by swordsmen and shared amongst the "rioni" (parts of the city) for a feast.

Today you can feast on the heavy Roman cuisine in the trattorias in the area. Shortly before sunset the traps of the *cavallari*, coach drivers, arrive—they live in Mattatoio—and stop for a chat. This is where the building workers, still the typical inhabitants of the area, doze in their free time. You can also see the first of the new inhabitants of the quarter, the theater directors, musicians, and actors, spending a little time here before rehearsing in clubs, in the tent theater **Spaziozero** or in the former cinema **Vittoria** in the Piazza S.M. Liberatrice.

An argument has been raging for years among Rome's political parties as to whether this splendid example of Roman industrial culture—the only one in this city with almost no industry—should be torn down or preserved as a cultural center.

raditional
lace to
eet:
iazza del
attatoio.

THE TIBER AND THE ROMANS

The Romans never had much to do with the river. The founding of the city took place on a hill—the Palatine. For many years the Tiber had remained a useful military obstacle—to the Etruscans on the other bank. Even when Rome was great and mighty, the inhabitants of this city never looked upon water as a means of transport. The Roman army was infantry and ships were mostly used to transport goods—the legions marched on foot on roads built by the consuls.

Bridging History

Only bridges made history. The first one was built 2,600 years ago. The *Pons Sublicae*—Volscian for wooden—led to Trastevere. The first stone bridge of Censor Aemilius Lepidus from the year 142 B.C. led there too. It was at another bridge that Constantine defeated Maxentius on Oct. 28, 312. The four central arches of the *Ponte Milvio* date from 109 B.C. and it was on a bridge that an angel appeared in 590, announcing the end of the plague. Now the bridge that once led to Hadrian's Mausoleum had a new name.

Classical Rome lay on "this" side of the Tiber, and the *Regio Transtiberium*, modern Trastevere, was expressly built for foreigners and sailors. On "this" side also lay the ancient harbors, intended only for transporting goods—the oldest landing place in the *Forum Boarium*, the new harbor *Emporius* (193 B.C.), with the warehouses of the Porticus Aemilia in modern Testaccio. The river was an artery bringing life to ancient Rome. Tirelessly boats brought in goods from throughout the Empire, but never penetrated the heart of Rome; they came in by the tradesmen's entrance. In A.D. 43 Claudius had the har-

bor transferred to Ostia, where the imperial fleet lay at anchor too.

Life by the River

In the Middle Ages the city regrouped and was concentrated in the bend of the Tiber, because this surrounded the city on three sides with water, providing essential water after the aqueducts had been destroyed. The river provided drinking water and fish, turned the floating watermills tied up between the banks and was a transport route that was safe from bandits, ever since Pope Leo IV (847-855) had built three towers at the Porta Portuense to protect the medieval harbor of Ripa Grande from attack by Saracens.

The river gave Rome hardly anything for survival, but it made the Romans suffer. The Tiber was also a "Cloaca Maxima", which led to plagues and epidemics. On top of that it flooded the city at regular intervals, so that Giuseppe Garibaldi's first and only project for the new capital of Italy consisted of only one word: embankments. These were built, and following the example of the Seine the river was forced into the high *Muraglioni*. From then on the river, which rises 246 miles (396 kms) away in the Tuscan-Emilian Hills, and which fitted into Mussolini's home region of Emilia because he had moved the boundaries, no longer existed for the Romans.

Only now that the dirt it unloads at Ostia has brought about a prohibition on bathing is there talk of "regenerating" the Tiber. The sewage of Rome is at present 80 percent untreated, this to be cleaned up for over a billion lire, and the banks are to be enlivened with cafés. So far the only opportunity for a boat trip comes in the summer, when plays take place in the Ostia Antica amphitheater. Then a boat, organized by the tourist office, EPT, will take on interested spectators to Rome itself.

THE WATER CULT

When the poet Petrarch sang of *"clear, sweet and fresh waters"*, he was referring to the drinking water of Rome. Even today Roman water still has an almost legendary reputation for quality. It flows day and night from all the fountains of the Holy City, from the great and famous "fontane" and from simple piped fountains, straight from the pipe down the drain, a never-ending display of Roman carelessness. So far the Romans seem to be able to get away with wasting so much water: the city gulps down 530 gallons (2,000 liters) per second.

But the carefree times of never-failing little fountains came to an end even in Rome. The city government, searching for ways of saving money, decided to put taps on the tens of thousands of steadily flowing piped fountains that enlivened the backyards with their steady splashing. Now water ought only to flow when required. Water experts reckoned that the steady loss from open pipes was too great. There was no great danger of summer water shortages such as in Naples or Florence, but the needs of this city of three million people were growing steadily and new wells were expensive.

Drinking at the Fountains

But still many of the countless little fountains flow. Often ornamented with a statue and splashing quietly to themselves, they are still the center of Roman daily life. Here people have time for a chat when they stop for a refreshing drink of water on their way through the dusty city. To drink from these fountains you need to take up a special position. The would-be drinker has to

Fontana dell' Orato in the Villa d' Este, Tivoli.

bend forward over the curve of the pipe and close the opening with one hand. A thin stream of water will then spray in a high curve out of the tiny hole in the top of the pipe and can now be comfortably drunk, without the unnecessary contortions that trying to get your mouth under the pipe calls for.

Visitors can take comfort from the fact that the mills of Roman administration grind extremely slowly. The water-saving edict of the city administration will probably soon be forgotten. And so the mini-fountains with their excellent water will continue to spray. There are no plans to fit the great fountains with taps; after all, they bring in prestige and tourists. We ought, of course, to agree with the city fathers in their attempts to save water, but the question remains whether seepage in the hundreds of miles of pipes isn't a more serious problem. Experts believe that, in order to secure Rome's annual water require-

ment of around 17 billion gallons (64 billion liters), the existing number of wells would have to be doubled. This fact also has something to do with the age of the water pipes. Most of the water system was built by the Romans and restored by the popes.

The popes' restoration of the ancient aqueducts helped Rome to conquer the water shortage which had been endemic since the destruction of the city. The Tiber was both a sewer and a source of drinking water, a situation that favored disease. The only wells dug in the Middle Ages were a few for drawing drinking water—the poor Romans of those times didn't feel like building elaborate fountains.

The popes skilfully combined the advantages of fresh water—Rome no longer suffered cholera epidemics such as those that raged in other European cities until well into the 19th century— with the beauty of the monumental

"spitting" fountain, "Sppedè quarter.

fountains, intended to proclaim papal might and splendor. We can see the last of these "acts of propaganda" in the shape of the **Fontana di Trevi**, the facade of which is an exact copy of an ancient triumphal arch. The Trevi fountain represents the final phase of the papal fountain-builders, who copied their Roman predecessors and ended the medieval era of utilitarian wells.

But no-one wanted to leave the heathen Roman fountains just standing there. Pope Sixtus V, the great builder, had the Septizonum Fountain of Septimus Severus demolished, although it was one of the most beautiful showpieces among the wall fountains of Rome. It stood at the foot of the Palatine, and from three niches water splashed down into a mighty basin. Mocking tongues claimed that Pope Paul V's fountain on the Janiculum was nothing but a late reparation for this vandalization of its predecessor, as it

was so like the Severus fountain.

The fountains of Rome not only made propaganda, they were also a source of scandal. The **Naiad Fountain** in the Piazza del Repubblica with its bronze sculptures by Mario Rutilli was only unveiled after massive public protest. The city fathers felt that the gestures of the nymphs were "lascivious". Water was also often used in landscaped gardens to very harmonious effect, as in the **Villa Aldobrandini** in Frascati or the **Vila d'Este** in Tivoli—these arrangements became famous throughout Europe. The Popes also took over with pleasure the ancient tradition of building some sort of showpiece, a "mostra", at the end of an aqueduct—this increased their fame and honor.

The revamped ancient water supply revived the cult of water, popular in ancient times. The first aqueduct to be repaired, in 1570, was the **Vergine** (virgin) water. It rises 16 miles (26 km) outside Rome and flows entirely underground. It flowed for the first time for the general Marcus Vipsanius Agrippa, who needed it for his luxurious baths. Today the Vergine still serves the Trevi fountains, the "Barcaccia" in the Piazza di Spagna and the Fountain of the Four Rivers in the Piazza Navona. The "Vergine" is even reputed to have medicinal properties, which is why Roman nobility always took a few carafes of this water on their travels.

The Popes then restored another three of the eleven classical aqueducts; first that of Alexander Severus, which was given the worldly name, Felice, of its restorer Pope Sixtus V—**Acqua Felice**. The "Felice" serves the center of Rome between the Termini station and the Quirinal Palace, residence of the State President. Once it also fed the Baths of Diocletian with their 3,600 bathers.

In 1611 Pope Paul V had the ancient aqueduct of the Emperor Trajan re-

Roman watering-hole.

stored. Now the water of the nearby **Lago di Bracciano** once more streams from the heights of the Janiculum down to the houses and fountains of Trastevere, naturally not without showing off a "mostra". The **Acqua Paolo** feeds the fountains of the Piazza Trilussa, the Tiber island and the Jewish ghetto.

Up until 1865 these aqueducts were sufficient for Rome. But now the expanding city was crying out for more water and papal engineers followed in the footsteps of the ancient Romans one last time. The **Acqua Marcia**, built from the remains of the **Acqua Claudia** of 52 B.C., brings water from the distant **Simbruine Hills** at the feet of the Abruzzi. The visitor can admire it in the Fountain of Naiads in the Piazza della Repubblica.

The crossing point of eight ancient aqueducts can be found at the **Porta Maggiore**, where a high position on the Esquiline eases the downflow into the city. For travelers coming in by train this is the most beautiful greeting from ancient Rome to its modern visitors.

The water cult lives on among modern Romans in the form of the arguments in the various quarters over who has the best aqueduct. However, the Acqua Marcia obviously has water of the first order. If you are lucky enough to have this flowing out of your tap, you will never need to buy mineral water in Rome. Those who aren't among the lucky ones nevertheless are usually able in their flats to point proudly to another "must" of the water devotee— a separate tap with *acqua diretta*, drinking water straight out of the aqueduct. This strikes us as a modern and ecological sensible separation, as most Roman families take their non-drinking water from another system that runs into a tank on the roof. This is almost an example for other cities, who have long given up learning from Rome, to copy.

eft, a
hild's
irst.
ight, by
e Fontana
Trevi.

THE ANCIENT CENTER

There is a legend that the end of the world will announce itself on the Capitol. *"When no more can be seen of the gilding on the statue of the Emperor Marcus Aurelius in the piazza, then the little owl will sing between the ears of the horse"* —and the end of days will draw near. It seems as if the time has almost come, for the statue, put up by Michelangelo in 1538, has had to be removed and the original will never see the open air in Rome again, otherwise it would crumble away, despite all the efforts of restorers. It was not disturbed even in the Middle Ages, as it was thought to be a portrait of Constantine (306-37), the first Emperor to be baptized on his deathbed.

The Capitol is 164 feet (50 meters) high, the smallest hill in Rome. In ancient times it looked quite different: the cliffs of tufa fell down steeply on all sides. You can see something of its original appearance in the park of Monte Caprino looking towards the **Theater of Marcellus**. You can see the two peaks of the hill from the Piazza Michelangelo looking towards the **Senatorial Palace**. Today the church of **S.M. in Aracoeli** stands on one, known in ancient times as the *Arx*. Here the ancient Romans honored the goddess *Juno Moneta*, the "warner". The goddess, to whom geese were sacred, is supposed to have warned the Romans of an attack by Gauls in 390 B.C. by the honking of her sacred animals. The mint also stood here, hence the use of the name *Moneta* for money.

The southerly peak is called Capitol and gave its name to the whole hill. Here stood the **Temple of Jupiter Optimus Maximus**, pictured standing with a bundle of lightning flashes in his hand. This is where the triumphal processions of victorious generals ended,

as they came in with red-stained faces—in imitation of Jupiter—to make the final sacrifice, while a slave whispered "Respice post te! Hominem esse te memento!" (Look behind you! Remember that you are but a man!)

Turn right at the end of the **Piazza Michelangelo** and up a flight of stairs to an arch, to come to the **Via di Tempio di Giove**. In front of the house wall on your right you see remains of the temple. Other parts of the walls are in the **Museo Nuovo**. The temple, big as a football pitch, was begun by the Etruscan kings and was dedicated in the first year of the Republic, 509 B.C. The passing years were recorded by hammering a nail into the wall.

The six-pillared front faced south. Behind it lay a great anteroom, from which the shrine of Jupiter led off to the center, and those for his wife Juno and daughter Minerva, goddess of wisdom, to the left and right. The temple, usually just called the Capitol, was the religious center of the state. Every New Year's Day the consuls were inaugurated in a formal ceremony and a white bull sacrificed in the presence of the Senate.

The triumphal processions of victorious generals followed the **Via Sacra**, the holy road, to this point, coming up the hill from the Forum. The remains of the basalt paving of this street can be seen quite well from the **Via di Monte Tarpeo**. The consuls had those guilty of treachery thrown from the Tarpeian Rock, the southern precipice of the Capitol.

To return to the Piazza Michelangelo—this place was once the **Asylum**, a sacred sanctuary which protected the persecuted and is supposed to go back to the founder of the city, Romulus. The **Tabularium** was built around the older **Veiovis Temple**. The best view of this building which served as a state record office from 78 B.C. on can be seen at the Forum, as today's Senatorial Palace covers the foundations. Two hundred

Preceding pages, Acqua Claudia aqueduct; view of the Colosseum. Left, Basilica of Constantine.

and thirty feet (70 meters) long, the front of the building had 10 arches opening on to the Forum; now all but three are bricked up. There were three further storys above. Even today, the city of Rome still keeps its archives in the Tabularium.

In the park on the way to the Forum you can still see the ruins of the Servian Wall. Almost seven miles (11 km) long, this oldest set of fortifications surrounding the city was built after the attack by Gauls in 390 B.C. and enclosed more than 1,000 acres (426 hectares). More notable remains can be seen in front of the **Stazione Termini**.

In the church of **S. Giuseppe dei Falegnami** you can see the *Carcer*, the state prison. Rome's most notable opponents, such as the Moorish king Jugurtha and Vercingetorix, who resisted Caesar's conquest of Gaul, were strangled here. Here also the Apostle Peter is supposed to have baptized many fellow-prisoners with water from a miraculous spring.

The Imperial Fora

A central part of the impressive complex of imperial buildings intended to glorify their builders are the **Imperial Fora**, which today are mostly buried under the **Via dei Fori Imperiali**. They are being partially excavated from fenced-in car parks next to the entrance to the Forum.

The first "imperial" forum was built in 51 B.C. by Julius Caesar. It was dedicated, albeit still unfinished, in 46 B.C. and only completed under Augustus (23 B.C.—A.D. 14). Following Hellenistic models, it was a square surrounded by pillars. On the west side stood the **Temple of Venus Genetrix**, of whom Caesar believed himself to be a descendent.

The **Forum of Augustus** was built

Piazza del Campidoglio and capitol.

on similar lines. In the center stood the temple of the war-god Mars Ultor. In the great apses of the square stood statues of the mythical ancestors of Augustus' family and of forefathers who had celebrated a triumph.

The Emperor Vespasian also didn't want to lose out on fame and glory of the Jewish War (A.D. 71) and had the **Forum Pacis** built, dedicated to the peace goddess Pax. The Forum was ornamented with spoils from Jerusalem, among them the seven-branched candlestick. Today the library of the forum is the church **SS. Cosimo e Damiano**. Here the marble map of Septimus Severus was kept, 59 feet (18 meters) by 42 feet (13 meters), recording the land ownership of Rome exactly to scale. Today parts of it are hanging in the gardens of the **Conservatory**. The narrow strip of ground between the Forum Pacis and the Forum of Augustus was added by Domitian as an open space to

the **Temple of Minerva**, goddess of wisdom, whom he honored. In A.D. 97 Nerva had the Forum dedicated, and it bears his name.

The **Forum of Trajan**, 1083 feet (330 meters) long and 607 feet (185 meters) wide, is the biggest of the fora. It was built between A.D. 107 and 113 to celebrate the victory of Trajan (A. D. 98-117) over the Dacians (in modern Rumania). To build this forum, with its equestrian statue of Trajan, a small hill between the Quirinal and Capitol was removed. To the northwest it was bounded by the **Basilica Ulpia**, a hall with five naves. In its western apse, the **Atrium Libertatis**, slaves were manumitted. Behind this, between two libraries, stood **Trajan's Market** 131 feet (40 meters) high, with the 656 feet (200 meter) long band of reliefs depicting the Dacian Wars (A.D. 101-102 and 105). The reliefs were brightly painted and visible from the balconies of the

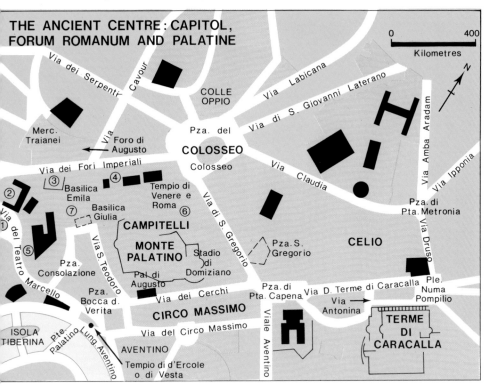

THE ANCIENT CENTRE: CAPITOL, FORUM ROMANUM AND PALATINE

libraries. In A.D. 177 a golden urn with the remains of the Emperor was buried in the base of the column. To make room for all this building, many market stalls had to be moved. Trajan's Market was built for them on the slopes of the Quirinal. This was a complex system of streets on various levels with shops, administrative offices and space for public grain distribution.

The Forum Romanum

The modern entrance by the Via dei Fori Imperiali leads down to the level of the ancient streets. When excavations began in the 18th century, all memory of the heart of the Roman Empire had been lost under nine feet of rubble, and the place was known as *Campo Vaccino,* the cow pasture. To the right lie the remains of the **Basilica Aemilia**, whose origins go back to the year 179 B.C. The censors M. Aemilius Lepidus and M. Fulvius Nobilitor had it built so that traders and customers could find shelter in bad weather. All great Roman public buildings of this sort were financed from the private pockets of rich Romans, who then earned the right to give them their own names.

The remaining ruins of the Basilica are those of the building restored after the fire in A.D. 410, when Alaric, leader of the Goths, conquered Rome. Even today you can still see the stains of coins burned into the floor. Up till 1500 most of the hall was still standing. Bramante had a lot of it carted away to build the **Palazzo Girau-Torlonia** in the Borgo quarter. On the steps you can see the modest remains of a temple of Venus, goddess of love. Here she had the cognomen *Cloacina*, for the small circular building marks the spot where the **Cloaca Maxima** divulges into the valley of the Forum. *Cloaca* comes from a

Restoration work on the Arch of Constantine.

Latin word *to rinse* and describes the sewers built to drain the Forum swamps. The sewers were built in the 1st century B.C. and are still in use today. They drain into the Tiber at the **Forum Boarium.**

Along western side of the Basilica Aemilia ran the **Argilentum,** not immediately recognizable today, lying under grass and shrubs, as the connecting route to the housing areas of the **Esquiline** and the **Forum of Nerva.** On the opposite side of the Argilentum stood a great brick building, the **Curia,** meeting place of the Senate and political center of the Roman republic, although less important in imperial times.

The Curia was begun by Julius Caesar in 44 B.C. and dedicated by the Emperor Augustus in 29 B.C. The building visible today was rebuilt by the Emperor Diocletian (A.D. 284-305) after a fire. In the Middle Ages it was consecrated as a church, which is why it remained standing and could be restored to its original condition in 1937. Since the 17th century, the original doors have made up the main portals of **S. Giovanni in Laterano**; those in the Forum are copies. The volume of the inner hall—89 feet (27 meters) long, 59 feet (18 meters) wide, 69 feet (21 meters) high—is impressive. On the ledges for the chairs of the senators, there was room for only 300 honorable gentlemen, although there were 600 senators; so even a half-empty house gave the impression of being crammed full. The public was kept informed, as meetings had to be held with the doors open. Still recognizable is the base for the statue of the goddess of Victory, a piece of booty from Tarento. Everyday dress for the senators consisted of a toga over a tunic and—of course—a golden ring on one hand.

In front of the Curia, under a protective roof, lies one of the most important sacred objects of ancient Rome, the **Lapis Niger**, the Black Stone. A dark patch of plaster marks the spot where the **tomb of Romulus,** founder of the city, is supposed to have been honored. According to other versions, his foster father Faustulus and the King Tullius Hostilius are supposed to have been buried here. The remains of an ancient monument from the 6th century B.C. have been excavated from under the Lapis Niger. While they do not prove the existence of the grave, they are evidence that Romulus was already venerated in early Rome.

Behind this looms the **Triumphal Arch of Septimus Severus** (A.D. 193-211). The arch is 76 feet (23 meters) wide, 37 feet (11 meters) deep and 68 feet (20 meters) high. It was built in A.D. 203 to honor the Emperor and his two sons Geta and Caracalla. Later Caracalla had his brother murdered in the arms of their mother and then placed him under *damnatio memoriae.* This "exile from memory" caused the deletion of all inscriptions to Geta from monuments. They were excised and replaced with laudatory titles of Caracalla. You can still see the chisel marks on the inscriptions, originally inlaid with metal. The reliefs on the arch depict the campaigns of Septimus Severus against the Arabs and the Parthians. In earlier years there was a statue of the Emperor in a four-horse chariot on top of the arch.

Next to it stood the **Rostra**, the speaker's platform of the Forum. It was built in its present shape by Augustus and had enough room for the Emperor and his immediate party. You can still see the drilled holes for the ships' prows taken from the Latins at the sea battle of Actium (338 B.C.). Trophies from Cleopatra's fleet are supposed to have been displayed here too.

Behind, to the right, is the **Temple of Concordia**, dedicated to the "unity" among the citizens that supposedly marked the end of the class wars in 367 B.C. The Emperor Tiberius (A.D. 14-

37) had it built and decorated with works of art from different countries. Occasionally the Senate met here, and it wasn't without reason that Cicero stood on just this spot, wringing his hands and urging the citizens to unite against the "public enemy" Catiline.

Automatically, without awkward problems of recognition, Rome's Emperors became gods after their deaths and had temples consecrated to them. This happened to Vespasian (A.D. 69-79) and his son Titus (A.D. 79-81). All that is left of their temples are three Corinthian pillars to the right at the back of the Rostra. Titus is known to history inspite of his short two-year reign. He conquered Jerusalem and thus drove the Jewish people into the Diaspora. The Emperor Vespasian's name, on the other hand, is permanently linked with pragmatism. To restore the disastrous state finances after the extravagance of the Emperor Nero (A.D. 54-69) he placed a tax on urine (a useful raw material for cleaning heavy woolens). When the astonished question was raised as to how he could make money with such a stinking substance, he replied *pecunia non olet*—money doesn't stink!

In the curved Podium of the **Temple of Saturn** in the northwestern corner of the Forum the Roman state treasury was kept. Eight upright pillars are all that remains. Saturn, next to Jupiter, was one of the longest serving gods in Rome. His temple was consecrated in 498 B.C. It was renovated for the last time at the beginning of the 4th century. In Saturn's honor the *Saturnalia* was celebrated in Rome at the end of every year. Masters and slaves were, for a short time, equal and gifts were exchanged—an ancient precursor of Christmas.

Not only does the Forum boast famous halls and temples, there are countless memorials and monuments. In front of the Rostra, the base of the **Decenalia Column** can be seen, set up in A.D. 303 to celebrate 10 years of rule by the two Emperors Diocletian and Maxentius. The relief on the base shows the *Souventaurilia*, the ceremonial state sacrifice of boar, ram and bull. Next to it is the **Column of Phocas**, the last classical monument in the Forum. It was put up in A.D. 608 by Smaragdus, Byzantine Exarch for Italy, in honor of the Eastern Emperor Phocas. Next to that, some letters inlaid in bronze are a memorial to one of the sponsors of the paving of the Forum, L.Naevius Surdinus from the last decade B.C. In a small space free of paving a fig tree, an olive tree and a vine grew here. Together with a statue of Marsyas they symbolized the justice of the city.

On the southern side of the Forum stood the **Basilica Julia**, 331 feet (101 meters) long and 161 feet (49 meters) wide. This was the symbol of Julius Caesar's family. The Basilica, with its

In front of the Temple of Faustina and Antonius.

e Circus
aximus
d the
latine,
at of the
perial
laces.

five naves, was used for court cases, was the seat of the Roman office of weights and measures and a meeting place for bankers.

Next to the Basilica a temple was founded to mark a legend. Roman chroniclers report that, in 499 B.C., during a decisive battle between Latins and Romans by the now unknown **Lake of Regillus** two young riders intervened, making victory possible for the Romans. The Romans saw the two friendly helpers watering their horses at the **Lacus Juturnae**, recognized them as the divine twins Castor and Pollux, and promptly built them the said temple.

Time has only left a few uninspiring reminders of another legend. In 44 B.C. the dictator Julius Caesar was murdered by conspirators in the vicinity of the **Theater of Pompey.** The grief of the people was so great that they kept his pyre burning for days with their own possessions, so the legend goes. After the cremation, Caesar's ashes were washed with milk and wine and buried. After his deification, a temple, now the **Temple of Caesar**, was built on the site of the pyre.

Behind the Temple of Caesar are the irregular remains of the walls of the **Regia**, the residence of the kings before the Republic. Later it was the residence of the *Pontifex Maximus*, the High Priest. The name means "he who makes a bridge to the gods". Today the Pope bears this title, as can easily be seen from the abbreviation on all papal buildings, "P.M." or "Pont. Max."

Nearby the round **Temple of Vesta**, goddess of the hearth and patron of the state, has been reconstructed. Here the Vestals kept the eternal hearth fire of Rome burning and watched over the **Palladion**, a sacred image of Minerva, saved, according to legend, from blazing Troy by Aeneas. The Vestals en-

tered divine service as young girls and lived a chaste life for at least 30 years in the **House of Vestals**. If a criminal condemned to death met one, he was freed. In the circus and in the theater they had seats of honor, and in the city, where wheeled traffic was forbidden, they alone had the right to travel in a carriage. If they lost their virginity, they were walled up alive in underground rooms—their blood must never be spilled. Their lovers were strangled.

Opposite is the **Temple of Antonius and Faustina**, dating from A.D. 141. Only its reconsecration as a church saved it, as it saved the Pantheon, from destruction. It is the only building in the Forum that gives an idea of the monumental size of Roman temples.

The **Basilica of Constantine** or **Basilica of Maxentius** was begun by the Emperor Maxentius (303-312) and completed by the Emperor Constantine (306-330). Designed as a hall of three naves, 328 feet (100 meters) by 213 feet (65 meters), only the northern side nave now remains. The central nave, 115 feet (35 meters) high, was crossed by cruciform vaults, each resting on eight side pillars, one of which has been outside the church of S.M. Maggiore since 1613. In Renaissance times the Basilica was the model for the new church of St. Peter. In the western apse a **Colossus of Constantine** was discovered in 1487, which now stands in the courtyard of the **Conservatory**.

From the Basilica you can turn straight to the **Arch of Titus**, which celebrates the victories in Palestine of the Emperor, who died in A.D. 81, and his father Vespasian (A.D. 69-79). The seven-armed candlestick is easily recognizable among the spoils from Jerusalem. Even today, Orthodox Jews still refuse to go through the arch. From the Arch of Titus your way will lead you to the **Palatine**, where the palaces of the

Mosaic in the Baths of Caracalla.

Roman emperors stood. During the course of history, the name Palatine took on the general meaning of a noble and wealthy house—"palace".

Legend claims that this is where Romulus is supposed to have founded the city and the remains of archaic houses were venerated here even in Roman times, evidence of the origins of the city. In republican times the hill was mainly inhabited by the Roman nobility. This is why the Emperor Augustus had fine houses built here for himself and his wife Livia. The wall paintings are worth a visit. His successor Tiberius (A.D. 14-37) had the first great palace built. Most of it is still unexcavated under the gardens of the **Villa Farnese**.

Later the palace complex spread out further to the south. The Emperor Domitian (A.D. 81-96) had the **Domus Flavia** built, an impressive complex with the Basilica, the Aurea Regia (in which he was honored by audiences as *Dominus et Deus*, Lord and God), a great Peristyle and Triclinium or dining hall. The imperial living quarters were in the Domus Augustana, at the heart of which was a courtyard. In the Circus Maximus, in the dip between the Palatine and the Aventine, there was an impressive Exedra which acted as an imperial box. This, the oldest circus in the city, was also the biggest—1,968 feet (600 meters) long and 492 feet (150 meters) wide. Typical entertainments here were the chariot races between various racing teams which wore different colors, e.g "the Greens", "the Blues" etc. In the film *Ben Hur* such a race is portrayed fairly accurately.

Between the Arch of Titus and the Colosseum is the **Temple of Venus and Roma** built by Hadrian (A.D. 117-138). In 307 it was rebuilt by Maxentius (306-312) after a fire. The building, 361 feet (110 meters) by 174 feet (53 meters) was the largest temple in Rome and consisted of two shrines placed opposite to each other, surrounded by pillared halls. This echoes Greek temple design and is typical of Hadrian, who was an admirer of Greek culture.

The Colosseum

However, the most impressive building of ancient Rome must be the **Colosseum**. In the **Amphitheatrum Flavium**, as it was known then, gladiatorial combats and animal shows took place. The "performers" were criminals, prisoners of war and slaves (and sometimes volunteers). The Emperor Vespasian had it built on the site of an artificial lake which had belonged to **Nero's Golden House**. The ground plan is elliptical, and it is 617 feet (188 meters) long by 512 feet (156 meters) wide. Following Roman architectural taste, Tuscan, Ionic and Corinthian pillars were placed one above the other. In A.D. 80 Titus opened the Colosseum with a hundred days of games. More than 5,000 animals are supposed to have been slaughtered. The theater had 80 entrances, and could seat between 55,000 and 73,000 spectators. The **Ludus Magnus** near the Colosseum was the training ground of the gladiators and was connected to the arena by an underground tunnel.

Gladiatorial combat was finally forbidden in A.D. 438 and the last recorded animal show took place in 523. On the lower ledges you can still read the names of the last senators to have reserved seats here, 195 names from the time of Odoacer (A.D. 476-483). Later it became the fortress of the Frangipani family and a quarry for the Palazzo Venezia, Palazzo della Cancellaria, the harbor of Ripetta and St. Peter's. The holes in the masonry are contemporary evidence of the medieval shortage of metal: the clamps have been knocked out. In 1744 Benedict XIV consecrated the amphitheater to the memory of the martyrs who died here, thus preserving it from final destruction.

Nearby is the **Arch of Constantine**, built in 312 after the victory over Maxentius at the Ponte Milvio. The loss of Roman craftsmanship is shown by the fact that most of the sculptures come from monuments from the times of Trajan, Hadrian and Marcus Aurelius. In 1988 restorers working on this recycled material came upon an inscription from the Colossus of the Emperor Nero, which was, according to the writer Gaius Suetonius Tranquillus, 117 feet (35.5 meters) higher than the Colossus of Rhodes.

Early in the morning the theater would be filled with spectators, mostly men. The lower seats were reserved for senators, civil servants in official dress and the Vestals. On hot days units of legionaries would spread an awning over the theater. Shortly before the games began the emperor and his followers would come in. The audience got up and showed reverence by rhythmical clapping, cheering, waving cloths and chanting the honorifics of their sovereign.

If one of the gladiators tried to draw back, he was forced forward with whips and red-hot irons—until he stumbled out of the underground chamber into the arena. A trumpet call was the signal to start the games, and the spectacle began with cries of "Hail Caesar, those about to die salute you." The gladiators mostly fought to death. If one fell wounded to the sand, he could beg for mercy by lifting a finger of his left hand. If the crowds waved their handkerchiefs, he was saved. Thumbs down meant his death. The bloodstains were sanded over by boys. The dead bodies were dragged off into a mortuary, where red-hot irons were applied to check if they were really dead. Anyone who still lived had their throats cut. After that, the wild beast show began. The arena was cleverly decorated with

Pollution turning marble into limestone.

stage sets—we can see the underground passages now, because the wooden floor is missing. Animals were either set to fight each other or human beings, armed or unarmed. The latter was considered particularly exciting. Christians tied to stakes and torn apart counted as a short piece in-between acts. On really special occasions the condemned were dressed in pitch-soaked clothing and burned.

Baths in Ancient Rome

Apart from the huge Baths of Caracalla, Rome had many others: those of Agrippa, Nero, Titus, Trajan, Diocletian and Constantine, to name only the largest. In addition, there were 856 smaller public baths in the 4th century alone, not counting the private baths, which didn't lag behind the public ones in magnificence. Roman bathing had nothing in common with dull tiled in-

door pools and chlorinated water. Together with the fora, baths played a central role in public life.

You went to the baths around mid-day. Children were let in free, women were often excluded. Slaves watched over your abandoned clothes and then you were free to enjoy yourself, first in the *tepidarium*, a lukewarm room, then in the hot *caldarium*. After the baths you could have a massage and be oiled, or indulge in further sensual pleasures. Your stomach's well-being was seen to by cooks, and those bathers more interested in intellectual pursuits could make use of well-stocked libraries.

The rather bare impression given by the Baths of Caracalla nowadays is wrong. At their height they looked like an over-designed Baroque church, decorated everywhere with statues of gods and bright mosaics, with clouds of steam from the baths and scents of perfumed oils wafting through.

ew of the rum, to e right the mples of ustina and tonius.

VIA APPIA ANTICA

In classical times the **Via Appia** began at the Circus Maximus and then passed the Baths of Caracalla on its way to the city gate (now Porta San Sebastiano) in the Aurelian Wall. Only outside the ancient Porta Appia does it bear its old name. At number 9 of Via di Porta Sebastiano, is the entrance to the **Sepolcro dei Scipioni**, the tomb of the famous family of the Roman Republic. In the family tomb the remains of more than 20 sarcophagi have been found. At the edge archaeologists have left, as a warning against vandals, a *calcara*, in which the marble of the monuments was burned to make lime.

Also at the city gate you will find the entrance to the museum of the Aurelian Wall. You can walk along a fair stretch of it. It was almost 12 miles (19 km) long and had 381 towers. In A.D. 403 its height of 20 feet (six meters) was doubled. It was now 12 feet (3.5 meters) thick and had 18 gates.

To save time, older buildings such as the Pyramid of Cestius, the Porta Maggiore, the Praetorian barracks, the aqueducts, the Castrense amphitheater and Hadrian's Mausoleum were incorporated into the wall. A walk along the wall will give you a view such as the imperial legionaries must have seen as they watched for the coming of the barbarian armies. Today, however, the view is mostly of concrete blocks, built by home-grown barbarians, except in the direction of the Via Appia, where the Campagna is still almost in original condition.

When it was extended as far as Capua by the Censor Appius Claudius in 312 B.C., the *Queen of Roads* at first followed the line of an existing road to the Alban Hills. It was the most important campaign route for the conquest of southern Italy. In 190 B.C. it was then extended via Benevento to modern Brindisi (Brindisium) and thus formed a direct connection with the eastern Mediterranean. After the fall of the empire the road fell into decay and was not used until the time of Pius VI.

Half a mile down the Via Appia, on the left, is the church **"Domine Quo Vadis"** ("Lord, where are you going?"), where the Apostle Peter, having succeeded in escaping from a Roman prison, met Jesus on the way to Rome. He asked him this question and Jesus replied "To let myself be crucified a second time." Peter understood and turned back.

To the left of the Church a little tarmac road, the **Via della Caffarella**, leads into the valley along the Via Latina. If the rubble trucks are not actually unloading at the moment the walk is well worth it to see the **Templo di Dio Redicolo**, which you will find just over a mile further up, on the hill to your

1 Church "Domine Qu Vadis"
2 Tomba di Ge
3 Tomba di Prescilla
4 1st Roman milestone
5 Colombario detti dei libe
6 Colombario liberti di Livi
7 2nd Roman milestone
8 1st Salesian
9 Tomba d. lib e.d. schiavi o Valussi
10 Entrance to Jewish Catacombs
11 School and tomb of the Silvanus
12 Jewish Catacombs
13 Church of S
14 3rd Roman milestone

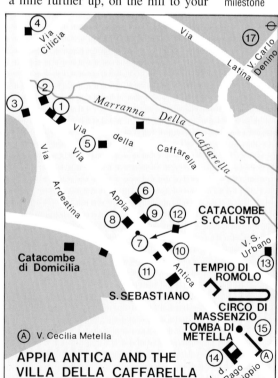

APPIA ANTICA AND THE VILLA DELLA CAFFARELLA

right. Further into the valley is another temple, now the church of San Urbano. Both temples, in good condition, are fenced off, but friendly visitors are allowed in. From the church of San Urbano you can see the **Sacred Grove**, but only three trees remain.

Now return to the junction of the side road with the Via Appia. To the right of the church is the **Fosse Ardeatine**. Here, on March 24, 1944, 355 Italian hostages were murdered in revenge for the partisan attack on the Villa Rasella. SS units under Hermann Kaplan led the victims, who had nothing to do with the attack, into the caves and shot them. Afterwards they blew up the whole network of caves. A memorial reminds passers-by of the massacre.

Back on the Via Appia, you will find on your right the **Catacombs of St. Callixtus.** These have a total length of over 12 miles (20 km), in four levels of about 1000 feet by 1300 feet. In the

Crypt of the Popes inscriptions of at least 10 different bishops of Rome from A.D. 3rd and 4th centuries have been discovered. Among them is the first documented use of the title "Pope" for the Bishop of Rome (dating from A.D. 298). Further catacombs are those of San Sebastiano, Domitilla and Priscilla. The dead of all faiths were buried in the catacombs, contrary to the tales of the guides. To save valuable space, burials were made underground.

Also worth seeing are the **Circus of Maxentius** and the **tomb of Romulus** (son of Maxentius), which dates from A.D. 309. Here the first open-air film shows in the early years of the Estate Romana were held. The tomb of **Cecilia Metella** (10 B.C.) was built for the daughter of Quintus Metellus Creticus, conqueror of Crete. She was later the wife of Crassus, son of the famous member of the Triumvirate of Caesar's time.

FAITH IN A PAGAN CITY

In Italy, if you have a resplendent and comfortable lifestyle, the Italians say you enjoy a *vita di papa*, which means "you have the life of a Pope".

Anyone who knows anything about Rome knows for certain that the city on the Tiber was for many centuries *the* seat of power of the ancient world and the center of the Catholic church. There has always been a pope at the head of the church, even though occasionally—in earlier years—there were several. The pope has absolute power to decide matters of Catholic doctrine— and also in other matters.

But the pope no longer leads "the life of Riley". The Borgia popes and their infamous extravagances belong to history. Temporal power was lost with the conquest of Rome by patriotic and democratic forces in 1870. The popes have permanently lost their role in making political history, but still try again and again to be the final authority on moral matters. Pope John Paul II is at present setting an example.

The "Flying Pope"

Since the time of John XXIII it has not been unusual for the once very lonely man to leave the Vatican, lay down his unapproachability and travel to the most distant parts of the world. Karol Wojtyla in particular has studied the real situation of the church in all parts of the world, so often that critics have referred to him as the "flying pope". On these trips the present pope holds a great number of addresses, sermons and audiences. The code *JP II* marks miles of tape reels in the office of Radio Vatican. The address is the main form of communication with the faithful, letters and encyclicals are much rarer. Pronouncements on dogma are extremely rare. The last one was from Pope Pius XII and pronounced the Assumption of Mary into heaven to be an article of faith.

The Curia, a kind of church government led by cardinals, assists the pope in fulfilling his worldly duties. Before the Second Vatican Council it was the prerogative of Italian prelates to form the Curia. Now only the Cardinal Secretary of State, something like a Prime Minister of the Vatican, Agostino Casaroli, is from Italy. All others are non-Italians. Decisions in the church are made by the Curia consulting with the bishops. For one thing, the bishops are required to come every five years *ad limina apostolorum*, to the tombs of the Apostles, to report. For another, conferences of bishops, so-called synods, are called to discuss important questions, for instance the role of lay helpers in the church.

If a pope dies, the cardinals with a right to vote assemble in conclave. Those cardinals under the age of 80 are eligible to vote. Every cardinal is at the same time a nominal member of the Roman clergy. This is because the pope is also Bishop of Rome and can therefore, according to canon law, only be elected by Roman clergy. For this reason every cardinal, as soon as he is appointed, has a titular church assigned to him, to make him a member of the Roman clergy.

When a bishop reaches the age of 75, he has to relinquish his office. There is only one exception: the Bishop of Rome, the pope himself. When Pope Paul VI crossed the two threshold years in 1972 and 1977, the question of abdication was discussed with interest. But any such speculation about John Paul II has to wait until the turn of the century.

Christian Charity

The ugly quarter of Magliana is where the most corrugated iron shanties

eceding
ges, Porta
Sebas-
no on the
a Appia.
ft,
trance to
. Paul .

crowd around the unattractive, hastily run up concrete tower blocks. Here, thousands of Christian charity doers work hard to ease life for the poor, the sick, the immigrants and the mentally handicapped; Vera is one such good Samaritan. When she goes there, happy children crowd around her. They are among the poorest of the poor. They only go to school now and then; this is reflected in their reading ability.

In this country, where people deeply mistrust the state, private charity is essential. Roman Christians always have been of the opinion that the Bible is not only a book for spiritual development, but a handbook for ordinary weekdays. There may be "Sunday Christians" in the middle-class parishes, but the grassroots groups in Sant' Egidio go in day after day wherever they are needed. The deserted convent dedicated to St. Clare, next to the church of S. Maria in Trastevere, is the headquarters of most of the young charity workers.

Help in Trastevere

Over the years their number has grown to 5,000, mainly in Rome, but also in Naples, Genoa and in the little Piedmontese town of Novara. In 1968 the first of them decided to do as the Scriptures required. At first they gave extra tuition to children from Sicily. Later they set up a center where Asians and Africans could get practical advise. They trained disappointed and cynical young people to help their neighbors.

In spite of many reverses, they tried to help drug addicts to lead a normal life. "We need to find a way back to life in this city that has grown inhuman," they say. Immigrants from Eritrea, Morocco, Ethiopa, girls from the Philippines, who over the last few years have grown into a slave labor force of 100,000, all find help in Trastevere.

In trouble with authority, having dif-ficulty with forms, problems with the law—the relief workers of Sant' Egidio are there to help. "We wouldn't dream of converting them," says Don Ambrogio, one of the priests of the grassroots group, "everyone should live with his own religion." So they organize Islamic festivals and Greek orthodox weddings for several hundred people.

City Poverty

Poverty in this city of three million is increasing from year to year. But also increasing is the number of relief organizations. "You can't starve in Rome," observes one German tramp. He ought to know. He's been on the road for three years. His wife and children have been living in Spain for years, but "for some stupid reason" he is not allowed back into the country. No-one asks why in the parish on the Via Appia with the long-winded name of *Navitá*

Roman domes at sunset.

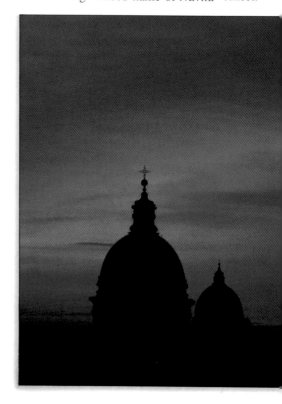

del Nostro Signore Gesù Cristo. Here, twice a week, friendly women cook for everyone who is hungry.

On this day there are 250 guests, as mixed a lot as you could imagine. Some are black, some unshaven, some carefully dressed. No money is given out, "Or those who don't just need a meal will turn up," says Don Pietro, the diminutive priest of this lively parish. Everything that gets put on the table on this Tuesday and on other days is financed by the collection box.

State Help

There is no state help for the church in Italy. But sometimes five million lire suddenly appears in the box, which is a considerable sum even in 1988. No-one should underestimate the willingness of the faithful to give. Sometimes one might harbor the suspicion that a businessman has been driven by conscience

because he has cheated the state of too much tax.

The old and the helpless often vegetate in shabby homes on the edge of the city, sometimes with the mentally handicapped as well. Human contact only exists for them because many of the charity workers spend hours every day with these deserted people. Bureaucratically minded administrators, however, see these workers as nuisances. Often these "spies" are barred from entering the homes.

There's not much that the grassroots Christians can do in this anonymous system that turns people into numbers. "But if the old people feel human again just for one hour a day," says one of them, "that's worth a great deal." There are not many in the pagan city of the popes who act according to the message of the Christ, but the few who do offer good and encouraging examples to the others.

The Synagogue in the ghetto.

The Waldensians

Hardly any other Christian church has a more critical attitude towards the pope or towards Catholicism as the Waldensians. This Protestant community, whose origins go back much further than the Reformation, still has about 50,000 members in Italy, about one per thousand of the population. The history of the eight centuries of their existence is one of bloody persecution. In the harsh struggle with Rome most of the notable Waldensians have died martyrs' deaths. Even the origins of this church were a clear signal that opposition from the Catholic "head office" in Rome was inevitable.

Because early Catholic and Waldensian sources are few and unreliable, little is known with certainty about Valdes (also known as Peter Waldo), the reputed founder. It is said that at the end of the 12th century Valdes, then a merchant from Lyon in France, divided his wealth among the poor. In succeeding years his followers spread to the whole of France, Spain, Flanders, Germany, and even reached Bohemia and Poland. The "Poor of Lyons" (as his followers were called) survived the time of the Counter-Reformation in the inaccessible Alpine valleys of Piedmont, which is still their heartland. These early Protestants, now members of the Reformed Churches, did not come to Rome till 1870, when the Bersaglieri of the House of Savoy had put an end to papal rule.

Lux lucet in tenebris, the light shines in the darkness, is the Bible text above the entrance of the largest Protestant church on Italian soil, only a hundred yards from St. Peter's. "We see ourselves as the southern Diaspora of Protestant Europe," says Pastor Franco Giampiccoli, the Moderator of his church in Italy.

The main church of St. Maria Maggiore.

The activities of this small congregation, in which each person seems to do the work of three, has made the name of the Waldensian church famous far beyond the borders of the country. Youth groups from the church were among the first to help the earthquake victims south of Naples in the early 1980s, and they stayed for months. But they are not present at the Day of World Prayer in Assisi or at the annual week of prayer for Christian unity. The Waldensians prefer to worship among themselves rather than in front of television cameras.

Many followers of Valdes have moved to Latin America with the wave of emigration over the past years. About 15,000 of them live there. Today the scattered communities are members of an Italian and a South American Synod, which meets alternately in Europe and in the New World.

The rules of their life together can only be changed by mutual agreement. "That's our way of overcoming our system of colonialism," says Giampiccoli. Rome's Waldensians work closely with the Methodists, and the Baptists are often included as well, leading to jokes being cracked about the "BMW-Union".

The Waldensians have only recently come to terms with the Italian state. How could they take seriously the paragraphs in the constitution guaranteeing religious freedom, when at the same time Catholicism was prescribed as the "state religion"? Recently the state has given a binding undertaking not to interfere in the activities and institutions of the Waldensians, for example their services, funding of schools, hospitals, old people's homes and the theological college.

The most notable of the "BMW-campaigns" are the peace demonstrations. In Comiso in Sicily long-stand-

me is the stination many rican migrants.

181

ing Protestant groups protested against the instalment of American missiles. They are also in the front line, along with other political groups, when pressing for reforms to protect the citizens. The amount of work often seems as if it would crush the Waldensians, but they comfort themselves with the paradoxical saying brought with them from their first home:

Jesus est le maître de l'impossible which means "Jesus is the master of the impossible".

Luther's Successors

There are many different groups of Protestant Christians in Rome. In 1930 the pastor of the German Embassy, Ernst Schubert, said of the reformer Martin Luther that "in these foreign lands he was doubly thankful for his German nature…" This sort of chauvinism seems ridiculous today, but Schubert also proposed a reason for its development. The tolerance exercised by the pope towards Protestants in life was denied them in death. "Heretics shall not lie in hallowed ground." They had to bury their dead outside the city, near Porta San Paolo and the pagan tomb of Cestius, in a cow pasture and at dead of night.

The non-Catholic cemetery is still there, but funerals are held publicly and in daylight. At first the only regular Protestant services were permitted in the chapel of the Prussian Legation in the Palazzo Caffarelli on the Capitol. There was something of an act of defiance about the group of diplomats, merchants and artists who met on Nov. 9, 1817 to celebrate Reformation Day in the home of the Legation secretary Bunsen, where it was said they not only sang the praises of God but also uttered "a prayer of thanksgiving for release from the Papacy".

These times of struggle are long over. Once Rome was integrated into the

Kingdom of Italy all non-Catholic Christians could worship publicly according to their own faith. The Palazzo Caffarelli no longer exists in its old form, but there is a new "Lutheran" church near the faded glories of the Villa Veneto. This Church of Christ, built according to designs by the German Emperor Wilhelm II, is of interest to modern art historians because of its medieval-Romanesque style.

It certainly didn't bring Catholics and Protestants closer together when the foundation stone of this church on the Via Toscana was laid on, of all days, the birthday of Pope Pius X. That end came closer to being achieved on the third day of Advent in 1983 when the Polish pope saw an end to the divisions shining "like the dawn".

Since that day Rome's pious Lutherans are in fashion. In the oldest seminary in the Eternal City, in the Piazza Capranica, they held a Protestant service for future priests. They are regular guests of the grassroots Christians of Sant' Egidio and active helpers in the *natività* in the Appia quarter, where a meeting was held between all Christian denominations, Islamic groups, Jews and Buddhists, long before John Paul II invited them to Assissi.

It seems as if heaven has no more borders, after all the centuries of often bloody conflict. Since the last war in particular, Rome's churches have become remarkably varied. There are German Lutherans, who now also have many Italian followers, as well as Swiss, Dutch, Austrians and other Europeans. There is even a small Swedish congregation.

The Salvation Army, *Esercito della Salvezza*, has done a lot of work with immigrants from the Third World. Two congregations of Adventists and the Anglicans make contacts with the English speaking people. The Pentecostal church has many followers and is today the most numerous non-Catholic

ft, the
eek-
zantine
onastery
Grotta
rrata.

group in the capital. At youth meetings with participants coming from all over the world the community of Taize shows itself to be very attractive. Two representatives of this ecumenical center based in the south of France are constantly in Rome. The Russian Orthodox community has a church in the center, the Greek Orthodox church even has a bishop.

The Jewish Community

The history of Jewish involvement with Rome began in the 2nd century B.C., when Simon Maccabeus made a treaty with the rising power in the center of the Mediterranean world. Horace mentions the followers of Moses, sold as slaves in the *urbs* after a lost war. Tensions with the Romans soon arose, but they increased when the center of the empire became seat of the popes. After the tolerance of the Humanist period, Paul IV forced the Jews to live in the Ghetto. Attendance at mass was enforced. But the aim of the church was not mere physical extermination, as was tried in other parts of Italy, but the cultural repression of the Talmud tradition as "unchristian" was its heart's desire.

Liberation came after three centuries of continuous oppression when Piedmontese troops moved into the city. The walls of the Ghetto fell, even though most Jews remained living near the Porticus of Octavia and around the Isola Tiberina. From 1938 on Mussolini's racial laws brought renewed oppression as Fascism gave in to German pressure. During the war, 2,091 Jews were murdered in Auschwitz and other concentration camps, only 15 returned. Seventy-five of their brethren were among the hostages killed by the SS in the Ardeatine Caves to the south of Rome.

The Basilica St. Paul by day...

Today you can see traces of the 2,000-year-old history of the Jews in Rome everywhere—in the Forum Romanum on the Arch of Titus, which shows the destruction of Jerusalem; on the floor of the Colosseum, partly built by Jewish slaves; on ancient sarcophagi, in many alleys of the old city and, in the last few years, in the excavations in Ostia Antica. It's hard to say how many Jews live in Rome today, but about 20,000 are members of the four synagogues in the city. Population movements within Italy, the move out of the countryside and the banishment of all Jews from Libya have increased their numbers.

Visiting a Synagogue

The chaotic system of streets makes a visit to the synagogue difficult. But on the Sabbath the men in particular are gathered in their synagogue on the banks of the Tiber. Prayer is a duty for women as well, but not attendance at the synagogue. Their area, according to tradition, is the family and the home. Among each other the Roman Jews speak Italian. The educated ones will speak Hebrew to foreigners. But by no means all still pray three times a day to the *Lord God Sabaoth*. Yet the synagogue is open to all the religious, according to the position of the sun. The fact that it is constantly guarded by carabinieri is a reminder of the bomb attack a few years ago which cost a child's life.

Nowadays it's chic to go and eat in the Ghetto. At "Gigetto's" you can get artichokes *alla giudea* and if you want you can try kosher fast food. The two restaurants, a snack bar and a butcher's, are inspected to see if they comply with the dietary laws. There's even a Jewish guide to Rome; it describes the Ghetto, this historic place where thousands have suffered, as "rather picturesque".

.and by ght.

GRAVES, GROTTOS AND BASEMENTS

During walks around Rome, it's best to look upwards first at the facades of the churches and palazzi, at the perspectives and views created by many city planners over the centuries. And even further up, because the blue Roman sky often displays a blaze of color, especially in the evenings behind the silhouettes of pines and palm trees.

The more you turn your nose up in Rome, the more you fit in with the inhabitants, and the more you get away from the smell of car exhaust, that tiresome modern incense. The earliest inhabitants looked upwards to see signs in the heavens. First Remus saw six eagles over the Aventine, then Romulus saw 12 over the Palatine. The consequences were far-reaching—a quarrel between brothers, murder and the origin of Roman historical dating *ab urbe condita*.

For the next chapter of the story, we ought to look down, for Rome has grown upwards over the years—66 feet (20 meters) in places from the fall of classical Rome to the present day. Looking at Rome from beneath you will gain deep insights, in more than one sense of the word. On every walk you will make discoveries—if you are careful not to stick slavishly to the rules and regulations. A police station dating from classical times, temple complexes—there are tombs and grottos in the basement.

Often they are locked up and neglected, because the building is dangerous or because there are insufficient staff, or there is a lack of money or of ideas. In short, they are only visible, if at all, to an unsatisfactory extent from outside and for that reason are often overlooked. With this totally subjective selection we would like to introduce the visitor to five places where Rome is nothing but underworld. For instance, in the German library **Kunstbibliothek Hertziana** near the Spanish steps, bibliophiles will find many manuscripts and books, if they are allowed in. But if they go down to the deepest basement they will get an extra treat—they will be able to touch the excavations of the place where Lucullus had his gardens.

Basilica di Porta Maggiore

An impressive and crazy scene: The roaring traffic in front of the **Porta Maggiore**, the trains clattering over the railway bridge, and in the railway embankment the door that leads to an underground secret. Unfortunately most visitors are put off by the fact that the door is locked. It's worth while going out of your way to the Piazza delle Finanze no. 1. Here you will find the **Soprintendenza Alle Antichitá Roma**, which gives out permits to visit sites, and organizes tours, usually on Sundays. Go back to the Porta Maggiore at the arranged time and, open Sesame, the door will open. You go down 45 feet (14 meters) into the building, discovered in 1914.

It is not known whether the building was a tomb or a temple or which religion it may have served. It is certain that it dates from A.D. 1st century and shows surprising features found later in Christian churches. It is believed that it is a shrine of some neo-Pythagorean cult. At any rate the basilica is an expression of the religious tolerance of imperial Rome, if you pay no attention to the few phases of persecution of those who did not share the ancient Roman-Etruscan religious horizons. The persecution of Christians has probably been given more importance over the following centuries by its undoubtedly biased chroniclers than the evidence will merit.

The Tomb of Peter

The Apostle Peter is supposed to have arrived in Rome during such a phase of persecution. According to legend, he was crucified head downwards at the edge of the **Circus Flaminius** and buried at the place where St. Peter's stands, probably the most important church of Christendom ever since the time of Constantine. Whether he really lies buried there or, as some religious historians claim, was never even in Rome, makes no difference. The propaganda effect has worked for nearly 2,000 years, strengthening Rome's claim to power over other communities, shaping Catholicism with its European ideas.

To get to this tomb in the necropolis of the Vatican is not easy (the Pilgrim's Office to the left of St. Peter's will give you information), but it is worthwhile. You will see a mainly pagan cemetery dating from A.D. 1st to 4th centuries. The supposed remains of the saint are enclosed in blocks of plastic. Directly over the tomb is the papal altar with the canopy by Bernini under the dome of Michelangelo, in the round of which can be read the verse from the gospel of Matthew which forms the basis of the Catholic church's claim to power, but the authenticity of which is much in doubt: *"And I tell you that you are Peter, and on this rock I will build my church. I will give you the keys of the kingdom of heaven."* As you can see, a visit under the ground can lead to unguessed heights.

The Sundial of Augustus

Not far from the hectic bustle of the Corso is another jewel on this tour of graves and grottos, but this time the way doesn't lead down. The church of **S. Lorenzo in Lucina** is worth a visit, not

**is,
ptian
of
th, in the
Giulia.**

just because of its fanciful priest, who would like to see Princess Grace of Monaco sainted and broadcasts from his private radio station to the Historic Centre. S. Lorenzo in Lucina would be worth seeing even without Don Piero Pintus, if only for the quality of light in this beautiful church, and its great glass door, which combines early Christian and Baroque styles in a surprisingly harmonious manner.

In the sacristy you can ask when "tours of the basement" are made. For underneath the church floor archaeologists have discovered the **sundial of Augustus** on the Campus Martius. To be exact, they have found part of the paving and bronze inscriptions. The Emperor Augustus had a rectangle 525 feet (160 meters) long by 246 feet (75 meters) wide paved with travertine, in the middle of which, on a base dedicated to the sun, stood an obelisk taken from Egypt as a marker. As things fall out in Rome, the sundial which Professor Edmund Buchner has excavated, and for which Don Piero now asks for a tip (I beg your pardon: a donation), isn't just Augustus' sundial. The remains belong to a restored sundial of Domitian's time, when the floor level was raised by about five feet (1.5 meters).

San Clemente

This church belongs to the core program of every detailed tour of Rome and is described in the smallest guide book, but it is such a fine example of the way underworld Rome is revealed to the light of day layer by layer that we really can't miss mentioning it here.

In a few short words, from the bottom to the top: in the deepest cellar you can hear the **Cloaca Maxima** gushing, that ancient drainage canal that was the main Roman sewer. Here are the remains of a Roman house and a shrine to the pagan god Mithras. Above this is the lower church, a building begun in the

4th century, dedicated to the Christian Clement and a real treasure house of Romanesque wall paintings. Above this is the upper church, added on top in the 11th century. This unfortunately filled in two thirds of the lower church. The choir with its floor portraying the Cosmos is among the most beautiful that medieval Rome has to offer.

S. Maria dell' Orazione e Morte

This is another place ignored by practically everyone going northwards along the Via Giulia. Skulls look grimly down from the facade at the passer-by, while on the edge of the church. Looking towards the Vatican, the bird beak of Osiris, Egyptian god of death, threatens. The church with its morbid name is unfortunately open only on Sunday for evening mass. If, taking this opportunity, you make a donation for the pious sisters, you may be lucky and be al-

Details of the church S. Maria de Orazione della Mor

lowed to come back the next day to see the dangerously dilapidated crypt. If again, you take this opportunity you will clearly see that Christianity is a religion of death, of triumph over death. The walls and the ceiling of the church are covered with reliefs and mosaics. Grotesque and fantastic arabesques of human bones, children's skulls, collar bones and ribs form the decoration of the walls.

The historian Gregorovius commented: *"It is strange how artistic form and aesthetic law have almost conquered the naturally morbid aspect. But that Art has here done such a deed, that it has taken that which appears to the living as most gruesome and which the earth should cover in kindly darkness, and made it into pictures and graceful arabesques, is truly too repellent and morbid. It seems to me to be the highest peak of fanatical contempt for life, a bizarre fantasy of the triumph over death and its horrors."*

Rome seen from below—there are famous sites such as the catacombs, unreachable ones such as the Baths of Decius and much that would bore the tourist, although of interest to the professional. But if you dig in Rome you'll always find something. That's what the builders of the Metro discovered, when work was interrupted again and again whenever a few splinters of history were discovered—and what isn't historic in such a city? So several tunnels, passages and escalators lead into that underworld in which the rubble and ashes of 2,000 years lie—the rubbish dump of our history. And of our civilization. Underneath the Stazione Termini, in the long passages between Metro and long distance trains the hideous face of drug addiction makes a mockery of all culture—and the triumph over death seems to turn into the triumph of death.

rum
manum.

Myths, Dragons and Treasures

The history of this city began with a myth, and of fabulous beings, messengers of the gods and evil monsters accompanied the ancient Romans throughout their lives. The supernatural was by no means unnatural as far as they were concerned. The protagonists of these dramas changed with Christianity, but the basic theme remained. A battle between the powers of good and evil, a path along the abyss between white magic and the black arts. Many memories have been lost, but some things have survived the centuries. The official church has suppressed much: the closeness of magic, miracles and signs of faith, so dear to the ancient Christians, is often denied, history is smoothed over to make it more palatable to the ideas of the moment, which it believes it ought to satisfy.

We would like to dig a little, not under the earth this time, to discover the endless number of Roman myths and secrets.

"In Rome anything can happen," as Seneca said, and indeed everything has happened here over the centuries, from blindfolded gladiators fighting naked girls to the ghosts in the Colosseum that drive the unsuspecting mad.

After the fall of the empire the knowledge of gods and ghosts soon disappeared. The ruins were populated with creatures of fable and exorcists like the sculptor Benvenuto Cellini, who in the 16th century boasted in his *Memoraria* that he had expelled the Devil from the Colosseum. It happened in this way: together with a Sicilian priest, Cellini went on a special wind-producing diet, and the subsequent digestive noises and smells caused the Devil to leave in a great hurry.

Temple of Vesta in th~~ Forum, where nearby a dragon is supposed t~~ have been buried.

Against the ghostly backdrop of Roman temples the ghosts of Emperors wandered about, paying for their innumerable sins and their bloody persecution of Christian martyrs; together with monsters of the most varied kind. But in these early Christian times the popes obviously still had spiritual power to put an end to the haunting, power that was missing from so many of their successors.

In the early 4th century a dragon frequented the Forum Romanum. Every day the monster ate several people, till at last Pope Sylvester I was asked to intervene by the people. Unafraid, the saint walked up to the dragon and commanded: "In the name of our Lord Jesus Christ I forbid you to bite people." With that the dragon lost all its teeth and died. The people shouted hosannas and buried the monster near the **Temple of Castor and Pollux**. As a reminder of events the church of

Santa Maria Antica was built, later renamed **S. Maria Liberatrice** to commemorate the liberation from the dragon. In 1903 the church was demolished during excavations in the Forum, but the foundations of the older building remain.

Infidelity Proven

The **Bocca della Verita**, the mouth of truth in the Forum Boarium, is less about the occult and more about marital fidelity. The medieval travel guide *Mirabilia urbis Romae* reports that the mouth once bit the hand of an unfaithful spouse. One woman, however, was more clever: her husband wanted to make her confess and brought her to the mouth. Her lover was already waiting nearby and the woman staged a fit of insanity, in order to be held by the lover, standing there as if by chance. When she did put her hand in the mouth, she

Bocca della Verita", the mouth of truth.

could say with a clear conscience that she had never been embraced by any man other than her husband and this gentleman, whom all had seen.

Talking Statues

There are also talking statues in Rome. The custom was begun by Cardinal Oliveiro Carafa, who, on April 25, 1501, had Latin sayings in honor of St. Mark hung on the classical statue of Menelaus in the **Piazza Pasquino.** But the Romans soon turned praise into *Pasquinate*, satires on the church and authorities. The first of these posters were found on the statue of *Pasquino*, a hunchbacked tailor. Later they appeared on other statues—*Madame Lucrezia* in the Piazza San Marco, Marforius in the Via del Campidoglio, *Abbot Luigi* in the Piazza Vidoni, the *water bearer* in the Via Lata (also known as *Luther*), *Babuino* (little

monkey) in the Via del Bambino. The threat of capital punishment, confirmed by Benedict XIII as late as the 17th century, hung over anyone, regardless of rank and including clerics, who put up such writings.

The tale of the hidden treasure is set in the **Campo Marzio.** In 1001 Pope Sylvester II noticed that a statue pointed at a stone in the middle of the square. The Pope stepped on the stone and behold—an underground cave opened. Before the eyes of the Pope and the astonished people stood dozens of golden statues. Sylvester warned the Romans not to touch the statues. "They are alive", he warned. But two men, greedy for gold, could not resist and were killed by the statues: whereupon the cave closed once more and has never been found again to this day.

The subject of countless legends are the 124 steps to the church of **Ara Coeli.** Women who suffer from infertility would go up the steps on their knees, praying. The steps were also the scene of a wicked trick played by Prince Pietro Caffarelli on a group of peasants. They were sleeping at the foot of the steps one night, when the Prince had heavy rocks rolled down. Many peasants died, but the Prince was not convicted, because the snoring of the peasants had disturbed his sleep. But the ghosts of the unavenged peasants drove the Prince insane.

Everyone who has ever crossed the **Piazza del Gesú** has noticed the strong wind there. The Romans have a theory for this: One day the devil and the wind were taking a walk together; as they passed the piazza, the devil said: "Wait for me, I've got a bit of business to do here" and went into the Jesuit church. The wind is still waiting.

The move of 4,000 skeletons of Capuchin monks must have been a strange sight. The brothers moved them in 1631 from the Quirinal to the church of S. Maria della Concezione dei Cap-

Rome's popular poet Trilussa.

pucini at the lower end of the Via Veneto, taking 300 wagon loads to do so. The living did not want to leave the dead behind, and so the latter came along as well. The brothers then decorated the underground chapels with the bones.

In the Piazza Vittorio Emanuele are the sorry remains of the once famous **Porta Magica**, the magic gate. This former glory of Queen Christina's garden now lies in a corner, behind barbed wire and rubbish. Christina invited the greatest magicians of her time to her court, and on the gate are cabalistic formulas such as:

TRIA SUNT MIRABILIA, DEUS ET HOMO, MATER ET VIRGO, TRIUS ET UNUS

("There are three wonders: God and Man, Mother and Virgin, Trinity and Unity").

Under the signs of the stars magical signs are inscribed, such as the one inscribed for Venus, the goddess of love:

SI FECERIS VOLARE, TERRAM SUPER, CAPUT TUUM, EIUS PENNIS, AQUAS TORRENTUM, CONVERTES IN PETRAM

("When you let the earth fly over your head, your scents will turn minerals into silver stones").

The earth was symbolized by sulfur, quicksilver and salt and "earth above your head" referred to a reversal of the natural order of things.

The only fitting conclusion to a trip through the secrets of Rome has to be a trip to Palestrina, outside the city. Here, behind the oracle of the goddess of fate, caves go deep into the hillside. Here all who want to know the last truths have to enter—but they never come out again, because they always want to wait for the final answer to the final question. And if you don't believe this, go down there and ask some questions yourself.

e secrets
Rome are
den from
se who
n't in the
ow.

VILLAS AND GARDENS

When a city starts to reflect on the amount of green space left to it, its growth has reached the point of no return. Rome is one of the European cities with the lowest amount of green space per head: 20 sq feet.

In earlier years, when Roman families took a trip to the surrounding countryside, they mostly went to eat and drink copiously. Today it does happen that people travel out into the country to walk, cycle or otherwise commune with nature. In Rome, the defenders of the trees are growing in number, and every building project in a green belt meets with bitter opposition from local people.

In the Archaeological Park, planned in Mussolini's time, between the Via Appia Antica and the Via Latina thousands of local people take part in walks organized by conservationists. They may be the same people who previously at this spot unloaded the rubble from the houses they were building, but now they are vehemently defending this one mile (two km) wide and six mile (10 km) long strip of green against the speculators.

Air Pollution

But first of all the trees themselves have to be protected. The terrible air pollution—the prevailing condition is close to smog level—threatens pine trees, the classic tree of Rome, especially. If you have seen the pine trees, intended to provide shade, just below the Capitol, you will be aware of the problem. Elms, oaks, pines, plane trees—a wide range of trees are dying. The glory of evergreen leaves lulled the Romans into a false sense of security, but the great snows of February 1986

ended that. The first six inches of snow had barely settled on the branches when the trees, rotten within, crashed down in their thousands. Also badly damaged, admittedly this time by cold, were the palms. They are newcomers to the city and only met the Roman climate after the unification of Italy. They were—for instance in the Piazza Cavour and the Piazza Vittorio Emanuele—supposed to give Rome some Mediterranean flair. At the same time the new showpiece avenues, such as the Viale Trastevere, were planted with trees.

Medieval Rome had no space for trees. City and surrounding country were sharply divided. The rediscovery of nature did not start until the Renaissance. Then the splendid villas of Rome sprang up in quick succession. Roman noble families complemented their palaces in the city with great gardens outside, in which their summer residences, the villas, lay. At the beginning of the 16th century Rome came nowhere near filling the space enclosed by the Aurelian Wall, so many villas were built quite close to built-up areas. Without a doubt, the model for the Roman villas is the beautiful Villa d'Este in Tivoli. Not all villas survived. The most famous, the Villa Ludovisi-Boncompagni, was a victim of the developers. But others were saved and opened to the "popolo romano".

The first villa to be opened, in 1818, was the **Pincio**, the hill above the Piazza Popolo (the name probably doesn't come from "people", but from the Latin *populus*, a poplar). The "Passeggiata del Pincio", the promenade on the Pincio, is based on a project by the French architect Joseph Valadier, who began work during the French occupation. Napoleon himself had approved of the garden, which was to beautify Rome as the "Jardin du grand Caesar". However, the Romans had to wait till 1902 for their next park, which straight away became their favorite.

eft,
ntrance to
ıe Villa
orghese.

Villa Borghese was founded at the beginning of the 17th century by Cardinal Scipione Caffarelli. The Cardinal was a nephew of Pope Paul V. Later the family bought and added more land, so that 100 years ago the park enclosed 193 acres (78 hectares). The area has a long history as a place of relaxation for the nobility. The noblest families in Rome, from Nero to Lucullus, had their *horti* here.

Property developers threw a greedy eye on the villa in 1870. This set off the first struggle to save the Romans' traditional society promenade—the Borghese frequently opened the park to the public. The King delivered a Judgement of Solomon—he bought the park and gave it to the Roman people. But they were not grateful for this gesture—the name *Villa Umberto I* never came into use. Now there is a path from the "Passeggiata del Pincio" which unites these two parks. They are the only two Roman parks to be closed at night. However, you still shouldn't miss watching the sun set from the terrace of the Pincio.

The park, laid out among hills with winding paths and "casine", flowerbeds, hidden here and there, also has a reptile house, a little race track (**Galoppatoio**) and lawns everywhere. On Sunday the people of Rome take over the park. Then every spot is full of playing children, whose fathers have their transistors pressed to their ears so as not to miss a single goal scored by "Roma". Here you can also find a another source of controversy, the **zoo.** We can really only recommend a visit out of pity for the animals, because there is no sign of the landscaped habitats supposedly modeled on Hagenbeck's Zoo in Hamburg. That is why the animal rights protestors demand that this unattractive zoo be closed, and they're probably right.

A little further into the park is a tiny lake, in the middle of which stands a reproduction of a Greek temple of Asclepius, and on which you can row. Nearby you will find the **Fountain of Women,** created in 1929 by Giovanni Nicolini. The gardens also contain an aviary and not least the **Villa Borghese** itself, which is famed for a most beautiful private art collection.

On show among others are works by Bernini (*Apollo and Daphne, David, the Rape of Proserpina*), then *The Victory of Venus*, the semi-nude portrait of Napoleon's sister, *Paolina Borghese* by Antonio Canova, *Venus and Cupid* by Lucas Cranach and the *Madonna of Palafrenieri* by Caravaggio, and finally *Sacred and Profane Love* by Titian.

Another jewel in the park is the **Museo delle Belle Arti** in the street of the same name which crosses the park. Inside is the **Galleria d'arte Moderna**, which displays mostly works by painters from the last and the start of the present century. This is where most of

Taking a nap on the Pincio.

the big traveling exhibitions, which Rome too doesn't want to do without, are displayed.

Even more interesting is the **Museo Nazionale di Villa Giulia**, set up in the villa of Julius II. Here the best Etruscan finds from northern Latium and Umbria are exhibited, among them the fascinating and mysterious sarcophagus "degli Sposi", of the married couple, from the excavations in Cerveteri; it dates from the 6th century B.C.

The biggest public park in the city is the **Villa Doria Pamphili**, for which Rome has to thank another papal nephew—Camillo Pamphili, nephew of Innocent X. The Villa Doria Pamphili, built in 1652, is far away enough from the center and has always been too big to be filled up with too many monuments, so that much of the natural wild landscape of the park is preserved. There was even a bit of a dust-up in 1849, when French troops defeated the

Villa Doria Pampheli.

defenders of the Roman Republic after bitter fighting. In the 1960s the park was bought by the city and the state and opened to the public. Areas such as the "Garden theatre" were planted with over 600 different plants by English landscape gardeners, but some remain almost inaccessible, hidden and overgrown. Here you will find another peaceful starting point for your evening.

Go to the place where, ever since 1960, the **Via Olimpica** divides the city. From here the setting sun illuminates the domes of the city and even the peaks of the Alban Hills, so that they glow almost like the Alps. Now it's time for the joggers, who trot into the villa as soon as the offices close. The park even boasts a keep-fit trail, unique in Rome.

If you take the exit by the Porta

San Pancrazio from the Villa Doria Pamphili, you will come straight to the entrance of the **Passeggiata del Gianicolo** via the Lago di Porta Cavalleggeri. This "promenade" is exactly opposite the one on the Pincio, the sea of houses in the valley of the Tiber lies between them. After the "liberation" of Rome from papal rule, the heights of the **Gianicolo** became a gathering place for the anticlerical citizens of Rome, for here their hero Guiseppe Garibaldi had fought for the freedom of Rome in 1849. A memorial was built to him and, later, to his wife, and busts of those of his most famous fellow fighters who came from Rome were set up in the park.

The lighthouse was given to Rome by Italians who had emigrated to Argentina. If you follow the walls of Urban VIII to the left of the Viale Garibaldi and, on reaching the **Via Goffredo Mameli**, turn right, you will get to the **Villa Sciarra,** which is decorated with statues from a 16th-century Milanese villa. Here is a playground, a rarity in Rome, and a fixed mini-funfair for children.

In a quite different corner of Rome there are two other villas which are worth special attention. The first, **Villa Torlonia** on the Via Nomentana, can be reached by Bus No. 36 from the Termini. After years of neglect it has been taken over by the city. It was the last great villa created in Rome. The Torlonia family, nouveaux riches by the standards of the time, wanted to copy the old Roman families and contracted the French architect Valadier to design their villa. A theater was built, a small lake, a guesthouse, a sports field and a Temple of Saturn. Underneath the villa lie about five and a half miles (nine km) of **Jewish catacombs**.

If you follow the Via Nomentana outwards for another two blocks, you **Along the Tiber.**

will come to the **Villa Massimo**, seat of the German Academy in Rome.

Follow the **Corso Trieste**, directly opposite the entrance to the Villa Torlonia, and then turn left into the Via Chiana to come to the **Villa Ada-Savoia**. This is really not a true Roman villa, as it was built by the Piedmontese royal family as a hunting estate outside the city. Rome's vigorous expansion has brought the estate with something of its country character into the city and made it into a park. Half the estate was bought by the government, the other half still belongs to the house of Savoy. At the northern end is the hill of **Monte Antenne**. The name comes from *Ante Amnes* ("before two rivers", Tiber and Aniene). This is where the Sabine settlement of the *Antemnae* is supposed to have stood, and from here the Romans, under Romulus, are supposed to have kidnapped the women. On the other side of the river is the **Islamic Center** with its mosque, the first in Christian Rome, for the Islamic population (numbering at least 100,000) of the city.

Outside the Gates of Rome

Any greenery in the suburbs and the surrounding countryside is hard to get to. Footpaths are rare, and when they exist, such as the path around Lago di Albano, they are very crowded at weekends. Even the pinewoods of Ostia, the famous Pineata, look more like an army under canvas than a peaceful place for relaxation. In other places, such as the stretch between the Tusculum and the Monte Caro, just pick out one of the overgrown woodland paths and trust your sense of direction. With a bit of luck you may even find one of the old Roman paths, a *via sacra*, a Holy Road.

The Park on the Gianicolo.

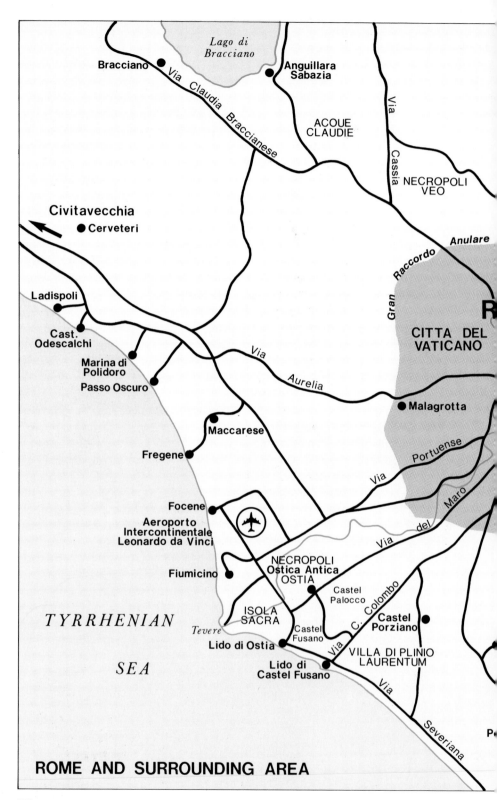

ROME AND SURROUNDING AREA

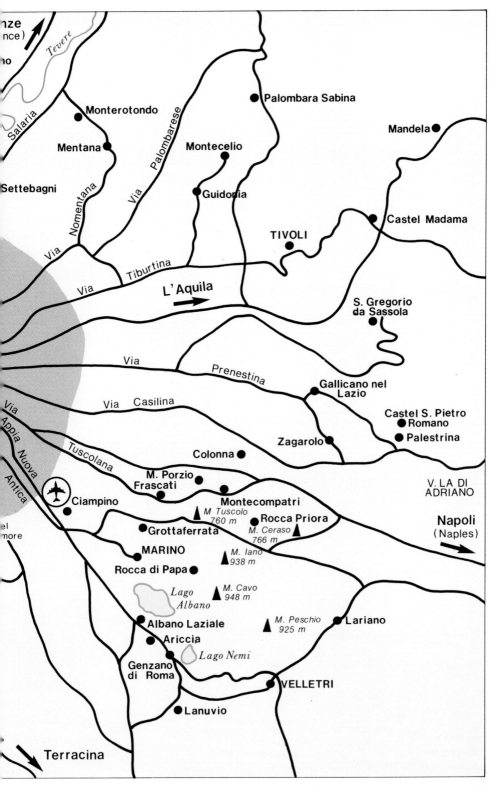

ROUND AND ABOUT

"One day the three of us walked the thirteen miles to Albano, fired by the wish to follow the ancient Via Appia, long overgrown and fallen into disuse. We started out at half past eight in the morning and within half an hour we were outside in the open Campagna. For twelve uninterrupted miles we climbed over hills and hummocks."
—Charles Dickens

"People pretend that the Roman Campagna, much loved by Goethe, is still the romantic wilderness, inhabited by shepherds and familiar from Pinellis etchings. In fact there are a hundred new housing estates out there, in which half a million people live in conditions comparable to those in the most impoverished areas of southern Italy."
—Giovanni Russo

The immediate environment of Rome is bounded by the Tyrrhenian Sea in the west, the Tolfa Hills in the north, the Pontine Marshes in the south and the Alban Hills to the southeast. It has not escaped the effects of the changes in the central city.

Yet a good deal of the "Roman" lifestyle survives here, more than in the city itself. If Charles Dickens were to walk along the Via Appia today, he would find ruins, as before, but also unfortunately a tightly packed row of 1950s villas, which have fenced in a number of historically important tombs without any concern for the public interest. In the evenings, beside bonfires made of burning car tyres, he would meet the *lucciole*, the prostitutes, whose ironic name for themselves means "glow-worm", for those creatures devour the male after mating.

One thing Dickens would not have found, unlike later travelers, would be the mountains of rubbish at the end of the Appia Antica. This debris of modern civilization, mostly rubble from building sites, is piled up in towers where the Antica joins its younger sister, the Appia Nuova—towers which obviously want to rival the tomb of Cecilia Metella in height. Dickens could come back with a quiet mind, for Judge Amendola has ordered the bulldozers in.

Goethian Campagna

The critic Giovanni Russo will still find those collection of houses flung together without any building plans—the phrase "housing estate" is really a euphemism—but if Russo were to look carefully, he would still see even today corners of Goethian Campagna, even along the Via Appia Antica. Just let him walk from the church "Domine quo vadis" in the Via della Caffarella and take a look: there is the Campagna, hilly, with its tufa caves, in which mushrooms are grown nowadays, a stream, a "maranna", herds of sheep and a 14th-century farmhouse.

The countryside around Rome offers such a variety of landscapes that it would be worth a holiday in itself. It is surprising that so few of the two million or so tourists who visit Rome every year find their way into the "hinterland romano", as it is called in Italy. The Etruscan graves near Cerveteri, the lakes of Bracciano, Albano, Nemi, the incredible remains of the pre-Roman shrine in Palestrina, the fountains of the Villa d'Este, the Byzantine Greek Orthodox abbey in Grottaferrata: the countryside has far more to offer than a two-hour trip to Frascati to stock up with wine. And there's even more to Frascati than white wine in taverns. A former summer residence for Roman nobility, Frascati has a delightful landscape, with its volcanic soil in which the vines flourish, is ideal for long walks.

ooling
ountains.

OSTIA ANTICA

Ostia, the "mouth" (of the Tiber), is supposed to have been built in the 7th century B.C. by King Ancius Marcius and the Romans consider it their first colony. However, archaeological evidence only goes back to the second half of the 4th century B.C. At that time **Ostia Antica**, a fortified settlement at the Tiber mouth, was built to protect it. From Ostia supplies of all essential commodities—especially grain— came up the **Via Ostiensis** to Rome.

The town had always been a port, and in 338 B.C. walls were built around it. Rome's dependence on its one connection with the sea was good news for Ostia's inhabitants—the town had a special status and its male population was freed from military service. Ostia grew with Rome—all the goods of West and East, which the monster Rome devoured, were traded here and the population had a luxurious standard of living. On hot summer days, when the stone streets of Rome practically blazed, Romans fled the big city to the fresh air of the sea resort. Today the less well-off Romans from the working class areas squeeze themselves into crowded trains to reach the polluted beaches, where swimming is often prohibited because of the filthy water.

But to return to history. The Emperor Augustus moved the Roman naval base to Misenium, so the town lost many of the free-spending sailors and the associated trade. But it was still the unloading point for the grain ships, for which Claudius (A.D. 41 -54) even had new docks built. Already the problem that was to destroy Ostia showed itself— silt. Not even the new harbor basin that Trajan (A.D. 98 - 117) ordered dug (it is now the airport of **Fiumicino**) could stop the silting up process. The coastline moved further west.

At the height of Ostia's prosperity in the early 2nd century A.D., its population was about 500,000. New buildings included tall brick apartment buildings and numerous temples. But its steady decline was strengthened by the move of the capital of the empire to Constantinople (modern Istanbul) under the Emperor Constantine (A.D. 306-337). Most of the population left the city, which covered 247 acres (100 hectares). The exodus was speeded up by pirate attacks, and in the early Middle Ages the Saracens made the Tiber unsafe up as far as Rome. In the Middle Ages, all that was left in the local marshes was malaria. At that time the coastline was four miles (two km) further inland than today. It was of course extremely lucky for the archaeologists that the city was never repopulated. Although the Roman ruins were quar-

The Decimus Maximus.

ried for building materials in the Middle Ages, about two-thirds of the Roman town can now be seen after extensive archaeological excavation. From the 19th century on, this archaeological treasure house has been systematically laid bare. The better finds went straight into Rome's museums.

At the entrance to Ostia the visitor has to follow the same road as the ancient Romans used. This leads to the city center. Worth looking at are the **Decimus Maximus**, the main shopping street, the **Baths of Neptune** and the **Amphitheatre**, used in summer for plays and worth a visit for its scenery. Also worth looking at are the **Piazza delle Corporazioni**, center of trade and shipping companies, the Forum and an old block of flats nearby, the public toilets, built as a place to meet friends and gossip, the School of Trajan, the Christian Basilica and the delightful square with three republican temples. A few miles away the tombs of **Isola Sacra** are worth a visit, for they give a better impression of ancient burial customs than the Villa Appia.

But before you turn back either to Rome or to the beaches of Ostia, you really shouldn't miss the chance to visit ancient Gregoriopolis. Today this place is called **Ostia Antica** and lies around the castle. The first name was given to this group of houses by Pope Gregory IV (827-844), who had a fortified settlement built here to protect against attacks by barbarians and Saracens. But the attacks, the increasing silting of the River Tiber and its frequent change of course soon drove the inhabitants away, until Pope Julius II had the Castello built. This was to be an outpost by the sea. In 1575 a change in the Tiber's course made it into a land castle, only usable as a customs station. In the castle barracks you can still see the bath for the soldiers.

Beach at Ostia.

CERVETERI

Cerveteri, Latin *Caere*, Etruscan *Cisra*, lies in the foothills of the Tolfa range, about 28 miles (45 km) northwest of Rome and only four miles (six km) from the sea. The oldest archaeological evidence dates back to the 9th century B.C. In the 7th and 6th centuries B.C. *Caere* grew to be one of the most important and powerful cities in Etruria. Its population was about 25,000. Although it was not all built up, the boundary of the city enclosed about 370 acres (150 hectares) and was about four miles in circumference.

The main sources of revenue were the rich ore deposits in the Tolfa Hills and trade with Greek cities and the Middle East via the ports of *Alsium* (modern Palo near Ladispoli), *Punicum* (today S. Marinella) and most of all *Pyrgi* (modern S. Severa).

Caere, probably ruled by a king, kept up good relations with Rome for a long time, until it was conquered by the latter in 358 B.C. Afterwards the city grew poorer, but was not finally abandoned till the Middle Ages. The population moved to Ceri and called it *Caere Vetus*, which developed into the modern name Cerveteri.

There is nothing visible left of the ancient city. But it is worthwhile going to look at the excavation of the necropolis on the hill of **Banditaccia**, where an archaeological park has been set up. Here you will find a great variety of different types of tombs, laid out along a main road and side roads like houses in a city, but all carved into the tufa rock.

From the simple *body tombs*, which were covered with a hill of earth, the *tumulus tombs* developed in the 7th century B.C. On a round foundation, up

Tumulus tomb in Cerveteri.

to 98 feet (30 meters) in diameter, a hill was built, on which rites for the dead were celebrated. Within the tomb were one or more burial chambers hewn out of the rock, copies of wooden houses of the living with windows, doors and pillars. As well as the chambers, furniture such as beds and chairs were carved out of the rock, giving a good impression of Etruscan everyday life. Worth seeing are the **Tomb dei Capitelli** and the **Tumulus II**, which contains four graves from one noble family, dating from the 5th century B.C. to the end of the 2nd century B.C. (Tomba della Casanna, Tomba dei Dolii e degli Alari, Tomba dei Letti e Sarcofaghi, Tomba dei Vasi greci, Tomba della Cornice).

In the 6th and 5th centuries the *cubic graves* became common. These rectangular buildings stand in rows in a regular network of streets and are a sign of social changes in the city. At that time,

prosperity had obviously spread to the lower classes and a social leveling-out had taken place. The tumulus tombs, appropriate to rustic huts, were replaced by the rectangular "council houses". At about this time, graves with many chambers gave way to graves with only one. On the one hand this was to save space, but on the other it was also a sign of a failing belief in an afterlife in which these graves could be used as houses.

Examples worth visiting can be found on so-called **Via dei Monti Tolfa** and the so-called **Via dei Monti Ceriti.** From the 4th to the 1st century B.C. the dead were buried in underground tombs, the *Hypogaea*. These were mostly plain and had space for many dead. The largest is the **Tomba dei Rilievi** of the wealthy family Matuna, dating from the 4th century B.C. It had space for 32 bodies and was decorated entirely with reliefs. There are carvings of weapons, tools, household implements, musical instruments and furnishings.

The members of the upper classes were buried in the big tombs. The poor people buried those of their dead who were dependents next to the tombs of the great, and others close to the edge of the necropolis. Finds from Cerveteri can be seen in the British Museum (London), the Louvre (Paris), in the Museo Gregoriano (Vatican) and the Villa Giulia in Rome, where you can see the famous sarcophagus of the married couple, the *Sarcofago degli Sposi.*

Finish off your visit to Cerveteri with a trip on your way back to Rome to the **Lago di Bracciano.** The palace of the Orsini is worth visiting. More idyllic are the two villages on the lake, **Trevignano** and **Anguillara.** These are hidden away along the shores of the lake, which covers 22 sq miles (58 sq km). Going back to Rome on the **Via Claudia**, take a quick look at **Veio.**

Tomba della Cornice" in Cerveteri, from the 7th century B.C.

CASTELLI ROMANI

When the grape harvest begins in October, when a laurel twig, a *frasca di lauro*, is displayed, when the smoke of the first woodfires mixes with the sweet scents from the vineyards, when a fat, fresh *porchetta* lies on the counter—this is the happiest time for Frascati, the "Queen of the Castelli Romani". **Frascati**—the name translates as "huts of leaves"—was made a town in 1197, when the population of ancient Tusculum fled the destroyed city on the Tuscolo and settled here.

Thirteen towns in the Alban Hills today bear the name "Castelli Romani", Roman castles because they were formed around the feudal castles of Roman patrician families or papal fortresses. During the last World War the Castelli suffered heavily from the fighting. Frascati, seat of the German High Command, was heavily bombarded, as were the other towns.

Frascati's trademark grows in the volcanic soil: a world-famous wine, mostly drunk by the "Frascatani" themselves, they like it so much. The stuff on sale in the supermarkets bears little relation to the drink served in taverns, which ranges from dark to pale yellow. The exported Frascati is no worse, it often doesn't even come from far away, but from places that have the bad luck not to be as famous as Frascati itself. This con-trick with the labels is the fault of the wine growers themselves. Instead of growing the more noble grapes such as *Malvasia* in limited quantities in order to obtain a good DOC (*Denominazione d'Origine Controlata*) and a really good quality, for which there is quite a demand, they invest in quantity. This is one reason for not letting the wine "travel".

Villa Aldobrandini.

You can get plain but good wine in every taverna. But start a walk around Frascati in the **Piazza S. Pietro**. From here you go through the little passage "Galerie" to the **Piazza del Mercato**. Here you can stock up with pieces of typical Castelli *porchetta*, suckling pig stuffed with herbs and spices. Go left past the market and you will find the wine shops in the **Via Regina Margherita** which allow you to bring *cibo proprio*, your own food. Some families come here equipped with a complete evening meal.

Here you can take a deep breath, for the whole Campagna lies spread out before your eyes—from the Tolfa Hills and the chimneys of Civitavecchia to the sea, with the setting sun reflected on its surface.

Frascati is not only famous for its wine or for its Children's Carnival but by its wealth of palaces with their gardens and fountains. Above the town rises the **Villa Aldobrandini**, built in 1602 for Pietro Aldobrandini, a nephew of Clement VIII. The most beautiful part of it is the park. There is a wonderful water display with Atlas balancing a "globe with a hundred thorns" on his head, and behind him a grove of bizarrely shaped oak trees.

The park of the **Villa Torlonia** is open to the public and lies to the right of the big bus station, the Piazzale G. Marconi. In clear weather you can even see St. Peter's from here. The beautiful villas of **Falconieri** and **Mondragone** are usually closed, but sometimes the tourist office *Azienda di Soggiorno e Turismo* will organize tours starting from the **Piazza Marconi**.

Another unusual secret lies hidden in the vineyards, south of Frascati. Here, in the **Via Enrico Fermi**, a young Jewish physicist exiled from Austria, Bruno Touschek, invented the first electron accelerator. This invention of

icnic on Tuscu-n.

the cyclotron in the nuclear laboratory in Frascati broke new ground, and later, in other research establishments such as CERN in Geva and DESY in Hamburg, the basic building blocks of matter, the quarks, were discovered.

The way to ancient Tusculum lies uphill along about three miles (five km) of asphalt road. There are no easily accessible footpaths, unless you want to trail around the long way following woodland paths—these tracks are not signed. The ancient city of the Latins (founded, according to legend, by Telegonos, son of Circe and Odysseus) was at first a monarchy, before it came into Rome's sphere of influence in the 6th century B.C. In 340 B.C. the city took part in the revolt of the Latins against the Romans. This ancient Etruscan foundation was still inhabited up until 1191, when Rome destroyed the town. This was an act of revenge for the military subjugation of Rome by the princely house of Tusculum, who had a strong political influence on Roman affairs from the 10th to the 12th century. From the cross on the summit you can see to your left **Rocca Priora**, the highest Castello (2,520 feet—768 meters). In winter it is often covered in snow, and has something of the character of a mountain fastness.

Settlement in this area is age-old, as is shown by the finds from iron and bronze age sites in the museum of the Greek Orthodox abbey **San Nilo** near the Piazza Cavour. The monastery, with its eastern rites, was founded by St. Nilus, a Greek from Calabria, fleeing northwards to find a site for a monastery that would be safe from attack by Saracens. Southern Italy was at that time under Byzantine rule and had a large Greek minority, descendants of which have survived in remote areas up till the present. The fleeing monks built their monastery on the remains of a

"Outing to the Castelli".

sepulchre dating from republican times, and Julius II later had the protective wall built. The church of the abbey has some impressively beautiful mosaics. After a visit, try the brothers' own wine, which is on sale to the public. On Sunday mornings the monks celebrate mass according to the Greek Orthodox rite—the chorales are unsurpassable.

Rock of the Pope

Only a few miles further on, but still steeply uphill, lies the town of **Rocco di Papa**, the "rock of the Pope", on the northern flank of the **Monte Cavo**, the highest peak of the Alban Hills (3,114 feet—949 meters). The medieval town has a "quartiere bavarese", named after Bavarian mercenaries who preferred the Alban Hills to their own and settled here. You are only a few miles away from Rome here, and yet the city, whose lights you see like a carpet of glowworms every night, couldn't be further away. The wine is excellent, and a delicious speciality of the area are the *sfogatelli* mushrooms.

If you want to, you can climb to the peak of **Monte Cavo** from here, following the Via Sacra through the oak woods (there is also a road, but you have to pay tolls). On the Via Sacra you follow the route of Roman generals who were due a "lesser triumph" along the basalt paving of the sacred way to the national shrine, also used by pilgrims from all cities. Above, disillusionment threatens, despite the fantastic view. The 2,500 antennae of the state and private radio and TV channels of Rome, plus military antennae, cover the remains of the ancient shrine of Jupiter of the 47 federated Latin cities and the more recent monastery. Try and imagine them out of existence. On top of all this, a struggle has been going on for some time to get all the antennae linked

iss
ards at
summer
idence
he Pope
Castel
ndolfo.

up in a system of dishes, which would be technically possible, if only the participants could agree.

The view from Monte Cavo is unsurpassable. To the north, lying close to the slopes, is Rocca di Papa and the fields of Hannibal, where, according to legend, the Punic general camped. In the distance, beyond Rome, you can see the **Tolfa Hills**, where the ancient Etruscans found their iron ore, and the Etruscan plain around Lago di Bracciano; further still lie the hills of Sabatini. You can even recognize the charter airport of Rome, **Ciampino**, quite well, and St. Peter's too—but in high summer the city is too damp to see anything. Further inland, looking northwards, you can see **Terminillo**, the skiing hill popular with the Romans every winter, only an hour's drive away but brushing the 6,000 ft (2,000 meter) mark. Further to the east lies the massif of **Gran Sasso d'Italia**, another skier's paradise, which can be reached by the motorway Roma-l'Aquila. The view to the south and southwest goes past Lago di Albano and Rocca di Papa to the former *Pontine Marshes*, where today they make the world-famous Mozzarella cheese from the milk of buffalo cows. You can see the coastline quite clearly and in clear weather even the islands of **Ponza** and **Palmarola**.

Now let's turn off to Marino, an unjustly somewhat neglected Castello. **Marino**, ancient Castrimoenium, is responsible for nothing less than the deliverance of Christianity from the Turks. The victor of the sea battle of Lepanto in 1571 was the Condottiere of the papal fleet, Marcantonio Colonna, Prince of Marino. In his honor a fountain was built which stands in the **Piazza Matteotti**—the name of the socialist leader murdered by Mussolini gives an indication of the political leanings of most Castellani—the **Fountain**

The Lago i▶ Albano, crater of a▶ extinct volcano.

of the Moor. The victor brought home dark-skinned human booty taken as spoil from the Turks. During the wine festival on the first Sunday in October the fountain runs with wine.

The church is worth a visit too. The **Chiesa Madonna del Rosario** is perhaps the most beautiful Baroque church in Latium, only to be compared with the works of Borromini. It was built in 1713, probably by Giuseppe Sardi. The construction of the nave, contrasting with the great circular altar space, is similar to S. Lorenzo of Guarini. Dominican nuns, living here in a closed community, are responsible for its excellent state of preservation, rare in these small provincial churches.

This Castello, Castel Gandolfo—Lago diAlbano, the one most often mentioned in the media, is beautifully situated on the edge of the crater of Lago di Albano. The ground beneath it was the setting for one of the most

ancient le-gends of the founding of Rome. Historians agree that this place, where up until now 27 popes have had their summer residence, was the site of ancient *Alba Longa* which was founded by Aeneas. The story is one of struggle between *Alba Longa* and Rome, and between the Horatian and Curatian families. The papal palace was built in 1624 on the ruins of a palace of the *Savelli* family. The gardens are closed to the public for security reasons. During the time of his summer residence, the Pope holds the traditional Angelus prayer every Sunday at midday on the **Loggia della benedizione**.

A supposed tomb of the Horatian and Curatian families can be seen in **Albano Laziale** on the **Via Appia** on the right-hand side going in the direction of **Ariccia**. In the communal park you can see remains of the **Villa of Pompey**.

But to go back to Castel Gandolfo—the victory of the three Horatian broth-

w of
ni.

ers gave Rome, under King Tullius Hostilius, the mastery over Alba Longa. The city was destroyed as a punishment for its treachery, but the temples were spared. They are rumored to have been exactly on the spot of the present papal villa.

Stendhal, Goethe, Winckelmann and Gregorovius were not the only ones to have a high opinion of Castel Gandolfo. Ordinary Romans of today love the place, particularly because it is so near to the Lago Albano. There is a delightful footpath, about six miles (10 km) long, around the lake. However, in summer the lake is as crowded as the seaside every Sunday and we can only advise against Sunday outings—a piece of advice that can be extended to all the Castelli.

The relatively clean water of this volcanic lake is an invitation to boating and surfing, a word of caution: In the middle, where the water is 558 feet (170 meters) deep, there are supposed to be dangerous currents.

The water level is kept constant by an outflow, the **Emissario**. A tunnel, just under a mile (1.4 km) long, takes up the water and drains into the Tiber.

The foundation of a medieval castle provided the starting point for this Castello, on the southeastern edge of the little lake of Nemi, as well. The city has been famous since the 16th century for its elm-lined roads, and it lives for two important occasions which have made it famous beyond Latium: the *Infiorata*. On the first Sunday after "Corpus Domini" the main street up to the church of the Virgin Mary is decorated with holy pictures made out of a single carpet of flowers. The central **Corso Gramsei** draws attention to another peculiarity of the "poor" town of Genzano. After the war, it was here that agricultural workers fought particularly bitterly for land reform, and

Small castl in the Castelli.

many a mayor who espoused the cause was deposed by the chief of police. They always were a rebellious lot, the hard-headed wine growers of Genzano.

Since the days of the October Revolution, the communists have had an absolute majority in local government. The town is also known throughout Latium for two cultural prodigies which almost raise it to the level of Rome itself. There is the annual dance festival, to which even the Bolshoi Ballet has been known to come, and a dance center with library attached, which offers young artists from the country around Rome a place to practice which they wouldn't find anywhere else.

A 30-minute walk along the **Largo di Nemi** will take us to the town of the same name and the sleepiest Castello. In spring it is famous for its fresh strawberries, which thrive in the warm climate along the low-lying lake shore.

The name was given to this community of 1,000 souls, beautifully situated by the cliff, by the goddess Diana. This region was sacred to her and known as *Nemus Dianae*, the sacred grove of Diana. The lake is unfortunately almost ecologically dead, due to intensive farming and untreated sewage. Here the Emperor Caligula had boats built for his excursions on the lake. The 1,446 boats discovered 69 feet (21 meters) down on the bottom of the lake were destroyed in June 1944 during battles between the German and Allied armies. Reproductions exist, but cannot be seen because the museum has been closed since the war. So go through the gate and follow the way to the right under the **Palazzo Cesarini** and you will come down into the small garden watched over by the statue of Diana. The little cafe sells excellent vanilla ice cream and the view spreads out over the volcanic lake to the sea.

the
rden of
ana above
e lake of
mi.

217

PALESTRINA

Unfortunately we know very little about the history of *Praeneste*, as Palestrina used to be called. Its origins must lie far back in the mists of time, for legend has it that it was founded by Telegonos, son of Odysseus. When Rome was in its infancy, Praeneste was already a flourishing city. The Romans conquered it in 338 B.C., and after the civil wars in 82 B.C. the Roman general Sulla, as a punitive measure, made it into a *colonia* and settled army veterans throughout the region.

Praeneste was famous but also feared for its shrine of **Fortuna Primigenia**. With its six terraces, one above the other, the mighty shrine still stands today. When the complex was richly adorned with statues and blazing with torches, which could be seen far over the countryside, it must have been impressive indeed. In the upper part of the shrine the goddess Fortuna was worshipped. The statue of the goddess stood in front of the semi-circle which now forms the entrance to the museum. For this reason the Roman patrician families of Colonna and Barberini built their palazzo neatly into the upper circle of the temple.

In the palazzo, now a museum, countless busts and other objects are on display, dedicated to Fortuna, and not only by Romans. On the top floor the **Nile Mosaic** is on exhibition. It was founded on one of the lower terraces of the shrine. It probably dates from the 1st century B.C. and shows the Nile valley after one of its fertile floods, in great detail, with peasants, fishermen and priests. In the lower part of the shrine, whose walls now enclose the old town of Palestrina, lies the secretive heart of the complex. In the central

The shrine of Fortuna Primigenia, Palestrina.

Piazza Regina Margherita is the **Seminario**, and this building incorporates the remains of the sacred place, the *area sacra*. Most archaeologists consider this to have been the entrance to the **Cave of the Oracle**. Here the citizen Numerus Sufficius, about whom nothing else is known, is supposed to have found the "sorti Preneste", thin wooden sticks with oracular powers.

If you wanted to consult the oracle, you had to draw one of the wooden sticks out of a box, and the priests of Fortuna Primigenia would prophesy from it. Cicero mentions the legendary fame of the oracle.

The worship of the goddess declined with the coming of Christianity, and with the prohibition of non-Christian worship in A.D. 4th century. Fortuna closed her gates. In the early Middle Ages the city was a much fought over bone of contention between Goths, Langobards, Byzantines and Popes. The latter finally conquered the town at the beginning of the 14th century and destroyed it all over again.

Apart from its goddess, lost in the mists of time, Palestrina can boast the composer Giovanni Perluigi da Palestrina, born here in 1525. As choirmaster of St. Peter's, he was responsible for a new expressiveness in Catholic church music, in the spirit of the Counter-Reformation, combining elements of polyphonic counterpoint with the new harmonious sound. His compositions fitted exactly with the current Catholic ideas of clerical dignity and compromise in favour of the pleasures of listening, required by the Tridentine Council. In autumn, gourmets are in hot pursuit of the local speciality, *funghi porcini*, a kind of mushroom.

The famous Nile Mosaic.

TIVOLI

There are two ways of getting to **Tivoli**, and both provide the visitor with a foretaste of the actual visit. From Stazione Termini the train travels through vineyards and past sulphurous springs. You can see the town, pressed against the hillside, from a long way off. From here you can turn back and look down on Rome and the Campagna, still relatively intact here.

The other possibility is to take the **Tiburtina** exit road. At first you drive through Pasolini's **Borgata Pietralata**, past the papal **Fort Tiburtino** into the countryside—a journey of contrasts. Here on the edge of Rome lies the prison of **Rebibbia**, which has many prisoners convicted of terrorism in its security wing. After nine miles (14 km) you come to the region where the spring for the **Acqua Vergine** rises, the aqueduct restored by the Popes which feeds the Fontana di Trevi. You carry on past the **Bagni di Tivoli**, acid, sulfurous medicinal springs, popular even in Roman times.

Before following the road up the hill to Tivoli, turn off right to the **Villa Adriana**, Hadrian's Villa. The Villa Adriana is the most magnificent country villa of Roman imperial times and even today, after centuries of systematic despoliation and decay, it still has an atmosphere of wealth and leisure.

When the Roman Empire flourished, ancient Tibur (**Tivoli**), lying in the low foothills of the Sabine Hills, was a favoured retreat for poets and for the wealthy. Among the guests of the splendid villas were Horace, Catullus, Maecenas, Sallust and the Emperor Trajan. In A.D. 117 the Emperor Hadrian started to build a luxurious refuge for himself at the foot of the hill on which Tivoli stands. The villa and park cover 111 acres (45 hectares) and were the most magnificent in the whole Empire. Hadrian is supposed to have tried to have monuments and places which impressed him most on his travels in the east rebuilt in Tivoli. However, Hadrian demanded more than mere copies of the originals. He was interested in creating a refined aesthetic pleasure, a contrast to functionalism and practical common sense.

Pride of place in the imperial souvenir collection went to Athens, the capital of Hellenism. Here Hadrian was impressed by the Lyceum, the Academy and the painted cloisters of the *Stoa Poikile* or **Pecile**, which got its name from the frescos decorating the walls. They are among the most important buildings, together with the **Canopus**, the copy of a shrine to Serapis near Alexandria, and the **Residence** of the Emperor.

The mighty surrounding wall, 761 feet (232 meters) long, of the **Pecile** has survived on the north side. Opposite on the inner side stood a covered, pillared entrance. The water basin, still filled on occasions, in the center of the Pecile has survived too. A notable feature of the villa was Hadrian's idea, a new concept at the time, of having the individual buildings scattered over the 148 acres (60 hectares) of the park, rather than in a central complex. However, as a protection against sun and weather all the buildings were connected by covered walkways. Excavations, first carried out to obtain marble, have turned up more than 300 statues since the 15th century. These are now in museums all over the world.

Tucked away is the **Villa d'Isola**, a little island in the middle of a circular building with a peristyle and concentric canal, the *Euripos*. This little villa, to which the Emperor or philosopher could withdraw, was reached by two swing bridges made of wood. Passing the olive grove, you can see the *Ninfeo*, and then the path descends to the enormous baths. From here you can get to what is certainly the most impressive point on the tour, the **Canopus**. A canal, nine miles (15 km) long, led from the Nile to the shrine of Serapis. The banks of the canal were lined with villas and statues, and this is the effect Hadrian tried to imitate here. Beside the banks of his 390 ft (119 meter) long canal lay sleeping rooms and taverns, countless copies of Egyptian statues stood to the left and right along the banks. On the southern bank there originally stood a copy of the Serapis shrine, on the spot where the big chunk of rock now lies in the water basin.

Hadrian's Collection

This eclectic collection of copies from Egypt and Greece was particularly useful for archaeologists as a pattern for the restoration of the originals, as happened with Phidias' *Amazon*, a copy of the original in the Temple of Diana at Ephesus. If you are tempted to smile at Hadrian's souvenir collection, just consider that sometime in the future the plastic models of a tourist from Texas may provide the pattern for rebuilding the Fontana di Trevi. Hadrian himself didn't enjoy his unusual collection for long, he died only four years after it was completed.

Carry on uphill from Hadrian's villa and you will come to the old town of Tivoli. Ancient Tibur is supposed to have been founded by the Siculi or the Latins. The town should not be visited for that reason only, but in order to witness the most beautiful water displays in the whole of Italy. The great Roman villas such as the Villa Doria Pamphili and the Villa Borghese were modelled on these displays, which have passed down to us almost unchanged— possibly because the fountains were so extravagant that later on changes

The Canopus at Hadrian's villa.

seemed impossible.

There was a convent built into the remains of an ancient Roman villa. Cardinal Ippolito d'Este, son of the famous Lucrezia Borgia and grandson of Pope Alexander VI, was made its governor in 1550 and included it in his family estate.

These gardens, with the largest number of fountains in Italy, were intended to help him become Pope. The Borgia descendant didn't succeed in his project. However, he left these incredible fountains to posterity. After the decline of the d'Este family the Habsburgs inherited the villa, but did not take particularly good care of it. In 1918 the town took it over.

The **Villa d'Este** was the model for whole generations of fountains. A walk through the gardens begins with a bang and gets better and better. In the **Viale delle Cento Fontane**, the avenue of a hundred fountains, a row of close-set thin pipes spray water into the air, an amazing spectacle. There in the middle of the road is the incredible **Fontana dei Draghi**, the dragon fountain. In honor of Pope Gregory XIII, the Cardinal had the emblem of the Pope's family (a short-tailed dragon) spraying water.

At the end of the Viale on the right is the **Fontana dell'Ovato** with eight nymphs in a semicircle. The river spirits above have already been overwhelmed by the vegetation—everywhere in the garden the rapidly growing plants lend it an almost magical air. Another remarkable feature is the great water organ. But Tivoli's watery attractions don't all lie in the Villa d'Este. The **Villa Gregoriana** is also worth a visit. Here the river Aniene falls in the famous **Cascate** cataracts. To round off your visit to Tivoli, you could have dinner in the garden of a restaurant in the center.

View of Tivoli.

222

THE CAMPAGNA

In this fertile hilly landscape, which now has billboards featuring Asterix and Obelix all over it, Rome fought to establish its precedence over Latium. After the defeat of the great rival Veio (396 B.C.) the Agro Romano was, at last, Roman. Soon the small farms were displaced by the *latifundia*, who used cheap slave labor to work the fields. Shortly before the fall of the Empire the Campagna blossomed once more. Everyone who could fled the city and lived in the country. Most of the ruins that are turned up by the farmers' ploughs date from this time. But after the collapse of the Empire the Campagna decayed and became a malaria-ridden marsh. The only people who dared come here were marble collectors.

The "Bonifica" of the Campagna was one of the first actions undertaken by the new Italian government, before the turn of the century. Appeals in earlier years to the Popes to have the Campagna drained and cultivated had been without success. At first only a stretch of some six miles (10 km) around the city was drained—this area has long since been completely built up—and the rest followed after the First World War. Later Mussolini found ideal sites for building his Borgate. Unfortunately most of the new inhabitants of the Agro were Romans from the inner city who knew nothing about farming.

In spite of all this, the Campagna still feeds most Romans, despite the inroads made by the city. Dairy farming, market gardening, strawberries, wine (of course), but also carnation growing and grain farming are among the types of agriculture that flourish. In spring the fields of rapeseed are in flower, and in autumn whole groves of olive trees.

Work in the fields near the Appia Nuova.

CINECITTÀ TO "LA REPUBBLICA"—THE MEDIA IN ROME

If you happen to need a Swedish actress who can speak good English, has forgotten all her German, can express herself in barely comprehensible French and can only manage "ti amo" in Italian, I would be prepared to come."

—Ingrid Bergman

From New York, Ingrid Bergman sent this declaration of love to the director of *Roma città aperta*. At the same time the person the letter was intended for was sitting in Anna Magnani's flat in Rome. "My dear Robertino does so like his spaghetti, with lots of sauce...here, take it, I'll give you some cheese, here, take the spaghetti..." Shrieking these words in a crescendo, la Magnani hurled the plate at his head. A scene like a comedy sketch from the lives of the protagonists in those years in which Cinecittà set out to conquer the cinemas of the world. As soon as la Bergman had seen *città aperta*, she wanted to come to Rossellini, and so began one of the most dramatic love stories in Roman cinematic history.

The fame of the Roman film metropolis may now be a little dusty, but has never faded completely. Its fascination lay with the Neo-Realism genre, which had among its famous directors Roberto Rossellini, Federico Fellini, Vittorio de Sica and Pier Paolo Pasolini. Amid the bare legacy of

Fascism and post-war wretchedness, they were stimulated by the newly emerging society to film the world of small thieves, of *malavita*, of desperate love. Their world lay among ruins, the black market and the rubbish tips of the suburbs. Cinecittà provided the right ambience, for in those years the city was pushing outwards with its slums, its high-rise blocks, its flimsy new buildings along the exit roads into the Campagna, nearer and nearer to Cinecittà. Films portraying the transition from Fascism to post-war Italy, such as *Campo dei Fiori* and *Roma città aperta*, were followed by Neo-

Left, Cafe Greco, above, entrance to Cinecittà.

229

Realism, such as Vittorio de Sica's *Bicycle Thieves*. The time of unrestrained economic growth, the early 1960s, saw the Roman films such as Pasolini's *Una vita violenta, Accatone, Mamma Roma*.

In earlier years directors, actors and all the hopefuls waiting for their big break had to take the tram. "Nannarella" Magnani, idolized by Rome, traveled this way, and so did Federico Fellini, who in his film *The Interview* portrays his beginnings in Cinecittà.

Uncrowned king of the film city was and

lochio, Nanni Loy and Carlo Verdone. This area of 717,594 sq ft (600,000 sq m) was intended to win world fame for the Fascist film industry, and was bought from the Vatican for this purpose. "Due to your foresight, Duce, Italian cinema is now an established and growing reality....But the gates of Italian cinema will be for ever closed to three factors: profiteering, bad taste and bourgeois corruption," the Minister for Popular Culture intoned during the opening ceremony for the *Centro Sperimentale di Cinematigrafia* in 1937.

is Federico Fellini. Here he made *La dolce vita, Oto e mezza, Satyricon, Amorcord, Cassanova, Roma, La nave, Ginger e Fred*. It would also be impossible to imagine the studios without Fellinis favorite actor Marcello Mastroianni and the unforgettable Anna Magnani.

Making an International Name

But other students and graduates of the Directors' School next door to the studios made their international names here, among them Liliana Cavani, Marco Bel-

It is one of the ironies of history that Mussolini's film city only achieved real recognition as a cinematic center through a number of truly bourgeois, commercial US-American huge epics, each laden with a fair-sized portion of schmalz. However, they made the name of Cinecittà a household word for an audience of millions all over the world. The unmistakable atmosphere of Cinecittà created *Quo vadis* with Robert Taylor and Deborah Kerr (1950), *Roman Holiday* with Audrey Hepburn (1953), *Ben Hur* with Charlton Heston (1957) and *Cleopatra* with Elizabeth Taylor (1960).

Meagre times followed the good years of the American epics. The crisis in Hollywood led to the decay of these once inexpensive studios. The glorious years of history, in which since the early years over a million actors, extras, technicians and directors had made more than 1,000 films; in which 16 theaters, an artificial pond and three restaurants were available—the whole long success story hasn't been able to stop the sworn enemies of the cinema getting their hands on Cinecittà. Today, apart from a few exceptions like a German film

able diversity, but Silvio Berlusconi from Milan soon rose to the top. He bought up three national TV companies: *Canale cinque*, *Retequattro* and *Italia Uno*. Since then Berlusconi and the three state-owned RAI channels are locked in a struggle of the giants over ratings and poach one another's stars. Around half of all the advertising money spent in Italy lands on Berlusconi's account. However, the programs are indistinguishable from one another and have led to a disenchantment with TV.

The first to profit from this TV overkill

on Baron Munchhausen, only TV films and commercials are made here.

In Rome the big cinemas have declined, and have been turned into theaters (in the best cases) or supermarkets (in the worst). When official permission was granted to the first private TV and radio stations in 1976 Italy's media scene was turned upside down. In the beginning there was considerable

were the radio stations, private (about 120 in Rome) and state-owned. The number of listeners grew. The print media also found new markets, primarily thanks to the Roman daily *La Repubblica*, founded in 1977. Its style lies somewhere between investigative journalism and "settled-down neo-revolutionary". The editor Eugenio Scalfari has managed to beat the honorable *Corriere della Sera* from Milan to top place as the best selling paper in Italy and has brought circulation up to over a million, although the first 20 pages often contain nothing but political articles and full-page commentaries.

Left, Marcello Mastroianni filming in the Piazza Navona. Above, filming on the Tiber.

NIGHTLIFE, THEATER, MUSIC

Roman night life really begins with the after-dinner *espresso*. Having met for a meal in one of the numerous trattorie in the Centro Storico, you stand at the bar drinking cafe and discuss what to do next. A decision isn't usually reached quickly—you generally go out in larger groups—so you leave the bar and go out into the piazza. Any decision is reached more quickly out there by the fountain. The fountain is floodlit, the water sparkles and people look forward to what the night will bring. In such company you prepare slowly and unhurriedly for the next few hours.

Some decide to visit one of the music clubs which are mostly found in the districts of Trastevere and Testaccio. Jazz and folk are mainly performed there, but fans of Latin American music can have their share too. Experimental rock groups are hard to find. They mostly perform only in the summer at open air concerts. Unfortunately you rarely hear live music in discos. Their repertoire is mostly confined to their own canned disco music, which tends to make a visit rather boring. Special effects, clever lighting and video try in vain to improve it. Not even the shows introduced in some discos, putting the latest designer fashion on the walkways, can make a visit more worthwhile; unless you want to move gently to and fro in a chic, elegant atmosphere—but for heaven's sake don't start to sweat.

Another group of night-lifers has decided to go to a late show in the cinema. They can choose either one of the big houses or one of the small independent cinemas, which often show good old films. You can sometimes get a special pleasure from a trip to an old cinema in Trastevere. There it is not just the film flickering on the screen, but it's the whole atmosphere that contributes to the spectacle.

You may find that a rather deaf old man from the quarter has decided to go to the cinema with his friend at 11 p.m. because he has admired the half-naked actress on the poster for days. It is she he hopes to see, and

until she comes on he holds a lively conversation with his neighbor. If you really want to see and understand the film, you do have to be a bit patient, especially as you may also be be disturbed by the snores of a woman sitting among her plastic bags, a leftover of the afternoon performance.

All those who have had their dose of culture—theater or music—in the early evening are looking for a seat in a birriera or paninoteca. Beer, hamburgers, wine, cheese, olives—you can satisfy every whim at this hour. In two hours time, it'll be more difficult.

Those with more unusual tastes and a different lifestyle will choose a cocktail bar. There they can lounge in kitsch red velour armchairs or sit on plastic stools in harsh neon light. The most cool sit on metal chairs against white walls.

Leave those people to their garish rooms and marble tables—the number of these style-conscious places has increased considerably lately—and follow the other *nottambule* enjoying themselves in the open air. The greedy walk through the alleys with huge ice cream cones—you can get a *gelato* till quite late at night in almost all parts of the city—and snack on delicious *zabaione*. You will meet all sorts of amusing night-time company.

Sounds of Roman Night

A few minutes ago, the Campo dei Fiori seems to have been declared a football pitch and the statue of Giordano Bruno looks, just for a moment, as if it would like to shout encouragement. A philosopher, astronomer, mathematician and occultist, Giordano produced books on magic and mathematics. He was regarded as a heretic and was burned to death.

But the statue of Giordano continues to stare silently at the Vatican, as if he knew that his *forza* wouldn't be heard, because a group of *ragazzi* on snarling mopeds are trying to see who can drive the fastest round the fountains of the Piazza Farnese. Loud cries of "Mario, Fabio, Mauro" sound through the night. Roman boys' names, simply have to end in "o", otherwise it would be impossible to draw out the last vowel when yelling.

They play more quietly in the Piazza Santa Maria in Trastevere. A frisbee whistles past your head, accompanied by occasional laughter and shouts of "attenzione". The first bars put up their shutters, and on the

bars and if you still feel like a pizza, you'll have to hurry to the Viale Trastevere to put your night-time hunger with a Margherita.

The taverns found on Trastevere have retained its simple charm, good wine and good songs. Here you will find quite a colorful collection of people. Some have come from work, others are returning from a midnight trip to the seaside, and if the atmosphere is good, the place may stay open till 3 a.m., longer during summer. But by this time the

street the black cars are back again. In each one sits a spruced-up Latin lover, his Hi-Fi turned on full blast, who still has not given up the hope of pulling a "bella ragazza", at least on the way home. They are the most unpleasant nightly phenomenon for many people, for their persistence knows no bounds.

They ring the bell for the last rounds in the

Above, the tent theater "Spaziozero" in Testaccio where a heavy snowfall in February 1986 caused performances to be delayed by as long as six months.

lights are out almost everywhere. The most romantic hours of the Roman night are just beginning.

When the City Sleeps

The city sinks into sleep. The noise level drops. Peace and quiet spreads out, even if it never gets absolutely silent. If you walk through the narrow streets of Trastevere now you will see Rome reconciled to its everyday chaos, wearing quite an unfamiliar face.

Stroll through the alleys of the Centro

Storico, turn the narrow corners and walk into enchanted squares. You would think time has stood still—it wouldn't be at all surprising to find Audrey Hepburn asleep on a bench near the Fontana di Trevi, like in the film *Vacanze Roma*.

The reddish facades, the street lights, the night sky above—the last of the night-lovers are not ready to go to bed. Now is the time to enjoy this very Roman night atmosphere in other squares, churches and monuments, using the Vespa, the motorino, the car. Go to the Ponte Sant' Angelo, St. Pe-

hood, one of the few that stays open very long hours. An espresso and a grappa always go down well together.

The streets are getting more lively again. The first delivery vans are bringing goods for the market in the Piazza Vittorio Emanuele. The new day dawns. But you can't possibly end your night's excursion without a fresh cornetto. You can buy one, sweet-scented, fresh from the oven. The last of the *nottambule* greet the Roman dawn with with a warm croissant with castor sugar and a filling of jam.

ter's Square, the Gianicolo, Testaccio, the Capitol.

Near the Colosseum at the foot of the slope of the Esquiline you can see the remains of a fire. The prostitutes have lit it to keep warm. Near S. Giovanni, too, you'll have to avert your eyes. But definitely by the time you see the statues of the Apostles stretching firmly and powerfully up into the night sky you'll know that as long as Rome stands, the whole world exists.

At peace, you can now go to bed, or to make the feeling of happiness last a little longer, go to a coffee bar in the neighbor-

Roman scenes

Slowly, with exactly matched movements, the two men move forward. They are wearing blue work suits. A group of three follow on their heels, taking over their way of walking and hand movements with a few small changes. They make a left turn and lean on their brooms. A group of four, precise as their predecessors, but with somewhat more expression, follows the prescribed route. They walk the gauntlet of those waiting to the left and right. Then two turn off left, two right, and they stop. The first two men in blue start again. The fascinating, orderly, concentrated and flowing motion begins once more.

This is no set piece by a Roman choreographer, and it doesn't take place on stage. The place is the Campo dei Fiori, the troop in blue are the refuse collectors. The market in the piazza is over, the stalls have been removed and the square is freed for Act Two of the spectacle. Act One was the morning market.

The theatricality of daily Roman life and the magic scenery of the city produce a play choice of performances make waves in the city. For instance, some people make snide remarks about the introduction of music matinees on Sunday mornings, claiming that these are a good idea because they distract from the poor evening productions.

Theater in the Early Days

There is no fixed company for the Teatro di Roma. A company is put together for each play, but they only work together for one theater season. Plays are cast so that actors

on their own. The theater of the piazze and the cafes is usually more interesting and lively, too, than performances on the official Roman stages.

One of these stages is to be found close to the Campo dei Fiori, the **Teatro Argentina**. It was opened in 1732 and today it is the seat of the Roman city theater **Teatro di Roma**. You can see some in-house productions, and touring theaters from other Italian cities or abroad. Polemics about the quality and

Left, the Roman theater group Remondi and Caporassi. Above, amphitheater in Ostia.

group themselves around a star, who is the real attraction of the piece. The audience sits happily and sleepily staring at Marcello Mastroianni or some beautiful actress and makes as dull and languid an impression as the theater itself.

Things were different in earlier years, as the chroniclers report. In 1816, during the world premiere of Rossini's *Barber of Seville*, the gallery resounded with hisses and whistles. The audience were indignant. Rossini, at that time house composer for the Teatro Argentina, had composed the opera under great pressure and musicians and sing-

235

ers had not had enough time to rehearse. But the work was already more successful during the second performance. The public demanded the Maestro. When he didn't appear (he had cautiously stayed at home) the delighted audience moved outside his house to honor him and his work.

The Argentinian Influence

If you have an interest in the theater, go round the corner of the Teatro Argentina to an ancient palazzetto with a small and beau-

the theater, text books, reference works, and letters, but there are also drawings, photographs, press cuttings, sculptures, costumes, posters, theater programs and handbills. One of these handbills is an order by the Milan police dating from 1815, prohibiting dogs, lit pipes and handwarmers in the theater. A pity—a few of those might liven up the Roman performances today.

But let's continue now with our theatrical and operatic walk in this area. On the left-hand side of the Corso Vittorio Emanuele we find the church of **Sant'Andrea della Valle**.

tiful inner courtyard. Here, in **La Biblioteca e la Raccolta teatrale del Burcardo**, you will find a library and a collection of theatrical items. In the 16th century the papal Master of Ceremonies, Johannes Burckard, lived here. He was born in Strasbourg, but as a holder of high clerical office he felt he had to add to his name the Latin word *argentinus*, which comes from the Latin name for his home town—*Argentoratum* or *Argentaria*. This name left inextinguishable traces in Roman life—the nearby square, the street and the theater were all called after it.

The library mainly contains literature on

This is where the first act of Giacomo Puccini's opera *Tosca* takes place. The fleeing consul reaches the chapel of the Attavanti, the first in the right hand side nave, and finds directions to help him find a secure hiding place.

Across the piazza, in front of the church in a small side street, is the **Teatro Valle**, even older than the Teatro Argentina. It was opened during the Carnival of 1727. Many architectural alterations over the years have turned it from a wooden building into a modern theater. However, it has still kept its charm. Until a few years ago it was surrounded on the outside by unassuming, shabby walls, which would hardly have led you to suspect that such a jewel lay behind them.

It's a picture book theater—heavy red velvet curtains, stalls, gallery and at the top, under the chandelier, the last rows of "the gods". The old peep-show stage has the same attraction as that of the Teatro Argentina. And when you sit on your seat, alone and dreaming, during one of the less well-attended performances, you could imagine spotting an actor or member of the audience in the box next to you who has been left over from the last century.

Unfortunately the repertoire of the Teatro Valle also leaves a lot to be desired. You're unlikely to find anything but usual middle-of-the-road stuff and badly produced classics. For a European capital, Rome attaches little value to traditional theater.

Interesting performances are more often found in the "fringe", because the guest performers are more likely to have some international standing. You have to distinguish between fringe theater groups, known in Italy as *Teatro di Ricerca e Sperimentazione* or *Teatro Avanguardia*, and the venues which make their performances possible. Supermarkets, former cinemas and cellars are turned into theaters. The best known are **La Piramide**, a little out of the center near the pyramid of Gaius Cestius in Testaccio, the **Trianon** near the Metro-stop Furio Camillo, the **Colosseo**, near the Colosseum, as the name indicates, and the **Teatro dell' Orologio** on the Corso Vittorio.

Roman Theater

One of the legendary names of the fringe theater is the **Spaziozero**, a circus tent in the Testaccio quarter. The highs and lows of the current Roman cultural scene always left their mark here. And the seasons haven't

passed the tent by without trace, either. The last unusually heavy fall of snow in Rome, in February 1986, caused the roof of the tent to collapse and held up performances for six months.

Spaziozero is a particularly good example of the lack of private initiatives in Rome, or at least of those that aren't partly financed by the city cultural assessors or the Ministry. There are other adventurous spirits, such as the women's theater group **La Madalena**, the fringe cinemas with their small film festivals or the music cooperatives. But they

get hardly any attention outside Rome.

Apart from a few exceptions, the theater-makers, even those of the fringe theater, are hardly any different. The former *avanguardia* directors, such as Meme Perlini, are stuck in their good-old-days style and wallow in it self-indulgently. The younger ones, such as the recently split up group *Gaia Scienza*, are more lively and open, even if they sometimes seem too much in love with modern technology, Hi-Fi and video.

However, the undoubted lights shining in the Roman theatrical darkness are those

Left, the Estate Romana in the Villa Massimo. Above, the dance group G.B. Corsetti, ex-Gaia Scienza.

groups on the border between theater and dance. They don't necessarily work from literature, language is not the central element. Their work is more physical, they use other means of expression and make other art forms part of the performance. Modern dance is also on the upturn due to the work of some younger choreographers.

Struggling to Survive

Money is not always the answer to a lack of artistic quality. However, the constant

swapped its sophisticated repertoire for banal comedies. This is particularly irritating because the comic and burlesque theatrical tradition has quite a history in Italy, but the warmed-up sketches in these productions have nothing to do with it.

There is no rosy future for theater life in Rome, either, for the once fresh breezes of the *Estate Romana*. The colorful activity of the "Roman Summer" was suddenly interrupted when the inventor, the long-serving cultural assessor Renato Nicolini, lost his post after the local elections in 1985. To be

struggle to survive, both for the groups and for the theaters, certainly doesn't improve the product. Repertoires and productions will continue to be dictated by chance and economic necessity, things will hardly change when the new law on theatrical subsidies is passed. On the contrary, the tendency will be towards cuts in the "non-established" area.

So theaters are looking for bigger audiences and nice, undemanding *spectacoli* fill the stage. The bitter moral is that bums on seats do make up for quality. An example is the **Teatro in Trastevere**, which has

sure, his successor Ludovico Gatto still talks about *Estate Romana*, but there is no longer a detailed plan to free Rome from its provincialism and keep the city alive throughout the summer with culture for all. This has given way to a shapeless collection of individual performances.

The protectors of historical monuments have meanwhile increased their power. It is no longer possible to hold performances in the Circus Maximus, among the delightful tombs along the Via Appia or in other beautiful places.

Troubled minds in Rome fear the ruin of

Roman buildings. But perhaps some cultural assessor should build up a lobby to put the counter-argument that sulfur dioxide emissions and the vibration caused by heavy traffic do a hundred times more damage to monuments than the performances taking place on their outer edges. And in any case this embalming process separates the Romans more and more from their monuments and therefore has lost its historical tradition in Rome.

This year the performances in the **Baths of Caracalla** are in danger. Here, where once people bathed, sweated and were rubbed with slippery salves and sweet-smelling oils, Roman opera companies have been holding productions for years. The atmosphere of these ruins by night, possibly even with a full moon, makes you forget the irritating performance on stage. Rome's opera companies are no credit to the city either.

The possibilities for open-air performances have been much limited by the prohibitive restrictions imposed by the blinkered patrons of ancient monuments. The most interesting place is still the **amphitheatre** in **Ostia Antica**. Here you really should combine a visit to the theater with a boat trip on the Tiber; the service has been specially arranged for this purpose. There's another place that will recompense you for the humid air of Roman summer days, the **Botanic Gardens**. You can look down on the lights of Rome or up to the stars and pass a few hours with music and theater.

To help out with the shortage of venues, the foreign academies have intervened in the cultural life of the Roman summer. The French **Villa Medici** and the German **Villa Massimo** have for some time opened their gardens to the public, in order to facilitate cultural exchange with Italy and provide a venue for visiting summer spectaculars. Rome does mourn the glories of past epochs a little, when audiences sat in the Circo Massimo watching the silver screen until

break of day. However, the times of the summer open-air cinema have not quite vanished from Rome.

The **Esedra** near the station and the **Teatro Nuovo** in Trastevere show films out of doors. The spirit of the times seems to be abandoning mass venues in favor of smaller dimensions, such as the delightful backyard atmosphere of the Esedra, where the neighbors can watch the film for free.

Shortage of Venues

Rome is short of performance venues, that much is obvious all over the city. Concerts held in halls with poor acoustics lose their value, and many a conductor has abandoned Rome. International exhibitions can't come, rock concerts have to be abandoned because the tent theaters have trouble with the neighbors again. The only big hall in the EUR district, the **Pala-EUR** has to be shared by artists, basketball players and political party conferences.

There are glimmers of light in some smaller places, and in the galleries, which are well conceived and make interesting use of space.

An example is the **Galerie Sala 1** in the Piazza S. Giovanni in Laterano. On the other hand, the **Campo Boario** (field of oxen) and the old **Mattatoio** the former slaughterhouse in the heart of Testaccio, are still empty. The city of Rome can't decide what to do with the buildings.

Years ago a project was begun to turn them into a center for exhibitions and all kinds of cultural events, and they were used for this purpose, but now silence seems to have fallen over the project. The city's indecisiveness means that the plaster is once more falling off the freshly renovated walls and all activity in the buildings has as good as stopped. Walking through the buildings, your heart bleeds to see such a treasure scorned in this way.

But Rome is a wasteful city. It has palazzos, piazzas, churches and sun in plenty, but apart from the sun it won't give anything voluntarily.

Left, puppet theater on the Gianicolo. Following page, cavallero's siesta.

TRAVEL TIPS

Traveling To Rome

By air: Travelers coming by plane either land at the international airport "Aeroporto Leonardo da Vinci" (Tel: 60121) in Fiumicino, or the charter airport in Ciampino (Tel: 4694). Private planes land at the "Urbe" airport, Via Salaria 825, Tel: 812 0524. There is a bus connection (ACOTRAL-bus) from Fiumicino to the Termini station, at about 10-minute intervals, costing 5000 lire and operating from 7 am to 11 pm. Depending on the traffic, the trip takes about 25 to 45 minutes. Going to the airport, the bus leaves from the right-hand side of the station (looking from the ticket hall)—Via Giolotti 36, Tel: 464 012. If you decide to take a taxi, choose a yellow one to avoid overcharging.

By train: Train travelers arrive at the main Roman station of Stazione "Roma Termini", which is right in the center of the city. You can get to all places of interest in the historic old city within half an hour by bus, taxi or Metro. Motorail trains come into the "Stazione Tiburtina".

Train time-tables: Tel: 4775.
Reservations (seats and couchettes):
Tel: 110
Sleeping car reservations through
Wagon Lit: Via Boncompagni 25,
Tel: 475 4941.

Collecting luggage (Termini):
Tel: 47 30 69 47.
Lost property: Tel: 47 30 66 82.
Railway police: Tel: 475 95 61.

By car: Car travelers reach the Gran Raccordo Anulare (abbreviated GRA) via the "Autostrada del Sole". The GRA is a lethal ring motorway, with a high number of serious accidents every year leaving several dozen dead. The section between the junctions of the Florence and Naples motorways is currently being widened to six lanes, causing more delays and accidents. There are no service areas or emergency phones (they are only now being built) along the GRA. During the rush hour there are mile-long traffic jams. The various roads into the city lead off from here. Most of the big hotels adjoin the

"Aurelia", which can be recommended as the best road into the center. Follow the white signs with the little "centre" circle, and not the blue signs leading to the exit "Aurelia"—these lead out of the city and there are just about no place to turn. Another example: the white sign "Appio" leads you into the Appio quarter on the Via Appia Nuova, i.e. into the city center, the sign "Via Appia" leads you to Ciampino on the Via Appia, i.e. out of the center. Once you have grasped the logic of these signs, nothing can put you off driving in Rome.

Conditions of entry: A British Visitor's Passport is sufficient if you don't want to stay longer than three months.

Practical Information

The city: The city of Rome, Comune di Roma, is capital of the Republic of Italy and has a population of 2.93 million living in a space of 8.2 sq miles (21 sq km). According to legend it was founded on April 21, 753 B.C. by Romulus. From then on it was the capital of the Roman Empire until Constantine's move to Byzantium in 330. In 410 Alaric and the Goths sacked the city, and the Western Roman Empire ceased to exist in 476. From 380 the Bishop of Rome was recognized within the Catholic church as "primus inter pares" and Pope. Invasions by Saracens and ongoing wars with German Emperors and the noble families of the city so undermined the position of the Popes that they spent the years from 1309 to 1377 in exile in Avignon. After that came the great years of the Papacy, which finally ended with the conquest of Rome by Piedmontese troops on September 20, 1870. Earlier, Italy's national hero Giuseppe Garibaldi had bitterly resisted the French allies of the Pope during the few months of the Roman Republic in 1849. Rome became the capital of the Kingdom of Italy, founded 10 years previously. In 1922 Benito Mussolini entered Rome as the head of his Blackshirts on the so-called "March on Rome" and made the city into the capital of a new, though somewhat smaller, empire.

In 1946 a referendum ended the monarchy, which had remained pro forma throughout the Fascist years. Ever since then Italy has been a republic, with Rome as its capital. The parliament has two chambers, the House of Representatives and the Senate. The State President has his residence in the Quirinal Palace in Rome. The strongest political party is the "Democrazia Cristiana", the second strongest "Partito Comunista", followed by the socialists. Since the end of the war the Christian Democrats have continuously formed at least part of the government.

The Roman inner city, the area inside the Aurelian Wall, is divided into 22 "Rioni". To these are added 60 "Quartieri", and outside these, adjoining the open country, there are 26 "Suburbi", known in earlier years as "Borgate". The area of the city of Rome is considerably larger than the built-up part, for the 41 communities of the "Agro Romano" are also included, so that the entire city area covers 58 sq miles (150 sq km). The province of Rome, which includes among others the Castelli Romani, covers 2,066 sq miles (5,352 sq km) and has its own independent administration.

The city has a mild Mediterranean climate and the coldest month is January with an average mean temperature of 8° Celsius. In August the temperature can easily reach 40°. The wettest month is October. According to statistics, the sun shines over 180 days in the year.

Only a minority of the population of Rome are of Roman descent. In 1870, when the city became capital of Italy, it had a population of barely 200,000. Since then people have come from all areas, mostly from the southern provinces.

About 99 percent of all Romans are members of the Roman Catholic church, but the number of practising Catholics is likely to be less than 50 percent. From the end of the war till 1976 the city government was formed by Christian Democrat led coalitions, until the Communists won the mayoral elections in 1976. In the local elections, which take place every five years, the Communists were defeated in 1985, and the Christian Democrats regained the position of mayor.

In the middle of the Roman inner city area lies the Vatican, which has been an independent and sovereign state since the Concordat agreed with Mussolini in 1929. The Vatican state covers an area of about 1.09 acres (0.44 ha) and has about 300 inhabitants who actually live there.

Tourist Information: You can get general information about Rome at the offices of the Italian State Tourist Office, *Ente Nationale per il Turismo* (ENIT).

Italian State Tourist Office
1 Princes Street
London W1.
Tel: 01 408 1254

The **Roman office of ENIT** is in a side street off the Stazione Termini:
Via Margharea 2/6, Tel: 49 771.
Information, Tel: 49 71 222.

Apart from ENIT, the *Ente Provincale per il Turismo* (EPT) offers excellent information, from leaflets about city tours to brochures and maps of Rome and Latium.

EPT head office: Via Parigi 5, Tel: 463748. Other EPT offices: In the "Atrio" of the Stazione Termini, Tel: 465461/475 0078; in the customs area of "Leonardi da Vinci" airport in Fiumicino, Tel: 601 1255/601 24471; and along the motorways before you get to the Raccordo Anulare, the Roman ring road:

A1 (Autostrada Roma- Milano)
Area di Servizio Salaria - Ovest,
Tel: 69 19 958.

A2 (Autostrada Roma - Napoli)
Area di Servizio Frascati - Est,
(in the summer)
Tel: 94 64 341.

Further information:
Agriturist: For tourists with "green" tendencies.
Corso Vittorio Emanuele II 101
Tel: 65 12 342.

Pilgrim associations:
Ufficio Informazione Pellegrini e Turisti
Braccio Carlo Magno, P'zza San Pietro
Tel: 69 84 466/69 84 866.

Peregrinatio ad Petri Sedem
Via della Conciliazione 10
Tel: 65 40 912.

Travel agents:
Thomas Cook
Via Boncompagni 25
Tel: 475 20 46.

Centro Turistico Studentesco e Giovanile
Via Barberini 23
Tel: 47 56 657.

Banks and exchange: You can change money right away in the station, or outside the Termini in the "Banca Nazionale del Lavoro" to the right. Banks are open from Monday to Friday from 9 am to 1pm and from 3 pm to 4 pm. Most banks are to be found in the stretch of the Via del Corso between Piazza Venezia and Piazza Colonna. On Saturday mornings you can change money at the airport, in the Termini Station and in the American Express branch in the Piazza Spagna. Nearly all shops and restaurants take credit cards. In general use are "American Express", "Visa" and "Eurocard". At present you can sign Eurocheques for up to 275 000 lire, and most banks will let you draw three a day. Credit card cash withdrawals on Eurocard are limited to 450 000 lire per day.

Foreign currency can be brought in unlimited quantities. The amount taken out is not supposed to exceed the amount brought in, but this is not subject to any controls. There are limits on the import and export of lire—your bank will be able to provide you with the details.

You can draw money from your post office account at the post office in the Via della Mercede, leading off the Piazza S. Silvestro.

Telephones: Using an Italian telephone is a somewhat unusual experience because of the Italian retention of the bip-beep, bip-beep ringing tone, but it is possible. Telephones are indicated by the yellow signs with a telephone on them. Often these are in ordinary shops, which have a payphone buried somewhere in their depths. Go in and ask: "Si puo telefonare qui?"

Payphones, if working, accept 100 and 200 lire coins and "Gettoni", special telephone chips. A local call starts at around 200 lire.

Long distance and international calls are expensive, so make them from payphones with unit counting displays, "contascatti".

You can find them in some bars. It's better to phone directly from a public telephone exchange of the Italian telephone company SIP:
Piazza S. Silvestro: open from 8 am - midnight.
Termini, basement: open 7 am - midnight.
Via Veneto, Villa Borghese car park: open 8 am - 9.45 pm.

Postal services

Direzione Provinciale:
Via della Mercede 96,
open daily 11 am - 12 noon.
Information: Tel: 160,
Open from 8 am - 8 pm.

Ufficio Vaglia e Risparmi:
Via della Mercede 96,
open: 8.25 am - 12 noon.
Sending money, drawing on savings account.

Ufficio Centro Corrispondenza:
Piazza S. Silvestro,
open: 8.25 am - 8 pm,
on Saturdays 8.25 am - 12 noon.
Post office, telegrams, poste restante.

Ufficio Centro Pacchi:
Piazza dei Caprettari,
open: 8.25 am - 3.30 pm,
on Saturdays 8.25 am - 12 noon.
Parcels, packages.

Telegrafo:
Piazza S. Silvestro,
Tel: 679 5530,
open 24 hours, telegrams by phone.
Tel: 67 90 623,
Telex, Telefax.

Opening times for the following:

Museums
Usually 9 am - 1 pm, Tuesdays and Thursdays often also 5 pm - 8 pm. Another day may be reserved for afternoon opening.

Shops
On weekdays from 9.30 am - 1 pm and 4 pm - 7 or 8 pm. The same times apply to Saturdays. In the summer, however, shops close on Saturday afternoons. General clos-

ing day is Monday. During August nearly all the shops are shut.

Galleries
10 am - 1pm.

Banks
9 am - 1 pm, in the afternoons 3 - 4 pm.

Official departments
8.30 am - 12 noon.

Parks
From 8 am till sunset, except for the Villa Borghese, which stays open.

Churches usually take a break at midday and close in the evenings from 7 pm on.

The Stazione Termini closes at night from 2 am till the first morning trains leave around 4.30 am.

Security and Crime: Rome has a bad reputation for thefts but statistics claim that as many cars are stolen in, say, Hamburg as in Rome. However, to prevent unpleasant surprises, put a car with a foreign number-plate in a garage overnight. Take your car radio out, even if your insurance company will replace it, because replacing a broken windscreen means wasted time and trouble. Don't leave any bags or other items lying around in the car, and leave the glove compartment open. When traveling in crowded buses only take essential money, in a purse, not loose in your pocket. Take care on bus routes frequently used by tourists; routes 64, 87. Keep an eye on small children, who crowd around you with cardboard boxes in their hands—under those are some surprisingly nimble fingers. But enough of this. If you keep to these few common sense rules you can walk around Rome, by day or night, without any worries.

Lost property offices
General lost property office:
Ufficio oggetti smarriti
Via Niccolo Bettoni 1
Tel: 581 0583
Open from 9 am - 12 noon.

ATAC bus company:
Via Volturno 65,

open from 9am - 12 noon

Railways:
Ufficio Oggeti Rinvenuti
Via Marsala 53
Tel: 473 06682.
Open from 7 am - midnight.

Shopping: Rome only has the one up-market department store, "la Rinascente" on the **Via del Corso**, level with the Piazza Colonna. Two simpler and smaller stores are "Standa" and "Upim". Apart from these, goods are mostly sold in specialist shops.

The classic window-shopping area is the area between the Via del Corso and the **Piazza di Spagna** and the **Via del Babuino**. Here you can find everything from jeans to jewelery, including imported foods, hats, shoes and paintings. Antiques can be bought better in the **Via Giulia** and the **Via Giubbonari**. Second-hand clothes can be bought in the shops along the **Via del Governo Vecchio** and in the **Via Sanno** market, and also in the **Porta Portense** fleamarket in Trastevere. Everything from food to cheaper brands of shoes is on offer in the market in the **Piazza Vittorio Emanuele II** and surrounding streets. Here you will also find the discount store "Mas". Don't forget the **Via Appia Nuova**, the "longest shopping street in Europe", between the Metro stops S. Giovanni and Re di Roma, where you'll find Standa, Upim and any number of clothes shops. Here you'll also find the largest sports shop in Rome.

Babysitting service

ARCI-Donna,
Tel: 31 64 49.:

Services for the disabled

C.E.O.S.
Tel: 581 8151.

Emergency:

Police: 113
Carabinieri: 113
Doctor: 475 67 41
Red Cross Ambulance: 51 00
Traffic police (Vigili Urbani): 676 91
ACI (breakdowns): 116.

Health: If you need emergency medical treatment you don't need any papers at first. Later, you will be asked to hand in Form E 111 available from British post offices.

If you need to see an Italian doctor, you will first need to exchange your E 111 form for an Italian "USL" cerificate (cf "hospitals"). Only a few officially appointed doctors accept the certificate—you can get a list of these doctors. Be prepared for long waits, or go to a private doctor, which is quicker but costs more.

All-night pharmacies

In the Quartiere Appio:
Primavera
Via Appia Nuova 213/a,
Tel: 786 971.

In the Quartiere Esquilino:
Cristo Re dei Ferrovieri
"Galleria Testa" of the Stazione Termini,
Tel: 460 776.

Lucci,
Piazza Cinquento,
Tel: 460 019.

In the Quartiere Ludovisi:
Internazionale
Piazza Barberini 49,
Tel: 462 996.

In the Quartiere Monti:
Piram
Via Nazionale 228,
Tel: 460 754.

In the Quartiere Ostiense:
S. Paolo
Via Ostiense 168,
Tel: 575 0143.

In the Quartiere Quadrao/Cinecittà don Bosco:
Cinecittá
Via Tuscolana 1258,
Tel: 742 498.

In the Rione Sallustino:
Doricchi
Via XX Settembre 47,
Tel: 474 1171.

In the Rione Regola:
Spinedi, Via Arenula 73, Tel: 654 3278.

Hospitals

Emergency ambulance:
Croce Rossa Italiana
Via Pacinotti 18,
Tel: 5100.

Health Service central offices:
U.S.L.,
Via Ariost 3/9,
Tel: 773 ol

Special clinic for traumatology:

Centro Tramatologico Ortopedico
Via S. N 21,
Tel: 517 931.

Ospedale G. Eastman
Viale Regina Elena 287/b,
Tel: 490 042.

Ospedale Figlie di S. Camillo
Via dell'Aqua Bullicante 4,
Tel: 273 141.

Ospedale Nuovo Regina Margherita
Via Morosoni 30,
Tel: 587 01.

Ospedale S. Camillo
Circonvallezione Gianicolense 87,
Tel: 587 01.

Ospedale S. Giovanni
Via Amba Aradam,
Tel: 770 51.

University clinic:
Policlinico Umberto 1
Viale Policlinico 225,
Tel: 499 71.

CONSULATES

Australia
Via Alessandria 215,
Tel: 841 241.

Canada
Via Zara 30,
Tel: 844 1841.

Federal Republic of Germany
Via Paisiello 24,
Tel: 86 40 03/86 40 06.

France
Via Giulia 215,
Tel: 656 5241/42/43.

German Democratic Republic
Via di Trasone, 56/58,
Tel: 83 41 94.

Great Britain
Via XX Settembre 80a
Tel: 475 5441/475 5551.

Iceland
Via Flaminia 441,
Tel: 399796.

Ireland
Largo Nazareno 3,
Tel: 678 2541.

Israel
Via M. Mercati 12,
Tel: 87 45 41.

Japan
Via Quintino Sella 60,
Tel: 475 7151/475 7323.8

Luxembourg
Via Guerrieri 3,
Tel: 578 0456.

Netherlands
Via M. Mercati 8,
Tel: 873 141.

Norway
Via delle Terme Deciane 7,
Tel: 575 5833/ 575 5995.

Portugal
Via G. Pezzena 9,
Tel: 80 22 60.

Sweden
Piazza Rio de Janeiro 3,
Tel: 86 04 41.

Switzerland
Via Barnaba Oriani 61,
Tel: 80 36 41.

Spain
Via Campo Marzio 34,
Tel: 678 4673.

Union of Soviet Socialist Republics
Via Nomenta 132,
Tel: 86 71 23.

United States of America
Via Vittorio Veneto 121,
Tel: 46 74.

AIRLINES

Aeroflot
Via Bissolati 27,
Tel: 48 66 19.

Air Afrique
Via Barberini 29,
Tel: 474 3041.

Air France
Via Vittorio Vento,
Tel: 46 55 63.

Air India
Via Barberini 50,
Tel: 475 1851.

Alisarda
Via Salandra 36,
Tel: 475 0057.

Alitalia
Via Bissolati 13,
Tel: 54 56, at night 60 10 37 46.

Austrian Airlines
Via Barberini 68,
Tel: 46 12 06.

British Airways
Via Bissolati 48,
Tel: 479 991.8

British Caledonian Airways
Via Piemonte 32,
Tel: 474 6353.

Eastern Airlines
Via San Basilio 41,
Tel: 48 45 97.

Egyptair
Via Barberini 105,
Tel: 47 42 641.

El Al
Via Bissolati 68,
Tel: 47 42 301.

Ethiopian Airlines
Via Barberini 51,
Tel: 47 59 374.

Finnair
Via Barberini 86,
Tel: 474 5839.

Interflug
Via S. Nicola da Tolentino 18,
Tel: 47 43 629.

Kenya Airways
Via Due Macelli 47,
Tel: 67 90 179.

KLM
VIa Bissolati 76,
Tel: 47 99 21.

Linee Aeree Olandesi
Via Bissolati 76,
Tel: 47 47 012.

Lufthansa
Via San Basilio 41,
Tel: 46 601/46 608.

Malev
Via V.E. Orlando 75,
Tel: 48 58 71.

Pan American
Via Bissolati 46,
Tel: 47 73.

Qantas
Via Bissolati 20,
Tel: 48 64 51.

SAS
Via G. Carducci 5,
Tel: 47 59 931.

Singapore Airlines
Via Umbria 7,
Tel: 47 58 943.

Somalia Airlines
Via Lucullo 5,
Tel: 47 59 041.

Swissair
Via Bissolati 4,
Tel: 84 70 555.

TWA
Via Barberini 67,
Tel: 47 211.

Varig
Via Sardegna 40,
Tel: 47 58 556.

Where To Stay

Rome offers countless places to stay in every imaginable category. For this reason we have limited this list to some hotels of the luxury and good medium class, together with a few plainer hotels near the city center. The Roman office of EPT will help you to book hotel rooms.

Luxury

Ambasciatori Palace
Via Vittorio Veneto 70,
Tel: 473 831.

Cavalieri Hilton
Via Cadlolo 101,
Tel: 31 51.
Situated right on the Monte Mario, a Roman holiday hotel with fine swimming pool, tennis courts and other comforts.

D'Inghilterra
Via Bocca di Leone 14,
Tel: 672 161.
Very old-fashioned and traditional. This is where Ernest Hemingway, Anatole France and Alec Guinness stayed. Good position in the business center.

Eden
Via Ludovisi 49,
Tel: 474 3551.
Near the Villa Borghese. A quiet, cosy hotel with excellent service and a roof garden restaurant.

Excelsior
Via Vittorio Veneto 125,
Tel: 47 08.

Especially popular with Americans. For almost a hundred years this hotel has been the meeting place of actors and famous people.

Forum
Via Tor de' Conti 25,
Tel: 679 2446.

This hotel is a little out of the way due to its situation in the middle of the Roman Forum, but from its roof garden it offers a lovely view of the city.

Hassler—Villa Medici
Piazza Trinta dei Monte 6,
Tel: 679 2651.

Beautifully situated above the Spanish Steps, for select guests.

The restaurant with its roof gardens and view of the city is particularly beautiful.

Jolly
Corso d'Italia 1,
Tel: 8495.

The usual excellent service, as in all the hotels in this chain.

Le Grand Hotel
Via Vittorio Emanuele Orlando 3,
Tel: 4709.

Situated between the station and the quarter around the Via Veneto, this hotel belongs to the CIGA chain and is run in corresponding style.

Lord Byron
Via G. De Notaris 5,
Tel: 360 9451.

Near the Villa Borghese. This first class hotel has the feel of a private club. Only 47 rooms, good restaurant (Le Jardin).

Parco dei Principi
Via g. Mercadante 15,
Tel: 841 071.

Modern, with swimming pool, near the Villa Borghese.

Raffael
Largo Febo 2,
Tel: 656 9051.

Popular with Italian politicians because of its nearness to the Piazza Navona, the Senate and the House of Representatives. The service is good but not first class.

Moderate

Gregoriana
Via Gregoriana 18,
Tel: 679 4269 or 679 7988.

Its attraction lies in the interior decor in Art Deco style, with room numbers designed by the fashion designer Erte in the 30s. Only 19 rooms, no restaurant.

Nazionale
Piazza Monyecitorio 131,
Tel: 678 9251.

This hotel, near the House of Representatives, is also known for its famous guests, such as Simone de Beauvoir and Sartre. It has 78 rooms.

Columbus
Via della Conciliazione 33,
Tel: 656 5436.

A second class hotel near St. Peter's, with old furniture and 107 rooms.

Dinesen
Via di Porto Pinciana 18,
Tel: 475 4501.

This very small hotel has a very good position: only a few steps away from the Via Veneto and very close to the Villa Borghese.

La Residenza
Via Emilia 22,
Tel: 679 9592.

A small, quiet hotel with only 27 rooms, near the Via Veneto.

Margutta
Via Laurina 34,
Tel: 679 8440.

Near the Piazza del Popolo. This hotel has only 21 rooms and no restaurant, but is still quite pretty.

Fontana
Piazza di Trevi 96,
Tel: 678 6113.

In a restored 13th-century monastery near the Fontana di Trevi.

Beautiful roof terrace with bar.

Economy

Abruzzi
Piazza della Rotonda (Pantheon) 69,
Tel: 67 92 021.

Hotel Pantheon
Via dei Pastini 131,
Tel: 67 95 305.

Campo dei Fiori
Via Biscione 6,
Tel: 65 40 865.

Coronet
Piazza Grazioli 5,
Tel: 67 92 341.

Della Lunetta
Piazza del Paradiso 68,
Tel: 65 61 080.

Albergo Sole
Via del Biscione 76,
Tel: 65 48 73.

Pomezia
Via dei Chiavari 32,
Tel: 656 13 71.

Youth hostels

Ostello del Foro Italico
Viale Olimpiadi 61,
Tel: 396 4909.
Reservations are advised, as this 350 bed hostel is the only one in Rome.

YWCA
(for female students)
Via C. Balbo 4,
Tel: 460 460 or 463 917.

Bed and board

Domus Mariae
Via Aurelia 481,
Tel: 620 576.

Domus Pacis
Via Torre Rossa 94,
Tel: 620 163.

Valehrad
Via delle Fornaci 200,
Tel: 636 256.

Agriturist
Corso Vittorio Emanuele II 101,
Tel: 651 2342.
Farm and vineyard holidays.

Camp sites

Capitol
Via Castelfusano 45 (Ostia Antica),
Tel: 56 62 720.

Flaminio
Via Flaminia 5.1 miles (8.2 km)
Tel: 327 9006.

Nomentana
Via della Cesarina 11, Nomentana corner.
Tel: 610 0296.

Roma Camping
Via Aurelia km 8.2 (5.1 miles),
Tel: 622 3018.

On The Move

On foot: The days in the city center should be spent on Shank's Pony, for you can comfortably walk through the actual center in the curve of the Tiber in three-quarters of an hour. Recently Rome's city fathers have made the attempt to ban private cars from the city center between 7 - 11.30 am and 3.30 - 7 pm. In Rome this may be less of a deterrent than the fact that there are only 3,000 parking places for the 1.3 million cars permitted in the center. And only the bravest tourist would join in the Roman custom of double and triple parking.

By bus and underground: The Roman buses provide an alternative form of travel, usually crowded but cheap. A single ticket costs 700 lire, and you have to get a new one every time you change routes. There are special passes for a morning, afternoon or a whole day. They are valid for all buses and trams. The weekly season for tourists, *Carta Settimanale per Turisti*, costs 10 000 lire.

These special tickets can be bought from the green kiosks at major bus stops. Single tickets can be bought in *tabacchi* shops, but are not always available. For 6000 lire, the bus 110 from Termini will take you on a tour of the city.

The buses begin their final trip out from the end of the line, *Capolinea*, at midnight. After that the night buses, *Servizio Notturno*, run. Their times are on notices at bus stops. In the daytime buses travel as schedule and traffic allows, usually every few minutes. You can work out the direction of travel from the names of the main streets and squares which are listed beside the bus number. You have to work out the rough route yourself from this information.

The Metro of this international city starts running at 5.30 am and finishes when the cinemas begin their late show—at 10.30 pm. The two lines of the *Metropolitana* cross at Termini. Route "A" runs from Ottaviano, near the Vatican, to Anagnina, one station past the film city Cinecittà. One station before that at Subaugusta, the buses of the ACOTRAL company start their outward routes to the Castelli Romani in the Alban Hills.

Taxis: The only official taxis are the yellow cars with the sign on the back saying *Servizio pubblico*. The unlicensed taxis are by no means cheaper! So take care at the Termini station and the airport. The basic fare is 3000 lire, at night and on weekends higher rates apply. If you drive outside the Raccordo Anulare, it will cost twice as much as within. Bargaining on individual fares is possible. A trip from the Stazione to the Campo dei Fiori should cost no more than 7000, to the airport no more than 40 000 lire.

Radio taxi numbers:

La Capitale:	49 94
Radiotaxi:	35 70
Roma Sud:	38 75
Cosmos:	84 33

Bicycles, mopeds, Vespas: You can hire a bicycle in the Piazza del Popolo, di Spagna, S. Silvestro and Argentina, in the Via dei Cestari, in the Largo Goldoni and an ever increasing number of other places. The yellow bikes cost 3000 lire per hour, 10 000 for the whole day.

The brave can also hire mopeds and Vespas:

Scoot-a-long:
Via Cavour 302, Tel: 678 0208.

Car hire: Inside the Termini station and at the Fiumicino airport there are counters for the companies AVIS, HERTZ, MAGGIORE.

Avis:
Piazza Esquilino 1, Tel: 47 01.
Via Sardegna 38a, Tel: 475 07 28.

Hertz:
Via Sallustiana 28, Tel: 46 33 34.
Maggiore: Via Po 8, Tel: 86 93 92.

Assistance for car drivers:
ACI breakdown service:
Tel: 116.

Service centre ACI-Roma:
Tel: 495 47 30.

FADAM Breakdown service:
Tel: 556 2896.
ACI outside Rome:
Tel: 748 1123.

Automobile Club d'Italia
Via Marsala 8,
Tel: 49 981.

Centro Assistenza Telefonica:
Via Magenta 5,
Tel: 42 12.

A few tips on traffic: To express it scientifically, the extent to which drivers in Rome pay attention to road signs is a direct function of the time of day. During the day most cars in the city center obey the traffic lights. The fact that the cars waiting at the traffic lights mostly stop right over the crossing is a minor point. The basic rules state that you may not drive into the side of the car which has its nose up front.

Cars double and triple parked are usually unlocked, so you can push them away when they block you in. There's no need to fetch the *Vigile* right away!

Pedestrians are remarkably well respected. You should cross the road with confidence, without obviously looking to the left or right, confident that the car driver will see you and stop, which—almost—always happens. If you look timidly about, they'll never let you across. Rome's car drivers only respect people who really want to cross the road, not pedestrian crossings *tout simple*.

In darkness these rules only apply in a limited way, because then people drive faster, drink more and see less. In Italy there are no alcohol or speed limits, and there is no requirement either to build in or ·wear seat belts.

Theft and towing away: If your car is no longer there where you left it (or your handbag has been stolen) you can go to the next police station, a Commissariato "P.S.", *Publica Sicurezza*, or to the Carabinieri.

A lot of cars are towed away in Rome — over 10,000 per year. Perhaps your car hasn't been stolen at all but only put in a safe place. The traffic police will tell you where this is. Getting it back will cost you around 100 000 lire.
Commando dei Vigil Urbani
Via della Consilazione 4, Tel: 67 6938.

Buses and trains around Rome

Stazione Ostense:
Piazzale dei Partigiani, Tel: 57 50 732.

Stazione Tiburtina:
Circonvallezione Nomnetana,
Tel: 49 56 626.

Stazione Trastevere:
Piazzale Biondo, Tel: 581 6076.
Connections to Pisa-Genoa, Nettuno, and Viterbo

Buses to the Castelli Romani leave from the Metro station Subaugusta.

Food Digest

Roman cuisine: Typical Roman cuisine is rich, not to say fatty. Offal such as tripe (*trippa*), plus oxtail (*coda alla vaccianara*) and veal trotters (*ossobuco*) make it rather indigestible. However, as a rule only the tratorrie and cheaper restaurants cook "au-

thentic" meals of this type, and even there the proprietors have got used to the fact that you don't have to eat all three courses:, pasta, meat course and fruit (*primo, seconda* and *frutta*). A plate of spaghetti followed by salad is ordered by Romans as well, especially those who can't take a two-hour nap after the meal.

If you're in a hurry there are *rosticcerie*, grills, on many street corners. Here you can buy *pizza a taglio* (wedges of pizza to eat on the move) and other takeaway food, all excellent value. Romans also eat snacks in coffee bars, where you can buy a sandwich (*tramezzino*) and freshly pressed orange juice (*spremuta di arancie*). Also, McDonald's have had two branches open in Rome for some time now, one in the Piazza di Spagna and one in the EUR district— and that's not counting the dozens of imitations. Hamburger deprivation is over in Rome.

But we ought not to miss out the good— and the best—cuisine. This list recommends a few restaurants which provide Italian cuisine of the best quality and also use particularly Roman ingredients with imagination. The prices (per head) are those current in early 1988.

Ai Tre Scalini
Rossana e Matteo,
Via SS. Quatro 30,
Tel: 73 26 95.
Closed Saturday evenings.
Excellent cuisine ranging from *couscous* to French fish soup.
(from 65 000 lire)

Alberto Ciarla
Piazza S. Cosimato 40,
Tel: 58 18 668.
Closed Sundays.
Well known for its famous fish dishes, best restaurant in Rome.
(from 80 000 lire)

Alfredo All'Augusto L'Originale
Piazza Augusto Imperatore,
Tel: 67 81 072.
Closed Sundays.
This is the realm of the king of *fettucine*, home-made Roman pasta ribbons (otherwise known as *tagliatelle*).
(from 45 000 lire)

Andrea
Via Sardegna 26,
Tel: 49 37 07.
Closed Sundays.
Hors d'oeuvres deserve a special mention.
(from 60 000 lire)

Checchino dal 1887
Via Monte Testaccio 30,
Tel: 57 46 318.
Closed Sundays.
Typical Roman cuisine.
(from 35 000 lire)

Chez Albert
Vicolo della Vaccarella,
Tel: 65 65 549.
Closed Sundays.
As you can see from the name, a restaurant
with French cuisine.
(from 40 000 lire)

Cul de Sac 2
Vicolo dell'Atleta 21,
Tel: 58 13 321.
Closed Mondays.
Italian cuisine and specialities from France,
Spain, Turkey, Greece and Egypt.
(from 35 000 lire)

Da Gingo
Vicolo Rosini 4,
Tel: 67 82 601.
Closed Sundays.
Family trattoria with dishes from the
Abruzzi.
(from 25 000 lire)

Il Drappo
Vicolo del Malpasso,
Tel: 687 73 65.
Closed Sundays.
Sardinian specialities.
(from 40 000 lire)

Il Gladiatore
Piazzale del Colosseo 15,
Tel: 73 62 76.
Closed Wednesdays.
Roman cuisine and dishes from the Castelli.
(from 25 000 lire)

La Cupola dell' Hotel Excelsior
Via Veneto 125,
Tel: 47 08.

International dishes. Also reputed to serve
the best *pasta all' amatriciana* in the whole
of Rome.
(from 80 000 lire)

Loreto
Via Valenziani 19,
Tel: 73 62 76.
Closed Wednesdays.
Good fish dishes.
(from 50 000 lire)

Margutta-Vegetariano
Via Margutta 119,
Tel: 67 86 033.
Closed Sundays.
Imaginative vegetarian cuisine.
(from 28 000 lire)

Osteria dell'Antiquario
Piazza S. Simeone 27,
Tel: 68 79 694.
Closed Sundays.
Dishes put together in an interesting way,
e.g. lasagne with aubergines and duck sauce.
(from 45 000 lire)

Papa Giovanni
Via dei Sediari 4,
Tel: 65 65 308.
Closed Sundays.
Food varies according to season, e.g. from
April to May you can get excellent artichoke
dishes.
(from 60 000 lire)

Porto di Ripetta
Via di Ripetta 250,
Tel: 36 12 376.
Closed Sundays. The proprietor—a
woman—is reputed to be particularly inven-
tive in combining dishes.
(from 80 000 lire)

Relais Le Jardin dell' Hotel Lord Byron
Via Giuseppe De Notaris 5,
Tel: 36 09 541.
Closed Sundays.
Not the usual hotel restaurant; in fact it's one
of the best in Italy.
(from 100 000 lire)

Taverna dei 40
Via Claudia 24,
Tel: 73 62 96.

Closed Sundays.
Cuisine and restaurant itself in the style of an old Roman osteria.
(from 25 000 lire)

Trattoria del Pantheon da Fortunato
Via del Pantheon 55,
Tel: 62 92 788.
Closed Sundays.
Refined Roman cuisine, fresh fish.
(from 40 000 lire)

Turiddu al Mattatoio
Viale Galvani 64,
Tel: 57 50 447.
Closed Thursdays.
Family trattoria right next to the old slaughterhouse, typical Roman cuisine.
(from 20 000 lire)

Pizzerie

Cristallo
Via del Cristallo.

Il Baffetto
Via del Governo Vecchio 114,
Tel: 65 61 617.
Closed Sundays.
Fast food and long queues.

Ivo in Trastevere
Via S. Francesco a Rip. 158,
Tel: 58 17 082.

Pizzeria
Viale Trastevere 57,
Tel: 58 97 555.
Closed Tuesdays.

Birriere
Via di S. Prassede 90,
Tel: 48 66 36.
Closed Mondays.

Peroni
Via Bescia 24/32,
Tel: 85 81 55.
Closed Mondays.

Tabasco
Piazza Capranica 52,
Tel: 67 93 977.
Closed Mondays.

The Fiddler's Elbow
Via dell'Olmata 43.
Irish pub. Closed Mondays.

Trilussa
Via Benedetta 19,
Tel: 58 13 448.

Cafes

Antico Caffe Greco
Via Condotti 86.
Favoured by Germans.

Alemagna
Via del Corso 181.
Generous lunchtime buffet.

Berardo
Piazza Colonna.
Has a view of the seat of government Pal. Chigi.

Cafe de Paris
Via Veneto 90.
A classic.

Canova
Piazza del Popolo.
Two beautiful cafes for sitting outside.

Gran Caffe Doney
Via Veneto 145.
Former meeting place of literati.

Rosati
Piazza del Popolo 5.

Activities

The best listings of coming events appear every Friday in a supplement of the daily *La Repubblica* which is called: *Trovaroma*. In here you can find details of everything scheduled for the next week in Rome and the surrounding area.

The city and an advertising agency together publish *This Week in Rome*, a tourists' diary with partially dated information.

The other dailies such as *Paese Sera* and *Il Messagero* also publish diaries of events for the traveler.

THEATERS

Adriano
Piazza Cavour,
Tel: 35 21 53.

Anfitrione
Via S. Saba 24,
Tel: 57 50 827.

Anteprima
Via Capo d'Afrika 5/a,
Tel: 73 62 55.

Arcar
Via F.P. Tosti 16/a,
Tel: 83 95 767.

Arcobalena
Salita S. Gregorio al Celio 3,
Tel: 73 28 53.

Argentina
Lgo Torre Argentina 52,
Tel: 65 44 601.

Aurora
Via Flaminia Vecchia 520,
Tel: 39 32 69.

Bagaglino
Via Due Macelli 75,
Tel: 67 91 439.

Beat 72
Via G.G. Belli 72,
Tel: 31 77 15.

Belli
Piazza S. Apollonia 21/a,
Tel: 58 94 875.

Bernini
Piazza S. Lorenzo Bernini 22,
Tel: 57 58 3000.

Brancaccio
Via Merulana 244,
Tel: 73 02 02.

Catacombe 2000
Via Iside 2,
Tel: 75 53 495.

Dell'Anfitrione
Via Marziale 35,
Tel: 35 98 636.

Delle Arti
Via Sicilia 59,
Tel: 47 58 598.

Delle Marionette degli Accettella
Piazza Gondar 22,
Tel: 83 19 681.

Delle Muse
Via Fiorli 43,
Tel: 86 29 48.

Dell'Opera
Via Firenze 72,
Tel: 461 17 55.

Dell'Orologio
Vie dei Filippini 17/a,
Tel: 65 48 735.

Dei Servi
Via Mortaro 22,
Tel: 67 95 130.
EliseoVia Nazional 183/d,
Tel: 46 21 14.

Flaiano
Via S. Stefano del Cacco 15,
Tel: 67 98 569.

Folk Studio
Via Gaetano Saacchi 3,
Tel: 58 92 374.

Ghione
Via delle Fornaci 37,
Tel: 63 72 294.

Giulio Cesare
Viale Giulio Cesare,
Tel: 35 33 60.

Goldoni
Viale Soldati 3,
Tel: 65 61 156.

Il Giardino Segreto
Via Panattoni 67,
Tel: 36 50 938.

Il Salottino
Via Capo d'Africa 32,
Tel: 73 36 01.

Il Torchio
Via Morosini 16,
Tel: 58 20 49.

La Maddalena
Via Campo Marzio 7,
Tel: 65 69 424.

La Piramide
Via G. Benzoni 51,
Tel: 57 61 62.

La Scaletta
Via del Collegio Romano 1,
Tel: 67 83 148.

Marionette al Pantheon
Via Beato Angelico 32,
Tel: 81 01 887.

Metateatro
Via Mameli 5,
Tel: 58 95 807.

Olimpico
Piazza Gentile da Fabriano 17,
Tel: 39 62 635.

Piccolo Eliseo
Via Nazionale 133,
Tel: 46 50 95.

Politecnico
Via Fracassini 18,
Tel: 36 07 559.

Quattro Fontane
Via Quattro Fontane 23,
Tel: 47 43 119.

Quirino
Via Minghetti 1,
Tel: 67 94 585.

Sala Umberto
Via delle Mercede 50,
Tel: 67 94 753.

Sistina
Via Sistina 129,
Tel: 47 56 841.

Spaziozero
Via Galvani 65,
Tel: 57 30 89.

Teatro dei Satiri
Via Grotta Pinta 19,
Tel: 65 65 352.

Teatro in Trastevere
V.lo Moroni 3,
Tel: 58 95 782.

Teatro delle Voci
Via E. Bombelli 24,
Tel: 68 10 118.

Tenda a Stricese
Via Colombo,
Tel: 54 22 779.

Trianon
Via M. Scevola 101,
Tel: 78 80 985.

Uccelliera
Viale dell'Uccelliera,
Tel: 85 51 18.

Valle
Via Teatro Valle 23,
Tel: 65 43 794.

OPERA AND CONCERTS

The season for the **Teatro dell'Opera** (tel: 474 2535) runs from December to June. The marvellous open air performances in the **Baths of Caracalla** only take place in July and August.

First-rate concerts are held from October to May in the **Auditorium of the National Academy of Santa Cecilia** on the Via della Conciliazione and in **Scala dei Concert** in the Via dei Greci (tel: 679 or 389)

Open-air summer concerts are also held in the **Basilica di Massenzio**.

In the **University auditorium of S. Leone Magna** (tel: 396 4777) and in the **Roman Philharmonic Academy** in the Via Flaminia 118 you can also hear concerts.

U.C.E Entertainment

A popular variation on the obligatory Roman evening entertainment *mangiare* (i.e. eating) is instead of (or after) going to an ordinary restaurant to find one that offers, besides food, music, a bar, video, gambling or simply an amusing atmosphere and interesting clientele. Some of the places listed below are open till late at night or even until dawn.

Action Club
Via Benedetta 23,
Tel: 58 94 016.
Restaurant and pub with courtyard garden.
Open: 8 pm - 1.30 am or later, closed Mondays.

Aldebaran
Via Galvani 54,
Tel: 57 60 13.
American bar, 250 cocktails.
Open: 9 pm - 2.30 am, closed Sundays.

Al 19
Via degli Avignonesi.
Piano in the bar, restaurant service.
Open every evening until 2 am.

Alfellini
Via F. Carletti,
Tel: 57 83 595.
Cocktail bar, live music, cabaret.
Open till 2 am, closed Sundays.

Arc-en-ciel
Via del Banco di Santo Spirito 45,
Tel: 65 61 513.
Wine dealer, creperie, snack bar, live performances and background music.
Open daily from 12 noon to 3 pm and from 5 pm to 2 am.

Ambush Bar
Vicolo del Cinque 60,
Tel: 58 95 913.
Video-bar, birreria.
Open from 8 pm to 3 am.

Bar Venerina
Via G. Vitelleschi 44,
Tel: 65 61 615.
Restaurant service, panini, beer and tobacconist.
Open till 2 am, closed Sundays.

Baronato Quattro Bellezze
Via di Panico 23.

Cocktails, wine, snacks and music.
Open: 2 pm - 2am.

Belle Epoque
Vicolo del Leopardo 31,
Tel: 58 95 540.
Piano bar.
Open from 9 pm to 1 am, closed Wednesdays.

Blatumba
Piazza in Piscinula 20,
Tel: 60 54 810.
South American style bar. Live music and poetry readings.
Open from 10 pm till late, closed Sundays.

Bibelot
Via G. Capponi 45,
Tel: 78 10 626.
Pub, cocktail bar, small restaurant, table games.
Open from 8.30 pm till 2 am and later, closed Wednesdays.

Blue Toscano
Via di Tor Margana 4,
Tel: 67 98 158.
Cocktail bar, buffet, music.
Open: 12.30 - 3 pm and 8.30 pm till far into the night, closed Mondays.

Bulli e Pupe
Via delle Cave 138-140,
Tel: 78 71 57.
Birreria, cocktail bar and cold buffet.
Open from 8 pm till 2 am.

Cafe le Folies
Via S. Francesco a Ripa 165.
Piano bar, tea room, creperie.
Open from morning till late at night, closed Tuesdays.

Calise
Piazza Mastai 7,
Tel: 58 09 404.
Panini, beer, long drinks, and background music.
Open from 7 pm to 3 am.

Camarillo
Via Properzio 30,
Tel: 65 48 471.
Piano bar, restaurant.

Open from the evening till 3 am, closed Tuesdays.

Carpe Noctem
Via dei Genovesi 30,
Tel: 58 95 186.
Cocktail bar, cold buffet.
Open from 10 pm to 3 am, closed Mondays.

Camelot
Via della Scala 45.
Cocktail bar, cold buffet.
Open from 10 pm to 2 am.

Contrasteo
Via Tor Millina 4/5,
Tel: 68 79 945.
Wine bar, restaurant, cold buffet, desserts.
Open from 8 pm till 3 am, closed Mondays.

Clarabella
Piazza S. Cosimato 39.
Cocktail bar, live Brazilian music.
Open from 9 pm to 2 am.

Coffee Shop No Stop
Piazza Euclid 43,
Tel: 80 37 51.
Pizzeria, restaurant, snack bar.
Open till 3 am, closed Mondays.

Cotton Club
Via Prenestina 44,
Tel: 77 98 08.
Birreria, Afro-Asian cuisine.
Open from 6 pm to 3 am.

Creperie de la Valle
Via del Teatro Valle 54.
Crepes, wine, cold buffet.
Open from 8 pm to 2 am, closed Mondays.

Crigio Notte
Via dei Fienaroli 30/b,
Tel: 58 13 249.
Cocktail bar, disco.
Open every evening from 8.30 pm till 3 am and later.

Dalmine Club
Via Dalmine 207-211 (Prima Porta).
Birreria, casino, live concerts and performances.
Open from 7.30 pm till late, closed every Sunday.

Doctor Fox
Vicolo de'Renzi 4,
Tel: 58 90 519.
Video bar, cocktails.
Open daily from 8.30 pm till 2 am.

Dr. Vagaps Studio
Piazzale Stazione Castelfusano 10 (Ostia).
Wine bar, afternoon tea room, live music.
Open from 5 pm to 4 am, closed Mondays.

Enoteca dell' Orologio
Via del Governo Vecchio 23,
Tel: 65 61 904.
Wine tasting.
Open all hours, closed Sundays.

Equatore
Via Rasella 5,
Tel: 47 42 413.
Tropical cocktail bar.
Open from 9.30 pm till 2 am or later, from 4 pm on Sundays.

Erasmo da Rotterdam
Via S. Maria dell'Anima 12,
Tel: 65 61 612.
Cocktail bar.
Open from 5 pm - 3 am, closed Sundays.

Feeling Club
Piazza S. Callisto 9/a,
Tel: 58 18 256.
Cocktail bar, haute cuisine, video.
Open from 8.30 pm to 3 am, closed on Mondays.

Fonclea
Via Crescenzio 82/a,
Tel: 65 30 302.
Music, pub, restaurant.
Open from 8 pm to 2 am, Mondays to Fridays at lunchtime from 11 am to 3 pm.

Giulio Passami L'Olio
Via di Monte Giordano 28.
Entertainment, wine, salads.
Open every evening from 8 pm till far into the night.

Goldfinch Club
Piazza della Pollarola 31.
Open from 8.30 pm to 2.30 am.

Glamour
Via S. Giovanni in Laterano 81,
Tel: 73 88 80.
Cocktails, buffet, music.
Open from 7 pm till 2 am, closed Mondays.

Gran Cafe dell' Opera
Via Torino 140,
Tel: 47 45 227.
American bar, restaurant, birreria, and to-
bacconist.
Open every evening till 3 am.

Gunilla's
Piazza S. Pancrazio 19-22,
Tel: 58 22 97.
Candlelit restaurant, tea rooms.
Open from 5 pm till midnight, closed on
Tuesdays.

Hangar
Via in Selci 69.
Tel: 46 13 97.
Video and cocktail bar.
Open from 9 pm till 3 am, closed Tuesdays.

High Five
Corso Vittorio 286.
Rock video bar, cocktails, and restaurant
service.
Open in the evenings till 2 am, closed on
Tuesdays.

Hemingway
Piazzelle delle Copelle 10,
Tel: 65 44 135.
Cocktail bar.
Open till 3 am.

Hungry Bogart
Borgo Pio 202.
Small restaurant, paninoteca, cocktails and
desserts.
Open every evening from 8 pm to 2 am.

Il Brutto Anatroccolo
Viale Paroli 18/20,
Tel: 87 93 09.
Cafeteria, tea rooms, creperie.
Open from 7 am till 1 am, closed Sundays.

Il Cantuccio
Corso Rinascimento 71,

Tel: 65 42 982.
Open from 8.30 pm till 2 am, closed on
Mondays.

Il Cicchetto
Via Nomentana 565,
Tel: 89 39 84.
Wine dealer, wine tasting and draught beer.
Open evenings till 3 am.

Il dito e la Luna
Via dei Sabelli 49-51,
Tel: 49 40 726.
Restaurant.
Open 7 pm to 1 am, closed Sundays.

Il Pelo nell'Uovo
Via A. Jandolo 9,
Tel: 58 00 625.
Cocktail bar with live music.
Open every evening till late at night

.Il Melarancio
Via A. Brunetti 25/b,
Tel: 36 14 149.
Piano bar, cocktails.
Open from 10 pm till 3 am, closed Mondays.

Il Piccolo
Via Emilia 48,
Tel: 46 56 31.
Restaurant, piano bar.
Open from 8.30 pm to 3 am, closed Sundays.

Il Tempo dei Giochi
Via Sestio Calvino 16.
Birreria, tea rooms, casino.
Open Mondays and Tuesdays from 7 pm to
3 am, on other days from 9 pm to 5 am.

I Tre
Via del Macao 10,
Tel: 47 46 218.
Birreria, paninoteca, restaurant.
Open from 8 pm to 5 am.

L'asino Cotto
Via dei Vascellari 48,
Tel: 58 98 985.
South American restaurant with live music.
Open till 2 am.

La Libra
Via dei Salumi 36,
Tel: 58 09 753.

Restaurant, birreria, video bar, live music on Fridays.
Open from 8 pm to 2 am, closed Tuesdays.

La Merlo Maschio
Via del Governo Vecchio 12,
Tel: 68 61 813.
Pub, small restaurant, creperie.
Open from 7 pm to 3 am, closed Mondays.

La Bagatelle
Via Alberico II 27,
Tel: 65 47 137.
Restaurant and piano bar.
Open from 8 pm to 3 am, closed Mondays.

La Pappagorgia
Via E. Vittorini 67,
Tel: 50 03 766.
Creperie, gelateria, long drinks and music to listen to.
Open from 11 am till midnight and later, closed Mondays.

La Rugantina
Largo A. Troja 2/3,
Tel: 58 03 579.
Rich cuisine, fish specialities, bar, musical meeting place.
Open from 8 pm till 2 am, closed Sundays.

La Tana dei Re
Piazza Re di Roma 49,
Tel: 75 77 762.
Birreria, restaurant offering national and international dishes.
Open from 7.30 pm to 2.30 am, closed on Mondays.

La Torta in Faccia
Viccolo delle Grotte 39,
Tel: 65 47 366.
Cocktails, buffet, live music Fridays, Saturdays and Sundays.
Open from 8 pm to 2 am every evening.

La Vetrina
Via della Vetrina 20,
Tel: 65 30 148.
Open from 8.30 am till late.

Le Cornacchie
Piazza Rondanini 53,

Tel: 65 64 485.
Cocktail bar, presentations and special events.
Open far into the night.

Le Donne
Piazza Cenci 70,
Tel: 65 64 008.
Restaurant.
Open in the evenings till 2 am.

Le Piramidi
Via Caio Mario 6.
Cocktail bar, classical music, pleasant to listen to.
Open from 9.30 till late.

L'Ombelico
Piazza delle Coppele 46,
Tel: 65 45 941.
Pub, snacks and cocktails.
Open from 9.30 to 2 am, closed Tuesdays.

Manaus
Via A. Pignatelli 21/a (Monteverde),
Tel: 53 78 563.
Tropical cocktail bar, music to listen to.
Open from 9 pm to 2 am, closed Mondays.

New Goldoni
Vicolo de'Modelli 51/a.
Rock pub, music to listen to.
Open from 9 pm to 2 am, closed Tuesdays.

No New York
Via dei Sabelli 62,
Tel: 49 40 612.
Cocktail and video bar, cold buffet.
Open from 6 pm to 2 am, closed, Sundays.

Only One
Piazza della Maddalena 4.
Cocktail bar, restaurant service.
Open far into the night.

Orient Express
Borgo Pio 161,
Tel: 58 09 868.
Cocktail bar.
Open from 8.30 pm to 1.30 am, closed Sundays.

Othero
Via Monte d'Oro 23,
Tel: 68 76 505.

Cocktail bar with "Liberty's" style decor. Open from 6 pm till late, closed Wednesdays.

Papillon
Via Crescenzio 2.
Pizzeria, birreria, restaurant.
Open from 12 noon till 4 pm and from 7 pm till 2 am.

Pinzimonio
Via degli Ombrellari 10,
Tel: 65 43 018.
Restaurant, cocktail bar, live music on Thursdays.
Open from 8.30 pm - 2 am, closed Mondays.

Rive Gauche
Via Clementia 7,
Tel: 47 57 007.
Pub, innovative music.
Open daily from 9 pm to 2 am.

Rive Gauche 2
Via dei Sabelli 43,
Tel: 49 56 722.
Pub, cafeteria, jazz music to listen to.
Open daily from 5 pm to 2 am.

Roma di Notte
Via Arco di Callisto 40,
Tel: 58 92 144.
Beer, cocktails, cold buffet and jazz music to listen to.
Open daily from 8.30 pm till 1.30 am.

Rock Subway
Via Giuseppe Peano 46.
Open from 8 pm till dawn, closed on Wednesdays.

Sax Notte
Via della Pigna 21,
Tel: 67 88 211.
Piano bar.
Open from 8 pm to 3 am, closed Sundays.

Sottosopra
Via Panisperna 68,
Tel: 48 39 61.
Cocktail bar, live music every evening.
Open from 10 pm till 4 am, Saturdays and Sundays tea rooms open from 5 pm.

Sam Michele aveva un Gallo
Via S. Francesco a Ripa 73,
Tel: 58 92 870.
Drinks, buffet, cultured and open-minded atmosphere.
Open from midday till late at night.

Sweet Movie
Via Rasella 146,
Tel: 49 53 969.
Birreria, cold buffet, tea rooms, table games.
Open every evening from 7.30 to 1 am.

Taverna Fassi
Corso d'Italia 45,
Tel: 84 41 61/85 82 75.
Birreria, snacks, cocktails, music to listen to.
Open from 8 pm to 3 am, closed Mondays.

Tango
Circonvallazione Casilina 43/45,
Tel: 29 07 80.
Cocktail bar with garden, live music.
Open in the evenings till 2 am, closed Sundays.

Tattoo
Via degli Scipioni 238,
Tel: 31 91 49.
Crepes, cocktails and soul music to listen to.
Open from 7 pm to 2 am, on Sundays from 6 pm, closed Wednesdays.

Teste Matte
Via dei Baullari 113.
Creperie, restaurant service.
Open from 8 pm to 2.30 am, closed every Tuesday.

Tulipano
Via dell'Orso 71,
Tel: 65 48 751.
Video, music, desserts.
Closed Mondays.

The Fox Pub
Via Monterone 19,
Tel: 65 78 89.
Open from 9 pm to 2 am, closed Mondays.

Versacrum
Via Garibaldi 2/a.
Cocktail bar, live music on Thursdays, Fridays and Sundays.
Open till late at night.

Vicolo 49
Vicolo dei Soldati 47,
Tel: 68 75 440.
Pub, cocktail bar, background music and live music.
Open every evening till late.

Why not—Perche No?
Via B. Tosatti 64,
Tel: 82 37 60.
Cocktails, beer.
Open from 9 pm till late, closed Mondays.

Why not
Via S. Catarina di Siena 45,
Tel: 67 93 33.
Cocktail bar.
Open in the evenings, till late, closed Mondays.

Ye's Brazil
Via S. Francesco a Ripa 103,
Tel: 58 16 267.
Open from 8 pm till 2 am, closed Saturdays.

Night life: The rest of the night life in Rome is not so very different from that in other big European cities. People meet in nightclubs and discos, to talk, dance or simply listen to the music. Below is a list of bars and clubs. The owners and the styles may change at short notice, but that shouldn't affect your enjoyment.

Acropolis
Via Luciani 52,
Tel: 87 05 04.
Disco, cocktail bar, restaurant.

Amnesty Club
Via Palermo 34,
Tel: 47 57 828.
Disco, piano bar.

Atmosphere
Via Romagnosi 11/a,
Tel: 36 11 231.
Disco, piano bar.

Bella Donna
Via Tuscolana 695,
Tel: 76 66 893.
Disco, piano bar, cabaret, "liscio" dance and live music.

Black Out
Via Saturnia 18,
Tel: 75 96 791.
Disco and live concerts.

Blue Music
Via Forli 16,
Tel: 86 27 75.
"Liscio" Thursdays and Sundays, disco Saturdays.

Club 84
Via Emilia 84,
Tel: 47 51 538.
Disco, piano bar, restaurant.

Concorede 2 Club
Via Nomentan (km 17.2).
Rock, Black and New Wave disco.

Dorian Gray
Piazza Trilussa 41,
Tel: 58 18 685.
From midnight restaurant service and disco with Afro-Latin-American music.

Dancin' Days
Via G. Neper 4,
Tel: 69 02 538.
Thursday to Sunday, "liscio" dance, orchestral accompaniment.

Easy Going
Via della Purificazione 9,
Tel: 47 45 578.
High energy disco, gay disco.

Ebrite Disco Club
Via Tuscolana 18,
Tel: 70 05 403.
Disco music, rock music on Thursdays and Fridays.

Evolution Club
Via Cincinnato 7.
Rock, funk, New Wave.

Executive
Via S. Saba 11/a (Viale Aventino),
Tel: 57 82 022.
Fashion shows, dance music.

Fabula
Via Arco dei Ginnasi 14,

Tel: 67 97 075.
Disco, cocktail bar.

Fantasy
Via Alba 42,
Tel: 78 80 741.
Afro-rhythm and concerts on Fridays, Saturdays and Sundays.

Free Time
Via Filomarino 10,
Tel: 84 49 22 54.
Afro-Latin-American music Thursdays, Saturdays and Sundays.

Galaxia
Largo Talli Virgilio 41,
Tel: 81 31 043.

Happy Club
Via Vassallo 14,
Tel: 43 91 764.
Saturdays and Sundays, disco music only.

Hysteria
Via Giovannelli 3,
Tel: 86 45 87.
Disco, cocktail bar, funk, soul and dance music.

Jackie'O
Via Boncompagni 11,
Tel: 46 14 01.
Disco, cocktail bar, restaurant La Graticola.

Jolie Coeur
Via Sirte 5,
Tel: 83 93 523.
Disco.

L'Alibi
Via di Monte Testaccio 44,
Tel: 57 43 448.
High energy gay disco.

La Cabala
Via dell'Orso,
Tel: 65 64 221.
Disco, piano bar, exclusive theme parties, presentations, special events.

La Makumba
Via degli Olimpionici 19,
Tel: 39 64 392
Disco, live Afro-Latin-American music.

L'Angelo Azzuro
Via Cardinal Merry del Val 13,
Tel: 58 00 472.
Gay clientele, disco and funk.

Le Stella
Via Beccaria 22,
Tel: 36 11 240.
Soul, funk, rap and dance music.

Life '85
Via Triofale 130/a,
Tel: 38 91 15.
Disco, revivals, folk.

L'Incontro
Via della Penna 25,
Tel: 36 10 943.
Disco, piano bar.

Magic Fly
Via Bassanello 15/b,
Tel: 36 68 956.
Soul, funk and dance music, parties and spectaculars.

M Uno
Via degli Avignonesi 7
Dancing, American bar.

New Life
Via XX Settembre 8,
Tel: 47 40 997.
Disco, young tourists, parties, rap and disco music.

New Scarabocchio
P. dei Ponziani 8/c,
Tel: 58 00 495.
Maxi-video, special events and VIPs.

Notorius
Via S. Nicola da Tolentino 22,
Tel: 47 46 888.
Disco, restaurant.

Olimpo
Piazza Rondanini 36,
Tel: 65 47 314.
Disco, piano bar, jet set performances, black music, new dance.

Open Gate
Via S. Nicola da Tolentino 4,

Tel: 47 50 464.
Disco, cocktail bar.

Over Club
Piazza Roncigliano 110/Cecchina,
Tel: 93 41 139.

Ovidius
Via Ovidio 17
Dance music, funk, soul and theme parties.

Revolution
Via del Bentivoglio 15,
Tel: 62 36 848.
New dance, funk, special effects.

Pape Satan
Via Tacito 43.
Disco, piano bar.

Gilda
Via Mario De'Fiori 97,
Tel: 67 84 838.
Disco, international acts, floor show.

Pinky Club
Via C. Lorenzini 65/c,
Tel: 82 26 04.
Disco, cocktail bar.

Piper '80
Via Tagliamento 9,
Tel: 85 44 59.
Disco, live concerts, Multivision video.

747
Via Kennedy 131 (Ciampino),
Tel: 61 18 319.
Disco.

Ti Odio
Via Carducci 8,
Tel: 48 69 34.
Music, fashion, novelty, disco on Friday evenings.

Vonna Club
Via Cassia 871.
Rock disco.

Veleno
Via Sardegna 27,
Tel: 49 35 83.
Disco, restaurant, personalities from the sports and entertainment worlds.

Zanussi
Piazza Tarquinia 5/e,
Tel: 75 93 859.
"Liscio" and "revival" on Fridays and Saturdays. Disco music and funk on Sundays.

MUSEUMS

Antiquarium Forense-Palatino
Piazza S. Maria Nova 53,
Tel: 67 90 333.
Opening hours: In summer 9 am - 6 pm daily, in winter 9 am - 3 pm daily, closed Tuesdays.
Early settlements on the Palatine.

Musei Capitolini e Pinacoteca
Piazza del Camidoglio 1,
Tel: 67 82 862.
Opening hours: 9 am - 2pm weekdays, also on Tuesdays and Thursdays 5 pm - 8 pm, additionally on Saturdays 8.30 pm - 11 pm, Sundays 9 am - 1 pm, closed Mondays.
Classical sculpture, paintings from the 15th to the 17th centuries.

Museo Barrafco die Scultura Antica
Corso Vittorio Emanuele 168,
Tel: 65 40 848.
Opening hours: weekdays 9 am - 2 pm, Tuesdays and Thursdays also 5 pm - 8 pm, Sundays 9 am - 1 pm, closed Mondays.
Egyptian, Greek and Roman sculpture.

Museo Civico die Zoologia
Via Aldrovandi 18,
Tel: 87 35 96.
Opening hours: In summer 8.30 am - 7.30 pm daily, in winter 8.30 am - 4.30 pm daily.

Museo del Collegio Teutonico e Camposante Teutonico
Piazza dei Protomartiri Romani - Citta del Vaticano 14th-century artists and Paleochristian objects.

Museo del Folklore e dei Poeti Romaneschi
Piazza S. Egidio 1/b,
Tel: 58 16 563.
Opening hours: 9 am - 1.30 pm daily, also 4.30 pm - 8 pm Tuesdays and Thursdays, closed Mondays.
Scenes of Roman life.

Museo del Fonografo
Via Caetani 32,
Tel: 68 68 364.
Opening hours: 9 am - 1 pm daily.
Rare radios, records, tapes.

Museo della Basilica di San Paolo Fuori le Mura
Piazzale S. Paolo,
Tel: 54 10 178.
Opening hours on request.

Museo della Civilta Romana
Piazza Agnelli 10,
Tel: 59 26 135.
Opening hours: 9 am - 1 pm, Tuesdays and Thursdays 4 pm - 7 pm., Sundays 9 am - 1 pm., closed Mondays and in August.
Marvellous museum of Roman culture.

Museo delle Anime del Purgatorio
Largo Tevere Prati 18, Chiesa del Sacro Cuore.
Open by appointment.
Prints of souls in purgatory in books and on clothing.

Museo delle Cere
Piazza S.S. Apostoli 67,
Tel: 67 96 482.
Opening hours: 9 am - 9 pm daily.
Waxwork figures.

Museo delle Mura
Porta S. Sebastiano,
Tel: 75 75 284.
Opening hours: In summer 9 am - 12 noon weekdays, Sundays 9 am - 1 pm, in winter 10 am - 5 pm weekdays, 9 am - 1 pm Sundays, closed Mondays.
History of the Aurelian Wall. Tour of the Wall.

Museo dell' Osservatorio Astronomico e Copernicano
Viale Parco Mellini 84,
Tel: 34 70 56.
Opening hours: Tuesdays, Thursdays, Saturdays 9.30 am - 12 noon, closed in August.
Collection of astronomical instruments from all ages.

Museo del Servizio Geologico
Largo S. Susanna 13,
Tel: 46 09 82.

Tours by appointment.
Mineral collection.

Museo di Geothe
Via del Corso 18, Tel: 36 13 356.
Opening hours: Weekdays 10 am - 1 pm and 4 pm - 7 pm, closed Sunday afternoon and Mondays.
Material from Geothe's famous stay.

Museo di Palazzo Venezia
Piazza Venezia 3, Tel: 67 98 865.
Opening hours: weekdays 9 am - 2 pm, Sundays 9 am - 1 pm, closed Mondays.
Objects and sculpture from the 9th to 19th centuries.

Museo di Roma
Piazza S. Pantaleo 10, Tel: 68 75 880.
Opening hours: Weekdays 9 am - 1.30 pm, Tuesdays and Thursdays also 5 pm - 7.30 pm, Sundays 9 am - 12.30 pm, closed Mondays.
City planning and the development of Rome.

Museo e Galleria Borghese
Piazza Scipione Borghese 3, Tel: 85 85 77.
Opening hours: Weekdays 9 am - 2 pm, holidays 9 am - 1 pm, closed Mondays.
Sculpture, paintings by Bernini, Titian, Caravaggio, da Vinci etc.

Museo Francescano dei Padri Capuccini
Via Vittorio Veneto - Chiesa di S. Maria della Concezione.
Opening hours: 9 am - 1 pm and 3 pm - 7 pm daily.
Macabre collection of 4,000 Capuchin monks' skeletons, used for decorating the crypt.

Museo Keats-Shelley
Piazza di Spagna 26, Tel: 67 84 235.
Opening hours: Weekdays 2.30 pm - 5.30 pm, closed Saturdays and Sundays.
Objects and pictures to do with the two poets.

Museo Napoleonico
Via Zanardelli 1, Tel: 65 40 286.
Opening hours: 9 am - 2 pm daily, Tuesdays and Thursdays also 5 pm - 8 pm, closed Mondays.
Mementoes of Napoleon.

Museo Nazionale dell' Arte Orientale
Via Merulana 248,
Tel: 73 59 46.
Opening hours: Weekdays 9 am - 2 pm,
Sundays 9 am - 1 pm, closed Mondays.
Excavated finds from expeditions to the
Middle East.

Museo Nazionale degli Strumenti Musicali
Piazza S. Croce 9/a,
Tel: 75 75 936.
Opening hours: Weekdays 9 am - 2 pm,
closed Sundays.
3,000 musical instruments from ancient
times to today.

Museo Nazionale dei Arti e Tradizioni Populari
Piazza Marconi 10,
Tel: 59 26 148.
Opening hours: Weekdays 9 am - 2 pm,
Wednesdays also 4 pm - 7 pm, Sundays 9 am
- 1 pm, closed Mondays.
Italian folklore and traditions.

Museo Nazionale Etrusco di Villa Giulia
Piazzale di Villa Giulia 9,
Tel: 36 01 951.
Opening hours: 9 am - 2 pm daily, in summer
9 am - 2 pm and 3 pm - 7.30 pm on Wednesdays, in winter 9 am - 6.30 pm on Wednesdays, closed Mondays.
Pre-Roman ancient times in central Italy,
finds from Etruscan tombs.

Museo Nazionale di Castel Sant'Angelo
Largo Tevere Castello 1,
Tel: 68 75 036.
Opening hours: Weekdays 9 am - 2 pm,
Sundays 9 am - 1 pm, closed Mondays.
Frescos, weapons collection.

Museo Numismatica della Zecca Italiana
Via XX Settembre 97,
Tel: 47 611.
Opening hours: Weekdays only 9 am - 11
am, closed Saturdays.
Wide-ranging collection of rare coins from
all ages.

Museo d'Arte Ebraica
Largo Tevere Cenci,
Tel: 68 64 648.
Opening hours: Modays to Fridays 10am - 2
pm and 3 pm - 6 pm, Sundays 10 am - 12.30
pm, closed Saturdays.
The history of the Jews in Rome.

Museo Storico dei Bersaglieri
Piazzale Porta Pia,
Tel: 48 67 23.
Opening hours: Tuesdays and Thursdays 10
am - 12 noon,
Scenes from the heroic dramas of Bersagli-
eri life.

Museo Storico della Lotta di Liberazione di Roma
Via Tasso 145,
Tel: 75 53 866.
Opening hours: Thursdays and Saturdays 4
pm - 7 pm, Sundays 10 am - 1 pm, closed in
August.
Documents from the struggle for the libera-
tion of Rome 1943-45.

Museo Storico dell'Arma del Carabinieri
Via Cola di Rienzo 294,
Tel: 65 30 696.
Opening hours: 8.30 am - 12.30 pm daily,
closed Mondays and in August.
Carabinieri museum.

Orto Botanico
Largo Cristina di Svezia 24,
Tel: 68 64 193.
Opening hours: In summer 9 am - 7 pm
weekdays, 9 am - 1.30 pm Saturdays, in
winter 9 am - 5 pm weekdays, 9 am - 1.30
pm Saturdays, closed Sundays.
Botanical gardens.

Raccolta Teatrale del Burcardo
Via del Sudario 44,
Tel: 65 40 755.
Opening hours: 9 am - 1 pm daily, closed on
public holidays and in August.
Masks, puppets and costumes from the 17th
to the 19th centuries.

Musei e Gallerie Pontificie
Vatican Museums
Viale Vaticano—Citta del Vaticano,
Tel: 69 83 333.
Opening hours: 9 am - 2 pm daily, last Sun-
day in the month 9 am - 1 pm with free entry.
Holy Week, July, August, September: 9 am
- 4 pm, Saturdays 9 am - 1 pm.
Original Greek sculpture, Raffael,

Michelangelo...the best, usually somewhat crowded museum in Rome.

GALLERIES

Calcografia Nazionale
Via della Stamperia 6,
Tel: 67 94 916.
Opening hours: Weekdays 9 am - 1 pm, Tuesdays also 3 pm - 5.30 pm, closed Sundays and public holidays.
Engravings.

Cineteca Nazionale
Via Tuscolana 1524,
Tel: 72 29 41.
Opening hours: Weekdays 8.30 am - 4.30 pm, closed Saturdays and Sundays.
Films.

Gabinetto Nazionale delle Stampe
Via della Lungara 230,
Tel: 65 40 565.
Opening hours: Weekdays 9 am - 1 pm, Tuesdays also 3 pm - 5.30 pm, closed Sundays and public holidays.
Drawings and prints from the 15th to the 20th centuries.

Galleria Colonna
Via della Pilotta 17,
Tel: 67 94 362.
Opening hours: Saturdays 9 am - 1 pm.
Italian and foreign painters from the 15th to the 18th centuries.

Galleria Comunale d'Atre Moderna
Piazza S. Pantaleo 10, Palazzo Braschi.
Opening hours: Wednesdays and Saturdays 9 am - 2 pm. 19th-century Roman painters.

Gallerai dell' Accademia Nazionale die S. Luca
Piazza dell' Accademia die S. Luca 77,
Tel: 67 89 243.
Opening hours: Mondays, Wednesdays, Fridays and the last Sunday in the month 10 am - 1 pm, closed during August.
Raffael, Rubens and others.

Galleria Doria Pamphili
Piazza Collegio Romano 1/a,
Tel: 67 94 365.
Opening hours: Tuesdays, Fridays, Saturdays and Sundays 10 am - 1 pm.
Works by Filippo, Lizzi, Titian, Velasquez and others.

Galleria Nazionale di Arte Antica
Via della Lungara 10 - Palazzo Corsini,
Tel: 65 42 323.
Opening hours: Mondays and Saturdays 9 am - 2 pm, Tuesdays and Fridays 9 am - 7 pm, Sundays and public holidays between 9 am - 1 pm.
Paintings of Italian schools from the 13th to the 16th centuries and foreign works.

Galleria Nazionale d'Arte Moderna
Via Belle Arti 1331,
Tel: 80 27 51.
Opening hours: Weekdays 9 am - 2 pm, Sundays 9 am - 1 pm, closed Mondays.
Italian and foreign sculptors from the 19th century to the present day.

Galleria Pallavivini
Via XXIV Maggio 43,
Tel: 47 57 816.
First Monday in the month, 10 am - 12 noon and 3 pm - 5 pm.
Pictures by Italian and foreign schools from the 15th to the 18th centuries.

Galleria Spada
Piazza Capo di Ferro 3,
Tel: 68 61 158.
Opening hours: Tuesdays to Saturdays 9 am - 2 pm, Sundays 9 am - 1 pm, closed Mondays.
Incomparable private collection dating from the 17th century.

SMALL GALLERIES

Arco Farnese
Via Giulia 180
Tel: 65 65 145.

Artevisive
Via Properzio 37
Tel: 65 41 672.

Bottega Quartiere Coppede
Via Renzo 26a.

Break Club
Via del Moro 1b
Tel: 58 10 788.

Galleria Giulia
Via Giulia 148
Tel: 65 42 061.

Galleria Pieroni
Via Panisperna 203
Tel: 45 67 06.

Incontro d'Arte
Via del Vantaggio 17a

Rondanini
Piazza Rondanini 48
Tel: 65 58 56.

Studio Soligo
Via del Babuino 51
Tel: 67 84 328.

ARCHIVES AND LIBRARIES

Archivio Centrale dello Stato
Piazzale degli Archivi,
Tel: 59 20 371.

Archivio di Stato di Roma
Corso Rinascimento 40,
Tel: 65 43 823.

Archivio Storico Capitolino
Biblioteca Roman Emeroteca
Piazza della Chiesa Nuova 18,
Tel: 65 42 662.

Biblioteca Accademia Nazionale dei Lincei
Via della Lungara 10,
Tel: 65 08 31.

Biblioteca Angelica
Piazza San Agostino 8,
Tel: 68 75 874.

Biblioteca Consiglio Nazionale delle Ricerche
Piazza A. Moro 7,
Tel: 49 93 33 85.

Biblioteca del Centro Sperimentale di Cinematografia
Via Tuscolana 1524,
Tel: 72 29 41.

Biblioteca e Discoteca di Stato
Via Caetani 32,
Tel: 68 79 048.

Biblioteca Fototeca Unione Architettura e Topografia dell' Impero Romano
Via Masina 5,
Tel: 58 18 770.

Biblioteca Germanica Goethe Instituto
Via Savoia 15,
Tel: 86 88 88.

Biblioteca Hertziana
Via Gregoriana 28,
Tel: 67 97 352.

Biblioteca Instituto Archeologico Germanico
Via Sardegna 79,
Tel: 46 56 17.

Biblioteca Instituto Nazionale di Archeologia e Storia dell'Arte
Piazza Venezia 3,
Tel: 67 97 739.

Biblioteca Keats-Shelley Memorial Association
Piazza di Spagna 26,
Tel: 67 84 235.

Biblioteca Nazionale Centrale Vittorio Emanuele II
Piazzale Castro Pretorio 105,
Tel: 49 89.

Biblioteca Teatrale del Burcardo
Via del Sudaro 44,
Tel: 65 40 755.

Instituto Gramsci
Via Conservatorio 55,
Tel: 65 54 05.

ACADEMIES

Accademia Americana
Via Angelo Massina 5,
Tel: 58 18 653.

Accademia Angelico Constantiniana de Lettere, Artie e Scienze
Via del Vantaggio 22,
Tel: 67 87 658.

Accademia Belle Arti
Via Ripetta 222,
Tel: 08005.

Accademia del Mediterraneo
Via Plinio 7,
Tel: 38 35 40.

Accademia Delle Scienze
Casina Pio IV - Citta del Vaticano,
Tel: 69 83 195.

Accademia di Francia
Viale Trinita del Monti 1,
Tel: 67 611.

Accademia Internazionale Burckhardt
Piazza S. Salvatore in Lauro 13,
Tel: 65 97 37.

Accademia Italiana della Cucina
Via Paolo die Dono 145,
Tel: 50 33 012.

Accademia Nazionale dei Lincei
Via della Lungara 10,
Tel: 65 08 31.

Accademia Nazionale di Danza
Largo Arrigo VII 5,
Tel: 57 32 84.

Accademia Nazionale di S. Cecilia
Via Vittoria 6,
Tel: 67 80 742.

Accademia Romana die Archeoligia
Piazza della Cancelleria 1,
Tel: 69 85 025.

Accademia Tedesca
Largo Villa Massimo 2,
Tel: 42 03 94.

BOOKSHOPS

Al Tempo Ritrovato
Piazza Farnese 103,
Tel: 65 43 749.
Women's bookshop—info on women's groups.

Feltrinelli
Via del Babuino 41,
Tel: 48 44 30.

Il Leuto
Via Monte Brianzo 86,
Tel: 65 69 269.
Bookshop specializing in theater and film.

Librogalleria
Via di Ripetta 64,
Tel: 67 93 555.

Remainder's Book
Piazza San Silvestro 27-28,
Tel: 67 92 824.

Rinascita
Via della Botteghe Oscure 1,
Tel: 67 97 460.

Rizzoli
Galleria Colonna/Largo Chigi 15,
Tel: 67 96 641.

CINECLUBS

Augustus
Corso Vittori Enamuele II 203,
Tel: 687 54 55.

Azzuro Scipioni
Via degli Scipioni 84,
Tel: 35 81 094.

Grauco
Via Perugia 34,
Tel: 755 17 85.

Labirinto
Via Pompeo Magno 27,
Tel: 31 22 83.

Novocine
Via Cardinale Merry des Val 14,
Tel: 581 62 35.

LANGUAGE SCHOOLS

Dante Alighieri
Piazza Firenze 27,
Tel: 678 11 05.
Good traditional school.

Torre di Babele
Via Bixio 74,
Tel: 70 084 34.
One of the best new language schools in

Rome, with outings and opportunites for accommodation.

SPORTS

Joggers meet in most of the parks, such as the Villa Doria Pamphili (also with keep-fit-trail), Villa Borghese, Villa Ada, usually after office hours and on Saturday mornings around 9 am.

Joggers also run in and around the stadium near the Baths of Caracalla, in the street of the same name.

Groups of footballers usually meet up spontaneously on the large lawns of the parks.

Swimming baths:

Piscina Coperta
Via Stadio Flamino, Tel: 39 98 12.

Piscina del Foro Italico
Lungotevere Marasciallo Cadorna, Tel: 36 08 591.

Piscina del Foro Italico
Tel: 36 01 498.

Football stadium of the clubs Lazio (2nd division) and A.S. Roma: Stadio Olimpico Viale dei Gladiatori - Tel: 39 94 50.

FESTIVALS

January: *Befana* (Epifania), the traditional witch festival. End of the big Christmas market in the Piazza Navona (6.1).

February: Summer fashion shows in the couture houses.

Carneval: processions in the Castelli Romani, towns and villages in the Alban Hills, a few celebrations in the streets of Rome.
Blessing of cars outside the church of S. Francesca Romana on the Via dei Fiori Imperiali. (9.3).

Festa die S. Giuseppe with pancakes, lardy cakes and fun fair (19.3).

April: the Spanish Steps are decorated with flowers.

Founding of Rome (21.4. 753 B.C.)

Liberation Day (25.4).

Maundy Thursday — washing of feet in the Basilica S. Giovanni in Laterano.

Good Friday: Stations of the Cross with the Pope by the Coliseum.

Easter Sunday: Blessing *urbi et orbi* in St. Peter's Square.

May: Labour Day (1.5).

June: start of the *Estate Romana* (runs till September), Roman summer cultural festival with music, theater, dance, film in the Orto Botanico, Villa Medici, Villa Massimo, Isola Tiberina, Aventine and on the beach at Ostia.

Festa di S. Giovanni (St. John's Eve): eating snails and fireworks near S. Giovanni (24. 7).

July: *Opera die Roma* in the Baths of Caracalla.
Concerts by the musical academy of St. Cecilia in the Capitol Square.

Theater performances in the amphitheater in Ostia Antica.

Bastille Day (French national holiday) with celebrations in the Piazza Farnese in front of the French Embassy (14.7).

Autumn and winter fashion shows in the couture houses.
Festa di Noatri: popular festival in Trastevere with music, fireworks and food (all the pizzerias put out tables and chairs in the side streets). Fairly commercialized.

August: the great exodus from the city. Most shops close. Rome is almost empty. *Estate Romana* takes a break till September, but there are still open air performances in the *Estrada* and *Teatro Nuovo* cinemas. Possible strikes on the ferries to the islands, usually to Sardinia, and threats of strikes by railway workers.

Festa della Madonna della Neve near S.

Maria Maggiore. Artificial snow to honor the "Virgin of the Snows" (5.8).

Ferragosto ("Feriae Augusti") roma life comes to a complete halt. Assumption of the Blessed Virgin Mary (15.8).

September: Rome comes back from its Vacaze and comes to life once more. "Estate Romana" recommences.

Tevere Expo by the Tiber. Sales exhibition of the Italian regions.

December: Christmas market in the Piazza Navona begins (8. 12).

Christmas Mass said by the Pope in St. Peter's Up to 60,000 churchgoers. Book tickets early and come several hours before the due time (24.12).

Veglione among the Romans, general celebratory meal in a restaurant or at home (31.12).

Further Reading

The modest list below can only make a few suggestions for further reading on the "eternal" subject of Rome (and Italy).

General

Michael Grant, *The Romans*, Nelson.
Suetonius, *The 12 Caesars*, Penguin Classics.
Allan Massie, *The Caesars*, Secker & Warburg; gives the same biographies as Suetonius plus plenty of background information.
Justine Davis Randers-Pehrson, *Barbarians and Romans*, Croom Helm; *The last years of the Roman Empire*.
Ferdinand Gregorovius, *History of the City of Rome in the Middle Ages*, London 1894-1902.

Benvenuto Cellini, *The Life of Benvenuto Cellini*, translator John Addington Symonds, Macmillan.
Marguerite Yourcenar, *Memoirs of Hadrian*, Secker & Warburg.

Travelers

Johann Wolfgang von Goethe, *Italian Journey*, translated by W.H. Auden & Elizabeth Mayer, Pantheon Books.
Ferdinand Gregorovius, *The Roman Journals of Ferdinand Gregorovius*, editor Friedrich Althous, translator Gustavus W. Hamilton, G. Bell & Son.
Stendhal, *Promenades dans Rome*, Paris 1893
Henry V. Morton, *A Traveller in Rome*, London 1957.
Peter Quenell, *Byron in Italy*, Viking Press, New York.
Christopher Hibbert, *The Grand Tour*, G.P. Putnam & Sons, New York.

Church History

Walter F. Murphy, *The Vicar of Christ*, Cassell.
John Whale (editor), *The Pope from Poland: An Assessment*, Collins.
Hans Kung, *The Church*, Burns & Oates, London 1967

Special Interest

Lydia Vellaccio & Maurice Elston, *Teach Yourself Italian*, Teach Yourself Books (Hodder & Stoughton London 1985).
Elizabeth David, *Italian Food*, Penguin Cookery Library.
Phillip Dallas, *Italian Wines*, Faber & Faber.
Henning Kluver/Peter Kammerer, *Rom - Anders Reisen*.

And .....

The Cambridge History of Classical Literature, Vol. II - Latin Literature.

ART/PHOTO
CREDITS

2/3	Patrizia Giancotti	47	AKG	91	Patrizia Giancotti
4/5	Patrizia Giancotti	48/49	Patrizia Giancotti	92	Patrizia Giancotti
6/7	Patrizia Giancotti	50	Patrizia Giancotti	93	Patrizia Giancotti
8/9	Patrizia Giancotti	52	Patrizia Giancotti	94	Patrizia Giancotti
10/11	Patrizia Giancotti	53	Patrizia Giancotti	95	Patrizia Giancotti
12/13	Patrizia Giancotti	54	Patrizia Giancotti	96	Patrizia Giancotti
16	Patrizia Giancotti	55	Patrizia Giancotti	98	Patrizia Giancotti
17	Gerd Pfeiffer	56/57	Patrizia Giancotti	99	Patrizia Giancotti
18/19	Archiv für Kunst und	58	Patrizia Giancotti	100	Patrizia Giancotti
	Geschichte Berlin	60	Patrizia Giancotti	101	Patrizia Giancotti
	(AKG)	61	Patrizia Giancotti	102	Patrizia Giancotti
21/21	AKG	62	Gerd Pfeiffer	103	Patrizia Giancotti
22	Ping Amranand	63	Patrizia Giancotti	104	Patrizia Giancotti
24	Ping Amranand	64/65	Patrizia Giancotti	105	Patrizia Giancotti
25	Ping Amranand	66/67	Patrizia Giancotti	106/107	Patrizia Giancotti
26	Ping Amranand	68/69	Patrizia Giancotti	108/109	Patrizia Giancotti
27	Ping Amranand	70	Gerd Pfeiffer	110	Ping Amranand
28	Ping Amranand	72	Gerd Pfeiffer	112	Patrizia Giancotti
30	Ping Amranand	73	Gerd Pfeiffer	113	Patrizia Giancotti
31	Ping Amranand	74	Patrizia Giancotti	114	Patrizia Giancotti
32	Patrizia Giancotti	75L	Patrizia Giancotti	115	Patrizia Giancotti
34	AKG	75R	Patrizia Giancotti	116	Ping Amranand
35	AKG	76/77	Patrizia Giancotti	117	Patrizia Giancotti
36	AKG	80	Patrizia Giancotti	118	Patrizia Giancotti
37	Patrizia Giancotti	81	Patrizia Giancotti	119	Patrizia Giancotti
38	AKG	82	Patrizia Giancotti	120	Ping Amranand
39	Patrizia Giancotti	83	Patrizia Giancotti	121	F. Hacourt
40/41	AKG	85	Ping Amranand	122	Gerd Pfeiffer
42	Archiv Gümpel	86	Patrizia Giancotti	123	Ping Amranand
44	Archiv Gümpel	87	Gerd Pfeiffer	125	Patrizia Giancotti
45	Patrizia Giancotti	88	Patrizia Giancotti	126/127	Patrizia Giancotti

128	Patrizia Giancotti	166	Ping Amranand	209	Patrizia Giancotti
129	Patrizia Giancotti	168	Patrizia Giancotti	210	Patrizia Giancotti
130	Ping Amranand	169	Patrizia Giancotti	211	Patrizia Giancotti
131	Patrizia Giancotti	170/171	Patrizia Giancotti	212	Gerd Pfeiffer
132	Bodo Bondzio	173	Patrizia Giancotti	213	Patrizia Giancotti
133	Gerd Pfeiffer	174/175	Patrizia Giancotti	214	Patrizia Giancotti
134	Ping Amranand	176	Patrizia Giancotti	215	Patrizia Giancotti
135	Ping Amranand	178	Patrizia Giancotti	216	Patrizia Giancotti
136	Patrizia Giancotti	179	Patrizia Giancotti	217	Patrizia Giancotti
137	Patrizia Giancotti	180	Ping Amranand	218	Patrizia Giancotti
138	Ping Amranand	181	Patrizia Giancotti	219	Patrizia Giancotti
139	Patrizia Giancotti	182	Patrizia Giancotti	221	Patrizia Giancotti
140	Patrizia Giancotti	184	Patrizia Giancotti	222	Patrizia Giancotti
141	Ping Amranand	185	Patrizia Giancotti	223	Patrizia Giancotti
142	Patrizia Giancotti	187	Patrizia Giancotti	224/225	Patrizia Giancotti
143	Patrizia Giancotti	188	Patrizia Giancotti	226/227	Patrizia Giancotti
144	Patrizia Giancotti	189	Ping Amranand	228	Bruno Flavio
145	Patrizia Giancotti	190	Patrizia Giancotti	230	Patrizia Giancotti
146/147	Patrizia Giancotti	191	Patrizia Giancotti	231	AKG
148	Patrizia Giancotti	192	Patrizia Giancotti	232	Bruno Flavio
150	Patrizia Giancotti	193	Patrizia Giancotti	233	Patrizia Giancotti
151	Patrizia Giancotti	194	Patrizia Giancotti	234	Patrizia Giancotti
152	Gerd Pfeiffer	196	Patrizia Giancotti	235	Heinz Vestner
153L	Heinz Vestner	197	Patrizia Giancotti	237	Patrizia Giancotti
153R	Patrizia Giancotti	198	Patrizia Giancotti	238	Bruno Flavia
154/155	Patrizia Giancotti	199	Patrizia Giancotti	239	Patrizia Giancotti
158	Patrizia Giancotti	200/201	Patrizia Giancotti	240	coop. cult. blond
160	Ping Amranand	204	Patrizia Giancotti	241	Hans Hoefer
162	Ping Amranand	206	Patrizia Giancotti	242	Gerd Pfeiffer
164	Patrizia Giancotti	207	Patrizia Giancotti	244	Ping Amranand
165	Patrizia Giancotti	208	Patrizia Giancotti	245	Patrizia Giancotti

INDEX